Bargaining over t

Can nuclear agreements like the Iran Deal work? This book develops formal bargaining models to show that they can over time despite apparent incentives to cheat. Existing theories of nuclear proliferation fail to account for the impact of bargaining on the process. William Spaniel explores how credible agreements exist in which rival states make concessions to convince rising states not to proliferate and argues in support of nuclear negotiations as effective counter-proliferation tools. This book proves not only the existence of settlements but also the robustness of the inefficiency puzzle. In addition to examining existing agreements, the model used by Spaniel serves as a baseline for modeling other concerns about nuclear weapons.

William Spaniel is an assistant professor in political science at the University of Pittsburgh. He previously served as a Stanton Nuclear Security Postdoctoral Scholar at Stanford University's Center for International Security and Cooperation. He is also the author of *Game Theory 101: The Complete Textbook*.

Bargaining over the Bomb

The Successes and Failures of Nuclear Negotiations

WILLIAM SPANIEL
University of Pittsburgh

CAMBRIDGE
UNIVERSITY PRESS

CAMBRIDGE
UNIVERSITY PRESS

University Printing House, Cambridge CB2 8BS, United Kingdom

One Liberty Plaza, 20th Floor, New York, NY 10006, USA

477 Williamstown Road, Port Melbourne, VIC 3207, Australia

314–321, 3rd Floor, Plot 3, Splendor Forum, Jasola District Centre,
New Delhi – 110025, India

79 Anson Road, #06-04/06, Singapore 079906

Cambridge University Press is part of the University of Cambridge.

It furthers the University's mission by disseminating knowledge in the pursuit of
education, learning, and research at the highest international levels of excellence.

www.cambridge.org
Information on this title: www.cambridge.org/9781108477055
DOI: 10.1017/9781108630610

First published 2019

Printed and bound in Great Britain by Clays Ltd, Elcograf S.p.A.

A catalogue record for this publication is available from the British Library.

Library of Congress Cataloging-in-Publication Data
Names: Spaniel, William, author.
Title: Bargaining over the bomb : the successes and failures
of nuclear negotiations / William Spaniel.
Description: Cambridge, United Kingdom;
New York, NY : Cambridge University Press, 2019.
Identifiers: LCCN 2018040081 | ISBN 9781108477055 (hardback) |
ISBN 9781108701846 (paperback)
Subjects: LCSH: Nuclear nonproliferation–International cooperation. |
Nuclear arms control–International cooperation. |
BISAC: POLITICAL SCIENCE / International Relations / General.
Classification: LCC JZ5675 .S686 2019 | DDC 327.1/747–dc23
LC record available at https://lccn.loc.gov/2018040081

ISBN 978-1-108-47705-5 Hardback
ISBN 978-1-108-70184-6 Paperback

Cambridge University Press has no responsibility for the persistence or accuracy
of URLs for external or third-party internet websites referred to in this publication
and does not guarantee that any content on such websites is, or will remain,
accurate or appropriate.

Contents

Tables

Figures

Acknowledgments

The inspiration for this book came in 2009. I spent a gap year between undergrad and grad school working at a coffee shop on the campus of UC San Diego, where I had majored in political science. We had a large television, and I watched President Barack Obama make a speech urging Iran to accept concessions in exchange for ending its nuclear program. Theories we had in international relations suggests such a deal would not work. Power drives concessions; without it, strong states have no reason to negotiate with the weak. It appeared Obama's speech was merely a ploy, one which Iran would never fall victim to. I set out to write a paper to demonstrate why power politics would certainly doom such diplomacy.

Formal theory has a nasty tendency to invalidate one's intuitions. Much to my surprise (and delight!), I was wrong. Concessions-for-weapons agreements work; Obama's desired diplomacy could be effective in theory. Of course, this created a more fundamental puzzle: if concessions-for-weapons works, why does any state choose to proliferate at all? I spent the next several years trying to figure out some answers.

I am indebted to five groups of people for helping me write this manuscript. My undergraduate education at UC San Diego primed me to think about puzzles in international relations. I would not have pursued a career in this discipline or begun training in formal theory had I gone elsewhere. Erik Gartzke, Cullen Hendrix, Ethan Hollander, Sam Kernell, Darren Schreiber, and Branislav Slantchev were all instrumental in starting my passion for research. I also thank Leo Acosta and Daniel Morales for tolerating my whims at The Village.

The bulk of the writing for this manuscript occurred at the University of Rochester. My dissertation was the basis of the manuscript. Randy Stone, Mark Fey, and Hein Goemans comprised my committee, and they have read more of this and provided more feedback than anyone else. Phil Arena, Peter Bils, Gleason Judd, and Brad Smith also spent substantial time with me revising the pitch and formal argumentation. Brad, in particular, first proposed creating the v data that I exploit in Chapter 5. I am also indebted to Matthew Blackwell, Maya Sen, and Svanhildur Thorvaldsdottir for their comments.

I refined the manuscript while serving as a Stanton Nuclear Security Postdoctoral Fellow at Stanford University's Center for International Security and Cooperation. I thank the Stanton Foundation for their funding. Scott Sagan and James Fearon helped revise the manuscript and prepare it for broader consumption. I also benefited from conversations with Ben Buch, Kate Cronin-Furman, Lynn Eden, Rod Ewing, Sig Hecker, David Holloway, Morgan Kaplan, Chris Lawrence, Terry Peterson, and Ken Schultz.

I finally completed the book while at the University of Pittsburgh. In particular, Despina Alexiadou, Michael Colaresi, Jude Hayes, George Krause, Michael Poznansky, and Burcu Savun all helped me finally get the manuscript out the door.

Lastly, I benefited from help outside of my home institutions. I presented many earlier versions of this paper at conferences of the American Political Science Association, Midwest Political Science Association, Southern Political Science Association, Peace Science Society, Triangle Institute for Security Studies, and the University of Buffalo. In addition, I benefited from conversations with Andrew Coe, Alexandre Debs, Matthew Fuhrmann, Ryan Jaimes, Alexander Lanoszka, Rupal Mehta, Nuno Monteiro, Harvey Palmer, Aishwarya Ramesh, Toby Rider, Zachary Taylor, and Scott Wolford.

Of course, the book finally came together through Cambridge University Press. I am especially appreciative to Robert Dreesen for his seamless oversight of the project. Thanks as well to the two anonymous reviewers whose comments greatly improved the manuscript.

1

Do Nuclear Agreements Work?

On September 25, 2009, President Barack Obama issued the following warning to Iran at a G20 summit in Pittsburgh, Pennsylvania:

Iran must comply with UN Security Council resolutions and make clear it is willing to meet its responsibilities as a member of the community of nations. We have offered Iran a clear path toward greater international integration if it lives up to its obligations, and that offer stands. But the Iranian government must now demonstrate through deeds its peaceful intentions or be held accountable to international standards and international law.[1]

For years, Western powers had extended such olive branches to Iran, offering various enticements if Tehran ended its (assumed) nuclear-weapons program. Almost six years later, Obama's plan finally came to fruition. On July 14, 2015, Iran and an international coalition led by the United States completed the Joint Comprehensive Plan of Action (JCPOA). Known colloquially as the "Iran Deal," the JCPOA mandated that Iran reduce its uranium stockpiles, divest portions of its nuclear infrastructure, and welcome back weapons inspectors. In return, the United States lifted economic sanctions and took the first step toward integrating Iran back into that community of nations.

Although the JCPOA may have dominated recent news cycles, it is not unique in its intention. The United States has attempted to reach similar agreements with North Korea. In early 2012, Washington and Pyongyang reached a food-for-nukes agreement, which called for the

---

[1] Obama 2009.

North to end its nuclear-weapons program and suspend long-range missile tests in exchange for millions of pounds of food. That plan fell through. So too did the 1994 "Agreed Framework," which would have traded energy concessions for similar divestments. Since then, North Korea has stubbornly continued testing nuclear weapons and fired missiles under the auspices of its fledgling space program.

There are reasons to be pessimistic about these types of agreements in general. Both sides appear to face commitment problems. The United States would only want to offer its opponents concessions if they end their respective nuclear programs in return. However, these states could take those concessions, continue constructing nuclear weapons, magnify their military power, and extract yet *more* concessions. If Washington worries they will adopt such a strategy, it might never give the concessions necessary to induce them to end their programs. Meanwhile, without a nuclear deterrent at the ready, potential proliferators must worry that the United States' policy concessions are temporary. Thus, even if settlements exist that leave both sides better off, credible commitment problems may lead to proliferation anyway.

Despite these important concerns, there is cause for cautious optimism about the potential success of nuclear deals. Similar conciliatory strategies involving other states have lasted over the long-term. Egypt's turbulent early relationship with Israel led Cairo to explore proliferation beginning in the 1960s. However, Egypt lost most of the incentive to acquire nuclear weapons when the parties signed the Camp David Accords, which returned the Sinai Peninsula to Egypt (Einhorn 2004 48–51). Anwar Sadat formalized Egypt's commitment by ratifying the Nuclear Non-Proliferation Treaty in 1981. Although Egypt continued pursuing nuclear technology (Solingen 2007, 230–231), he and successor Hosni Mubarak never made a serious attempt to proliferate thereafter. Indeed, any nuclear experimentation would have put US foreign direct aid – tied to good relations with Israel per the Accords – in jeopardy (Arena and Pechenkina, 2016). Proliferation could have provided Egypt with benefits, but the net gain could not have exceeded the value of the deal that Egypt had already obtained.

Egypt is not the only historical case of nuclear forbearance. The end of the Cold War presented the United States a large-scale nuclear conundrum. Although the nuclear stockpiles in Belarus, Kazakhstan, and Ukraine remained under Moscow's control (Miller 1993, 71–74), each of these countries had the technological proficiency to proliferate. Negotiations between the United States and the successor states led to the Lisbon Protocol. Belarus, Kazakhstan, and Ukraine became parties to the Nuclear Non-Proliferation Treaty. Contingent on the terms, the United States offered assistance with civilian nuclear-energy projects, provided substantial aid at a time of financial crisis, and issued security assurances.[2]

The United States even offered concessions to its own Cold War allies. At various points, Japan, South Korea, and Australia explored a nuclear deterrent. The United States publicly extended its commitment to those countries in each case. Rather than risk destroying their good relationships with Washington, each backed down.

Of course, negotiations do not always lead to nonproliferation. Ten countries have proliferated; nine still maintain nuclear arsenals.[3] What separates Egypt, Belarus, and South Korea from the Soviet Union, Pakistan, and North Korea? Why do negotiations sometimes succeed? Why do they sometimes fail?

In the wake of the Iran Deal, this may be the most important question today regarding nuclear politics. Proponents of the Iran Deal envision it as a framework for future negotiations. That being the case, it is critical that policymakers understand what features of the agreement drive compliance. Meanwhile, critics of the deal suggest it is only a matter of time until Iran violates it. If so, it is crucial to identify the agreement's shortcomings and rectify them if possible. And if these deals are hopeless, then policymakers need alternatives to curtail future nuclear proliferation.

The possibility that deals may actually succeed has a broader implication for the nuclear politics literature. Fewer than five percent of countries possess nuclear weapons. A common research question is why more states have not yet developed a bomb. This project can answer that. If bargaining works, then the shortage of nuclear countries has a simple explanation. Rather than build weapons, potential proliferators prefer taking buyouts instead, and their opponents are happy to offer those concessions.

Unfortunately, we do not yet have a full understanding of whether states can bargain over the bomb and how they do that. This book fills that void.

[2] Foreign aid to recipients not allied to the donor is somewhat common. See Uzonyi and Rider 2017.

[3] South Africa held deliverable nuclear weapons from 1982 to 1990 but eventually acceded to the Nuclear Non-Proliferation Treaty due to a combination of structural change to the international system and internal political strife (Albright 1994). See Gartzke and Kroenig (2009) for a list of nuclear powers and when they entered the club.

TABLE 1.1. *Some Successful and Unsuccessful Nonproliferation Agreements*

States	Deal	Year
Soviet Union	US Concessions	1945–1948
Worldwide	Atoms for Peace	1953
Worldwide	IAEA Technical Cooperation	1957
Worldwide	Non-Proliferation Treaty	1968
Australia	US Guarantees	1970
Japan	US Guarantees	1970–1976
Pakistan	US Guarantees	1972–1998
South Korea	US Guarantees	1976–1981
Taiwan	US Guarantees	1977–1978
Egypt	Camp David Accords	1992
Argentina/Brazil	Guadalajara Accord	1991
Soviet Successors	Lisbon Protocol	1992
North Korea	Agreed Framework	1994
Iran	Tehran Declaration	2003
Libya	Libyan Disarmament	2003
North Korea	Six-Party Talks	2003–2007
North Korea	Leap Day Agreement	2012
Iran	JCPOA	2015

1.1 THE CENTRAL ARGUMENT

The main subject of this book is nonproliferation agreements, which I define as any transfer from one country to another with the intent to make the latter less likely to acquire nuclear weapons. Table 1.1 includes a list of salient agreements, some successful and others less so.[4] The definition is broad and the examples cast a wide net, but both are intentional decisions. The core model demonstrates that mutually preferable transfers exist between would-be proliferators and their rivals. Furthermore, the model demonstrates that *any* transfer has that effect. Nuclear-specific agreements, like the Joint Comprehensive Plan of Action, qualify. But so do broader agreements that do not seem to have a direct connection to nuclear weapons, like the Camp David Accords and American inducements to the Soviet Union following World War II. Regardless of whether nuclear weapons are in the headlines, these agreements intend to reduce tensions between states in discord, which reduces the value of a nuclear arsenal.

---

[4] See Bas and Coe 2017 for a similar list.

However, the possibility of such agreements does not guarantee feasibility. States may be misinformed about each other's capabilities or cannot credibly commit to such agreements. The presence of these bargaining frictions determines whether a state pursues nuclear weapons. In five words, proliferation is a bargaining problem.

Understanding nuclear proliferation is a two-step process. First, this book shows that there exist concessions-for-weapons agreements, or *butter-for-bombs* settlements, that leave the parties with no incentive to build nuclear weapons or declare war. The book then describes the circumstances under which opponents refuse to offer such settlements or potential proliferators reject them, perhaps leading to the construction of nuclear weapons or preventive action.

More specifically, this book presents a proliferation inefficiency puzzle. When nuclear weapons are too expensive or the rival's threat to launch a preventive strike is credible, reaching nonproliferation settlements is straightforward. Outside these cases, proliferation may seem inevitable, as the potential proliferator's temptation to build might prove too strong. However, such intuition fails to empathize with the potential proliferator's incentives. Nuclear weapons are exceedingly expensive. The costs start with building nuclear infrastructure to create weapons-grade material. Then the state must construct the physical weapons and the corresponding delivery systems. And once completed, the proliferator must maintain the weapons and delivery systems over time, which can be the most burdensome part of all. As a result, perhaps it is not surprising that Schwartz (1998) estimates that American expenses related to nuclear weapons totaled $8.9 *trillion* from 1940 to 1996 (in 2016 dollars).

Nuclear weapons must provide some sort of benefits for potential proliferators to bother with the whole operation. That being the case, why can't rival states concede most of those benefits up front and avoid the nuclear outcome? Under such terms, potential proliferators benefit by achieving the majority of their goals without having to pay a dollar; opponents benefit from not sacrificing the entire policy in dispute and avoiding the spread of nuclear weapons. It therefore appears that the inefficiency of proliferation incentivizes *both* states to reach an agreement.[5]

The main theoretical section of this book proves the credibility of butter-for-bombs settlements. Under these agreements, the rival state makes immediate concessions to the potential proliferator. The potential

---

[5] This argument is similar to war's inefficiency puzzle (Fearon 1995), except applied to costly weapons construction instead of war.

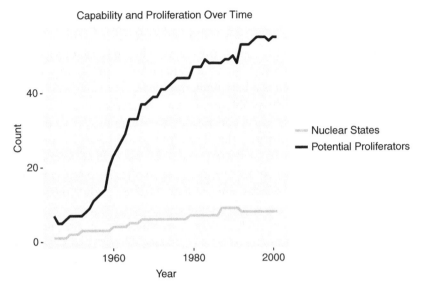

FIGURE 1.1. Nuclear Capacity and Weapons over Time

proliferator accepts the concessions and never builds. Surprisingly, nuclearizing would yield further concessions for the potential proliferator.
However, the additional concessions do not compensate for the cost of
proliferation. In turn, the potential proliferator has no incentive to break
the deal.

This has an important implication for the nonproliferation regime. By
some accounts, the Nuclear Non-Proliferation Treaty is one of the most
successful international organizations ever created.[6] Only four countries
have never signed (India, Israel, Pakistan, and South Sudan) and only
one (North Korea) has ever withdrawn. The model shows that concessions from rival states cause potential proliferators to abide by the treaty;
absent those concessions, many more states would leave the NPT and
develop a nuclear deterrent. This helps explain the discrepancy between
the number of nuclear-capable states and the number of nuclear-weapons
states seen in Figure 1.1.[7]

Going deeper, Figure 1.1 shows the universe of cases that this study
addresses. Note that these are *states*, not nonproliferation agreements.

---

[6] See Sagan 1996; Dai 2007; Rublee 2009. Mearsheimer 1993 provides an opposing
viewpoint.
[7] Figure adapted from Smith and Spaniel 2018.

This is for two reasons. First, explaining both the successes and failures requires cases where deals were successful, deals that failed, and deals that never even materialized.[8] These agreements span over time and may be adjusted according to shocks to relations, so it is important to consider them in their broader context. Second, despite the temptation to focus on agreements that are explicitly nuclear (e.g., the Iran Deal), the Camp David Accords case suggests that any sort of concession made to an adversary could override a state's need for nuclear weapons. Table 1.2 gives a comprehensive list of these nuclear-competent states with the year they first obtained a proficiency higher than North Korea's in 2001 and the year they first obtained that proficiency. Countries in bold have pursued nuclear weapons according to Bleek's (2010) data.

Figure 1.1 also suggests a bigger puzzle. Although most of these states opt not to proliferate, some do. Insofar as negotiations can reduce a state's desire to proliferate, these are the cases of bargaining failures. The task then is to explain these instances of proliferation within the context of the inefficiency puzzle. Why do potential proliferators nuclearize when nonproliferation settlements exist that improve both parties' welfare?

This book provides three causal mechanisms. First, commitment problems preclude a deal when the potential proliferator expects to lose the ability to develop nuclear weapons in the future. Opponents would like to promise concessions over the long term to convince the potential proliferator to forgo nuclear weapons. However, because the threat to proliferate drives those concessions, the potential proliferator knows it will lose the deal once nuclear weapons are no longer an option.[9] In turn, this dynamic forces the potential proliferator to invest while it can to coerce concessions in the long run.

Second, incomplete information leads potential proliferators to challenge rivals in the absence of a butter-for-bombs offer. Weak rival states have incentive to act tough and make no concessions, relying on the threat of a preventive strike to induce the potential proliferator to yield. Thus, the potential proliferator may develop nuclear weapons to test the rival's credibility. Stable butter-for-bombs agreements still exist here.

---

[8] Studies often overlook the cases where states never reached explicit nuclear negotiations, which means the conclusions are only useful for understanding how to solve a problem once it has started. Instead, I parse the cases at countries with nuclear capacity. This is similar to the empirical strategy in Bas and Coe 2017.

[9] Note that the potential proliferator does *not* face a commitment problem here. As later chapters will show, it is willing to accept concessions, even if it could freely proliferate after receiving a bribe.

TABLE 1.2. *List of Nuclear-Proficient Countries and the Year They Achieved Proficiency*

Country	Year	Country	Year
Germany	1939	Finland	1964
United States	1939	Portugal	1964
United Kingdom	1941	Turkey	1964
Soviet Union/Russia	1943	Bulgaria	1967
Canada	1944	Colombia	1967
Japan	1944	Greece	1967
France	1945	Venezuela	1967
Sweden	1948	Netherlands	1969
India	1949	Thailand	1969
Yugoslavia/Serbia	1953	Mexico	1970
Norway	1954	Iran	1972
China	1955	Pakistan	1972
Israel	1955	South Africa	1974
Australia	1956	Iraq	1975
Switzerland	1957	Chile	1976
Belgium	1958	Indonesia	1980
Brazil	1959	Peru	1980
Czechoslovakia	1959	Philippines	1980
East Germany	1959	Algeria	1983
Romania	1959	North Korea	1983
West Germany	1959	Bangladesh	1988
Argentina	1960	Belarus	1992
Poland	1960	Kazakhstan	1992
Spain	1960	Ukraine	1992
Hungary	1961	Lithuania	1992
Italy	1961	Slovenia	1992
Austria	1962	Czech Republic	1993
South Korea	1962	Uzbekistan	1995
Egypt	1963	Slovakia	1996
Taiwan	1963	Syria	2000
Denmark	1964		

However, because weak rivals have incentive to bluff, the potential proliferator sometimes challenges the status quo.

Third, imperfect information has mixed effects. If the rival cannot monitor the potential proliferator's decision to build, the potential proliferator faces great temptation to defect from a deal. When the cost of proliferation is high, the opponent prefers overpaying the potential proliferator to ensure compliance. In contrast, when the cost of proliferation is low, the required overpayment becomes too large.

Instead, the opponent sometimes launches preventive war to quash the nuclear option. Both parties are worse off in the second case. Consequently, potential proliferators benefit from voluntarily *increasing* their costs of nuclear weapons, whether through divestment, inspection regimes, or domestic constraints.

1.2 ALTERNATIVE EXPLANATIONS AND WHY THEY ARE INSUFFICIENT

My theory draws on previous state-level explanations for proliferation. The model confirms many existing necessary conditions for nuclear development. However, it also shows that some conditions the literature currently believes are sufficient fall short. In sum, conventional wisdom (Sagan 1996, 57–61; Debs and Monteiro 2017) holds that the following assumptions explain proliferation behavior:

1. Nuclear weapons increase a state's coercive power.
2. There is a zero-sum point of contention between a state and a rival.
3. The costs of proliferation are smaller than the coercive power gained by proliferating.
4. Preventive war is not a viable option.

The first two components form the backbone of most security-based explanations for proliferation. If nuclear weapons do not increase coercive power, then they are merely a radiation threat to their possessors. Fortunately, a long literature dating back to Schelling (1960, 187–204) suggests that states are more likely to back down on an issue when facing a nuclear-armed opponent. More recent empirical evidence indicates that nuclear-weapons states prevail more often in conflict (Beardsley and Asal 2009). And even critics who argue that nuclear weapons provide little to no compellent power still believe in their deterrent power (Sechser and Fuhrmann 2013, 177–178).[10]

Likewise, if a state is not involved in a coercive bargaining relationship today and does not expect to be at a later date, then there is no reason to invest in nuclear weapons. This is the "demand side" of nuclear proliferation. States with protracted disputes or enduring rivalries participate in proliferation behaviors (Singh and Way 2004; Jo and Gartzke 2007). Thayer (1995, 486) goes further, concluding that "security is the only necessary and sufficient cause of nuclear proliferation." Alternatively,

[10] I further explore the coercive power of nuclear weapons in the next chapter.

proliferation is just another form of "internal balancing" against external threats (Lavoy 1993, 196).

Recent research has paired the traditional security explanations with practical and political barriers. These form the cost component. Indeed, "supply side" theories recognize the high price of nuclear weapons and see technological hurdles as major determinants of nonproliferation. Countries with lower levels of nuclear proficiency are less likely to pursue nuclear weapons (Jo and Gartzke 2007; Smith and Spaniel 2018), especially if no status quo nuclear power offers assistance (Kroenig 2009a; Kroenig 2009b; Kroenig 2010; Fuhrmann 2008; Fuhrmann 2009). Low-proficiency countries can overcome their technological barriers, but they still will not do so when the ultimate bang is not worth the buck.

Domestic political explanations for proliferation fit into a broader conceptualization of the cost of nuclear weapons. Pure technical capability must be paired with competent program management, which takes some countries out of the proliferation equation (Hymans 2012; Braut-Hegghammer 2016). Leaders who care little about international economic integration are more willing to bear the opportunity costs of nuclear weapons than outward-looking regimes (Solingen 2007). Likewise, countries with normative aversions to nuclear weapons have a higher perceived cost of proliferation (Tannenwald 1999; Rublee 2009). In contrast, leaders with oppositionalist psychological profiles take threats more seriously and therefore internalize the costs of proliferation at lower values (Hymans 2006). If a state falls on the wrong side of each of these issues, they may find the price of nuclear weapons too large relative to the benefits and therefore decide against proliferation.

The final component delves deeper into strategic interactions in the shadow of nuclear weapons. For the proliferation process to run its course, the developing state must have some minimal ability to defend itself. Otherwise, recognizing the disadvantageous shift in power to come, the opponent would launch preventive war. Internalizing the threat, the potential proliferator passes on nuclear weapons (Debs and Monteiro 2014). Combining these components together, Debs and Monteiro (2017, 66) thus state that "high relative power is, together with a high level of threat, sufficient to cause proliferation."

I incorporate all of these components in my main model. However, the model demonstrates that these assumptions are *not* sufficient to explain proliferation. To be explicit, suppose a country faces an intense, zero-sum security issue, as the traditional, realist theories of proliferation require. Imagine that country is technologically proficient and can properly manage the process. Furthermore, it does not care about international economic integration, taboos against nuclear weapons, or the standards the nonproliferation regime promotes. It can also defend itself from preventive strikes. According to the literature, this is the perfect storm for proliferation. Yet I show that there is still no reason that the parties cannot bargain their way out of the proliferation problem.

What does the literature miss? In truth, many scholars have laid the groundwork for bargaining over nuclear weapons. Indeed, the works of Reiss (1988; 1995), Paul (2000), Rublee (2009), and Volpe (2017) all incorporate negotiations and policy concessions into theories for why countries ranging from Argentina to Ukraine to South Korea have passed on the nuclear path. This suggests bargained settlements are sometimes possible. But negotiations sometimes fail. Unfortunately, these works cannot distinguish whether bargaining fails because (1) no mutually preferable settlements exist or (2) such mutually preferable settlements exist but for whatever reason the parties do not reach one.

Much as Fearon (1995) showed the existence of agreements that are mutually preferable to war, formalizing the problem will help verify the existence of mutually preferable nonproliferation settlements. Of course, this book is not the first work to formalize power shifts and negotiations in the shadow of nuclear proliferation. However, in trying to answer the above question, three issues with the formal literature stand out. First, many previous models of shifting power have focused on the outbreak of war as the dependent variable of interest. In fact, the original models of shifting power treat the process as exogenous (Fearon 1995; Powell 1999; Powell 2006; Bas and Coe 2012). The decision to construct arms does not appear in these models, and thus they provide no leverage in explaining what causes states to develop nuclear weapons.

Chadefaux (2011) critiqued the exogenous setup and noted that states have the ability to negotiate over future distributions of power. However, many papers in this endogenous-power-shifts literature maintained war as their dependent variable of interest (Debs and Monteiro 2014; Jelnov, Tauman, and Zeckhauser 2017). This has been useful in explaining inefficient conflicts. When states have the ability to limit their future strength, preventive war is less likely – states simply develop in a manner so as to convince others not to stop them militarily.[11]

---

[11] Fearon (1996) provides the closest exception. However, in his model, power is inherently tied to the bargaining good and not produced as a part of an inefficient process. The focus here is on why states might produce power given that efficiency.

However, this focus has resulted in a second issue. Models of war make predictions about proliferation behaviors as well. But the robustness of those proliferation results are a secondary concern. Whether those results withstand assumptions geared toward the dynamics of weapons negotiations has not been well studied.

That said, Bas and Coe (2016; 2017) focus specifically on proliferation as their dependent variable. But like Debs and Monteiro (2014), the main interest is in understanding how the threat of preventive war interacts with a declining state's inability to observe a proliferator's investment decision. Deals can occur in these models. However, the direct inefficiency of nuclear weapons plays no role. Indeed, in both of these papers, Bas and Coe assume that the cost of nuclear weapons is free.[12]

Nevertheless, this is the third issue with the current literature. Preventive war is not always a credible threat. Many nuclear negotiations transpire under conditions when preventive war will not occur in the absence of a deal. For example, when the USA bargained with Japan and South Korea during the Cold War, it would not have plausibly launched a military strike against its own allies to stop nuclear development. Meanwhile, in the midst of an economic recovery following World War II, American policymakers believed that a preventive war to stop the Soviet Union's nuclear ambitions was either impractical or too costly (Silverstone 2007, 51–75).

This may not spell doom for deals, however. The cost of weapons alone may open up a bargaining range that could result in an agreement. In fact, Debs and Monteiro (2014) include the cost of weapons in their model and encounter the effect in an extension.[13] And the many of the aforementioned scholars have also recognized the importance of bargaining over weapons on an *ad hoc* basis (Reiss 1988; Paul 2000; Levite 2003; Rublee 2009; Rabinowitz 2014; Volpe 2017).

Taking stock, the literature has handled nuclear agreements in a piecemeal fashion. No existing work brings together the disparate concepts central to nuclear bargains. The security benefits of proliferation, the cost of nuclear weapons, the strategic dependence between proliferator and opponent, credible commitment, and information problems all need to be treated together. Without that, we do not have a complete picture

---

12 This is not a criticism of the assumption. Bas and Coe acknowledge that nuclear weapons are costly in practice. Rather, they make the assumption to show that their mechanism functions in a world where the nuclear weapons are costless.

13 See pages 7–8 of their appendix.

to understand whether and how these deals work. I bring these elements together and find that agreements succeed despite many the many hurdles that stand in the way, though some bargaining problems can lead to negotiations breaking down.

As a final note, other explanations for proliferation exist outside of the state-level framework. My findings do not diminish their importance: leaders, principal-agent problems, and domestic constraints all influence proliferation behaviors.[14] Nevertheless, exploring state-level explanations in isolation is still fruitful for two reasons. First, if leaders weigh personal gains versus state interest, state-level results still apply (to varying degrees) when domestic forces return to the model (Slantchev 2011, 9–10). Second, and perhaps more compelling, principal-agent problems may be the source of commitment problems or incomplete information, which later chapters integrate into the bargaining environment.

1.3 ROADMAP

Going forward, I use game-theoretical models to understand the origins of nuclear proliferation. Formalization is particularly useful for this subject for three reasons. First, bargaining is a key determinant of nuclear behaviors. However, the logic of bargaining can grow convoluted quickly; formal modeling provides "accounting standards" that ensure claims maintain internal validity (Powell 1999, 29–34).

Second, few states have ever made serious attempts to proliferate; even fewer have actually acquired a nuclear weapon. This poses a problem for cross-validation, especially for an outcome that occurs through many causal pathways. For example, we cannot easily verify the logic of a theory for the Soviet Union's decision to proliferate by process-tracing a second case. Formal theory again mitigates the problem through its accounting standards.

Third, nuclear programs are closely guarded state secrets (Levite 2003, 64–66). This creates two sub-issues. For opposing states, it means having to act without the knowledge of the other side's intended behavior. Modeling these dynamics helps avoid the "Robinson Crusoe" fallacy, in which analysts overlook how changing one player's incentives has a second-order effect on another's behavior (Tsebelis 1989). For scholars of international politics, secrecy creates a discrepancy between the analyst and behemoth intelligence organizations. Formal theory resolves

---

[14] See Sagan 1996; Fuhrmann and Horowitz 2015; Way and Weeks 2014.

some of these issues by elucidating states' incentives given a commonly understood set of assumptions.

In sum, models do not provide a perfect solution to all of the challenges facing a scholar of nuclear proliferation. But they do give a useful starting point for the analysis. I thus accompany the formal models with case studies throughout the chapters. These case studies serve a number of purposes. Primarily, they motivate the formal theory; without them, the numerical excursions are cumbersome, opaque mathematical expositions. With them, game theory answers critical questions about foreign policy. Understanding why Iran sought nuclear weapons, for example, first requires recognition of its strategic constraints. The models show that an opponent's inability to commit to concessions often drives nuclear development, not irrational belligerence from the potential proliferator.

Next, the case studies provide new explanations for historical proliferation and preventive war behaviors. For example, the Soviet Union's decision to proliferate in 1949 seems to be an obvious byproduct of rising Cold War tensions. Likewise, Israel's strike on Iraq's nascent nuclear reactor appears to be a straightforward cost-benefit analysis of allowing the program to continue versus intervening. Applying the logic of the formal models raises strong objections to the validity of these and other theories. Simultaneously, the models produce compelling alternative mechanisms.

Finally, the case studies illustrate the underlying logic of the formal models. Game theory provides wonderful accounting standards but often lacks straightforward application. Consequently, each model has a corresponding case study that operationalizes critical explanatory variables. These case studies make a plausible argument that states behaved as the models predict. In essence, they serve as an existence test of the models by plausibly demonstrating that the logical constructs have real world applications.

To that end, this book's discussion of the successes and failures of nuclear negotiations consists of eight additional chapters. The next chapter explores some of the idiosyncracies of nuclear weapons. I pay careful attention to their costs, their technological challenges, and the barriers to using them coercively. The last of these is a particular challenge. The standard bargaining model of war (Fearon 1995) often conceptualizes the ability to win concessions in war as the probability of victory. Yet some scholars (e.g., Sechser and Fuhrmann 2017) cast doubt on whether countries can use nuclear weapons in a compellent manner.

Fortunately, I show that the probability of victory in these models is equivalent to the average outcome of war, and thus traditional nuclear deterrence theories have sway over that value. This allows me to unlock the bargaining model of war as a tool to analyze the broader issue of bargaining over nuclear weapons.

The third chapter introduces the core theory of the book. Without bargaining frictions, I show that only three outcomes occur when states negotiate over nuclear weapons. First, if the threat to proliferate is not credible – either because an opponent would launch a preventive strike or the cost of nuclear weapons is large – the potential proliferator receives no concessions. If proliferation is a reasonable option but the costs are still prohibitive, an opponent offers immediate concessions and convinces the potential proliferator to pass on nuclear weapons. Proliferation only occurs when the threat to obtain nuclear weapons is credible and the costs are low. But even then, potential proliferators have incentive to increase the cost of nuclear weapons to avoid this outcome.

Broadly, the main theory claims that the potential to build nuclear weapons is good enough to win concessions from an opponent. Is there any large-n statistical evidence to support this assertion? The fourth chapter looks at target behavior during militarized interstate disputes. If a target worries that resistance today might cause proliferation tomorrow and a dispute under worse terms, it might not reciprocate the initiator's belligerence. Indeed, this holds quantitatively: states with high levels of nuclear proficiency are about 26 percent more likely to induce their opponents to back down than states with low levels.

Statistical evidence is useful for establishing general trends. However, it lacks the fine-grained diplomacy of individual case studies, and it cannot show what mechanism drives the results. Thus, the fifth chapter reviews the success of butter-for-bombs negotiations in practice. Specifically, the chapter applies the theory to Egypt, a set of American Cold War allies (Japan, South Korea, and Australia), and the nuclear-proficient Soviet successor states (Belarus, Kazakhstan, and Ukraine). Each of these countries had nuclear temptations. But other actors offered concessions and convinced them to forgo the possibility, just as the butter-for-bombs model predicts.

Combined, Chapters 3, 4, and 5 create a proliferation puzzle that the remainder of the book addresses. Chapter 6 investigates the stability of nonproliferation agreements in the shadow of war exhaustion. Proliferation opponents sometimes fluctuate in their resolve to handle various international crises. This opens up windows of opportunity for nuclear development. Indeed, potential proliferators may choose to build today if they expect that their opponent will launch preventive war at a later date. The opponent's inability to credibly promise future concessions sabotages arms deals in the present. I illustrate the mechanism using the Soviet Union's decision to proliferate in 1949.

Chapter 7 transitions to information-based explanations, beginning with when an opponent cannot monitor a potential proliferator's decision to build. Without bargaining over weapons, this uncertainty leads to preventive wars and nuclear development (Debs and Monteiro 2014; Jelnov, Tauman, and Zeckhauser 2017). However, incorporating butter-for-bombs bargaining allows the opponent to sidestep the monitoring problem by making generous offers. Negotiations only fail when the extent of the power shift is great. But even then the parties mutually benefit from raising the costs of proliferation. This helps explain the features of many arms agreements, including the Iran Deal. It also suggests that weapons inspections may be less about providing information and more about creating a nuisance for potential noncompliance.

The eighth chapter introduces uncertainty regarding the cost of preventive war. Even when preventive war is unattractive, opponents might offer no concessions, hoping that the possibility of a strike will induce compliance from the potential proliferator. However, due to incentives to misrepresent, the potential proliferator sometimes challenges its opponent by investing in nuclear weapons. Thus, investment occurs even though the opponent would retroactively prefer a butter-for-bombs deal. The chapter then traces the logic using Operation Opera, Israel's 1981 raid on an Iraqi nuclear reactor.

The ninth chapter concludes the book, highlighting overall lessons, investigating policy implications, exploring the generality of the models, and discussing future challenges for the nonproliferation regime.

2

How Are Nuclear Weapons Special?

The previous chapter made the case for negotiating to disincentivize proliferation. Later chapters will speak to the validity of that argument. Before advancing there, however, this book must carefully consider the important features of bargaining over nuclear weapons. After all, models only scrutinize the logical consistency of an argument; they cannot speak to the empirical usefulness of the interaction analyzed. This chapter therefore details the critical moving parts of negotiations that I include in the models.

Readers will recognize that nuclear weapons share characteristics with many other types of weapons programs. Thus, the assumptions I argue for below will apply to negotiations beyond nuclear proliferation to varying degrees. Identifying similarities across strategic scenarios is one of the best reasons to use game theory, and I welcome readers to think beyond the nuclear realm. Nevertheless, a variety of factors have led to the development of a nonproliferation regime especially worried about nuclear weapons. Consequently, I highlight these features of proliferation below.

Three topics drive the discussion. I begin by describing the direct costs of nuclear weapons; these create large inefficiencies that states can negotiate over. Second, I discuss the technological idiosyncracies of nuclear development. Finally, I explore how the standard bargaining model of war can incorporate deterrent power into its parameters.

2.1 THE COST OF NUCLEAR WEAPONS

As noted in the introduction, nuclear weapons are extremely expensive. For the moment, cast aside the costs a potential proliferator may incur in the event that an opponent initiates a preventive war. These are sizeable and include the lost capital of the program, military personnel and scientists who die in a strike, and any economic instability that results from a dispute. I return to these in the next chapter. Instead, consider four facts that illustrate the enormous *direct* costs of proliferation:

- The United States spent $8.9 trillion on its program from 1940 to 1996 (Schwartz 1998).[1]
- This was 11% of the United States' federal budget over that time period.[2]
- The only governmental programs that cost more were conventional military spending (across many different programs) and Social Security.
- There are implicit (and large) costs that these estimates exclude.

Readers may not have expected such a high price given that many potential proliferators tout a low cost of development. Given the bargaining framework I develop below, it is unsurprising that states underreport their estimated proliferation cost. The deals that opponents make in part incorporate this development cost; intuitively, the more nuclear weapons cost, the less opponents need to offer to satisfy the potential proliferator. Potential proliferators consequently have incentive to claim that nuclear weapons are cheaper than they actually are. It is therefore worth explaining the discrepancy.

Nuclear weapons and their direct infrastructure comprise the majority of the total cost of proliferation. Estimates of nuclear proliferation tend to speak exclusively to the creation of an explosive atomic reaction. But even then, creating a nuclear arsenal is not cheap. The United States spent $622 billion on its efforts. And this is purely a line-item expenditure. A true social price would also factor in the opportunity cost of development. Given that a successful nuclear program usually requires the brightest scientific minds a country has to offer, the foregone gains could be substantial.

Nevertheless, development costs pale in comparison to the price of delivery. Strategically, the creation of a nuclear explosion means little

---

[1] I calculate these figures in constant 2016 dollars. Schwartz uses constant 1996 dollars, to which I apply a 53.6% cumulative rate of inflation to reach the 2016 amounts. About a sixth of Schwartz's figure is for nuclear defense. It is unclear how much one should include this in the price of proliferation.

[2] By comparison, the Netherlands' entire government spending is roughly 11% of American expenditures.

compared to the capability to offensively deliver it. Deployment requires a second program to develop the appropriate technology. And unlike the construction of a bomb, deployment is not a one-time expense: a nuclear-weapons state has to consistently pay to maintain the capability. In that light, it is unsurprising that American expenditures on deployment, targeting, and command and control totaled ten times the cost of building the bomb (Schwartz 1998, 4).[3]

The above summarized realized costs that the United States has paid. It does not account for three types of hidden costs also worth discussing. First is disposal. As the American arsenal ages, at some point the nuclear materials will need to be retired. This requires careful planning given the radioactive hazards. Schwartz (1998, 3) estimates that this adds another $492 billion to the price tag.[4] This aspect of the costs of proliferation has received greater attention in the twenty-first century due to fears that a terrorist organization could acquire nuclear materials and construct a dirty bomb.

The risk of accident is more concerning. Although the United States has gone more than seven decades without major incident, there have been a number of close calls; a US Department of Defense study found 32 accidents involving nuclear infrastructure from 1950 to 1980 alone.[5] Near-misses come in two flavors: domestic disasters and unintentional nuclear war. Domestic risks are usually the result of transit failures. If failsafes break down, civilians on the ground face danger. International risks have graver implications. Throughout the Cold War, officials in both the East and West remained on high alert, knowing that the other side could launch an attack in minutes, leaving little time to identify it and select a response.[6] The result could be a mistaken nuclear counterattack. This is a serious issue. Pessimists estimate that the odds of such an

---

[3] Part of what drives these high costs is the large scope of the American program. Although a potential proliferator could save on the cost by developing a few dozen bombs (as opposed to a few thousand), this would also reduce the impact on the balance of power. Also note that the United States' superior industrial capacity has facilitated an easier route to its nuclear arsenal. A state trying to replicate the American effort may have to spend a large amount just to catch up to that point.

[4] Time discounting reduces the price of this at the moment of construction.

[5] https://nsarchive.files.wordpress.com/2010/04/635.pdf.

[6] The 1983 Soviet false alarm is emblematic of this problem. On September 26, a Soviet early warning installation misinterpreted reflecting sunlight as an incoming intercontinental ballistic missile. The timing invited suspicion: a few weeks after the Soviet Union shot down Korean Air Lines Flight 007, killing US Congressman Larry McDonald. Fortunately, Stanislav Petrov, the officer overseeing the installation, opted to not inform his superiors, against orders (Scott 2011, 770).

accident during the Cold War were greater than 50% (Lundgren 2013). Because non-nuclear states do not face this risk, the expected loss is thus an additional implicit cost of proliferation.[7]

Overall, then, the financial costs of nuclear weapons are considerable. But the claim of this section is not that nuclear weapons are so expensive that no state would rationally build them. Ten states have, and numerous others have spent large sums to bring themselves closer to proliferation. Rather, the takeaway here is that the cost of nuclear weapons incentivizes states to negotiate. Although the same incentives exist for cheaper weapons programs, the huge price means that the inefficiency is more likely to trump domestic hurdles, bureaucratic issues, and transaction costs. And although the proliferator primarily pays for the weapons, bargaining looks equally attractive to their opponents, as these opponents could potentially extract a large surplus through negotiations.

2.2 THE TECHNOLOGICAL IDIOSYNCRACIES OF NUCLEAR WEAPONS

Despite the potential for massive efficiency gains, agreements on nuclear weapons pose challenges unique to the technology. Yet, on further inspection, some of these peculiarities further incentivize agreements.

First, without any advanced research and development, a non-nuclear state is unlikely to proliferate over the course of a war.[8] If a state could quickly put together a nuclear weapon after rejecting its opponent's offer and starting a war, proliferation is no different than drafting an army and sending them to combat. There would be no opportunity to launch preventive war and no period of vulnerability that the opponent could exploit. The standard bargaining model of war tells us everything we need to know: the probability of victory incorporates the forthcoming nuclear arsenal, and the states adjust their bargaining strategies accordingly.

However, nuclear weapons do not function like this for most states. If a country wishes to proliferate, it must outlay a substantial budget to the project, wait for its scientists to overcome various challenges and

---

[7] Of course, part of the budget for command and control intends to limit the chances of such an accident. But even well-intending agents make mistakes, and creating incentive structures to eliminate all risk of accident is impossible. Thus, there are limits to safety (Sagan 1993).

[8] The United States is an obvious counterexample, but it is also the exception that proves the rule: it proliferated during the bloodiest war in history, spent years on the project, succeeded where other states had failed, and was the most technologically sophisticated country in the world.

technological hurdles, and hope that no opponent targets the operation in the meantime. Put simply, nuclear weapons are an investment in the future, giving states a large period of time in between to negotiate an alternative solution.

Second, the scientific progression toward nuclear weapons perversely promotes preventive war. Proliferation is a concentrated enterprise. Successful programs gather a country's top scientists and engineers into clustered locations. Once there, they spend years developing precise machinery to lay the groundwork for a weaponized atom. Duplicating these procedures is not usually feasible, due to both costs and lack of qualified researchers. A single, well-targeted operation against a nuclear installation can therefore delay a proliferator for years or decades. Indeed, Israel has executed two such missions, bombing an Iraqi facility in 1981 and a Syrian facility in 2007.[9] In the present day, a single computer virus like Stuxnet can cause major setbacks as well.

The potential for preventive war therefore creates a second, indirect cost for pursing a nuclear weapon. Failure to reach an agreement – and build credible enforcement mechanisms for it – means that a potential proliferator could pay an investment cost only for the program to go up in smoke. This outcome may be better than the alternative for the opposing state, but it also has to pay the cost for the preventive strike. In turn, both sides may wish to find a negotiated solution.

Yet the small footprint of some modern nuclear programs can create monitoring problems for opposing states. If intelligence is poor, a proliferator could work toward a nuclear weapon without its opponent's knowledge (Debs and Monteiro 2014). Even if a rival state can identify nuclear facilities, it may still struggle to understand what is happening there. Iran, for example, built its Fordow nuclear facility under a mountain. At its core, this is the classic "dual use" dilemma in nuclear technology. Countries wanting to pursue peaceful nuclear technologies take similar steps as those with more nefarious endgames. Thus, it is a challenge to know whether a potential nuclear state is complying with nonproliferation norms. An opponent could mistakenly fight a preventive war against a state not actively proliferating. Ironically, this in turn justifies a state's decision to build military fortifications around their nuclear facilities, even if there is no intent to weaponize the technology.

---

[9] Along these lines, the United States chose Los Alamos National Laboratory as key site for the Manhattan Project because the surrounding highlands were suitable for defensive fortifications for the lab.

These monitoring challenges would seem to doom agreements entirely. But to the contrary, they encourage states to reach more expansive agreements to overcome the problem. The International Atomic Energy Agency's budget dwarfs other international organizations geared toward disarmament, and providing information is one of the IAEA's main responsibilities. This suggests that potential private proliferation does not doom negotiations. Yet it also creates additional complications, as states must not only negotiate over nuclear weapons and the policy in contention but also the extent of the IAEA's activities.

2.3 LEVERAGING NUCLEAR WEAPONS

The nuances of nuclear weapons continue once a country has obtained a functioning bomb. Ostensibly, states with nuclear weapons perform better in military conflicts than without. By virtue of this additional strength, nuclear possessors therefore fare better in negotiated settlements than those without. International relations scholars have converged on the bargaining model of war (Fearon 1995) as a useful theoretical tool to analyze this type of coercion in the shadow of conflict. It would therefore be useful to adopt the framework as the book pushes forward for two reasons. From a practical perspective, doing so will facilitate comparisons with existing results. And from a theoretical perspective, negotiations allow states to endogenously choose offers; thus, such models avoid situations where conflict occurs due to some sort of indivisibility built into the game's extensive form.

However, there is an issue with this approach. One of the central parameters in the bargaining model of war is a state's probability of victory. Let this probability be p_R for the potential rising state. How this term interacts with nuclear weapons may or may not be problematic. On the non-problematic side, many scholars believe that nuclear weapons have direct military value in terms of a country's ability to win a conflict. That is, nuclear weapons behave much like conventional weapons and *compel* other states to give concessions.

Many mechanisms can lead to this conclusion. One is the sheer destructive force of nuclear weapons – they can decimate an opponent's infrastructure and beat them into submission. A second mechanism is "brinkmanship," escalating crises and increasing the likelihood of an unavoidable nuclear strike against military or civilian targets. Although such threats are difficult to make credible, the "threat that leaves something to chance" nevertheless encourages rivals to give up during a conflict and end the possibility of disaster. Moreover, because nuclear weapons are so destructive, the likelihood of quitting may be high even if the chance of nuclear disaster is small at any given time.[10] And more generally, Beardsley and Asal (2009) find empirical support for nuclear-weapons states prevailing more often in conflict. The overall takeaway from this perspective is that nuclear weapons create direct military benefits and allow their possessors to win wars more frequently.

Operationalizing all of these mechanisms into the bargaining model of war is easy: give a country nuclear weapons, and its probability of victory will be higher afterward than beforehand.

A second perspective is skeptical of whether nuclear weapons have direct military value in a confrontation between two states. Instead, they theorize that nuclear weapons only *deter* rivals; in other words, proliferation is merely useful in preserving the status quo.[11] Using nuclear weapons to directly win a war is challenging because they lack tactical applications (Sechser and Fuhrmann 2013, 177–178). For example, because nuclear explosions poison the surrounding land with radiation, a state cannot credibly threaten a nuclear attack on an enemy occupying a valuable territory. This forces the aggressor to instead utilize countervalue strategies; namely, a nuclear-weapons state could threaten to bomb its rival's capital unless the rival surrenders the land. But given the taboo against nuclear weapons (Tannenwald 1999), such countervalue strikes strain credulity according to this line of thought due to the risk of international backlash. These nuclear skeptics also have some support among policymakers (Trachtenberg 1985, 137).

How to operationalize the deterrent power of nuclear weapons in the bargaining model of war is unclear, especially as war itself is a black box in these models. Opening up that black box may provide some answers but could imply something very different from a shift in the probability of victory.

Taking stock, this debate is problematic because it seemingly forces the modeler to make a decision. Are nuclear weapons useful for increasing the probability of victory? Or are they only useful for deterrence? A

---

[10] This literature is extensive. Schelling (1960, 187–204) gave the first discussion of brinkmanship and threats left to chance. Other theorists have refined the concept (Jervis 1989; Powell 1987; Powell 1988; Powell 1989; Powell 1990), but a common theme remains: nuclear weapons force concessions. And outside of the theoretical literature, policy makers have believed that nuclear compellance is an important bargaining strategy (Gaddis 1987, 108–110; Truman 1955, 87).

[11] Compellence and deterrence date back to Schelling (1960, 193–199; 1966, 69–72).

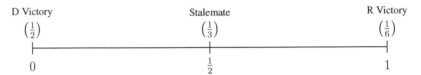

FIGURE 2.1. Outcome Probabilities for a Hypothetical War

model that speaks to one side might not speak to the other, forcing the modeler to develop two separate theories or risk alienating one side of the debate.

Fortunately, a simple reinterpretation of p_R resolves the dilemma. Rather than think of this as a probability of victory, it is more precisely the *average outcome of war*. Despite having a substantively different meaning, these two conceptualizations are mathematically identical. And unlike the probability of victory, it is easy to see how deterrent power can have an effect on how a war may end.

A simple numerical example will help illustrate the connection. Suppose bargaining has broken down between a rising state named R and a declining state named D. In accordance with the standard model, they fight a war over a strip of territory standardized to value 1. Imagine three outcomes are possible: (1) R completely defeats D militarily, (2) D completely defeats R militarily, or (3) the parties fight to a stalemate. In the first two cases, the winner is free to divide the strip of territory in any manner; naturally, without any other relevant considerations, the winner will take everything and leave the loser with nothing.[12] In the case of a stalemate, both sides split the territory evenly.

For further concreteness, as Figure 2.1 illustrates, suppose D wins with probability $\frac{1}{2}$, R wins with probability $\frac{1}{6}$, and the sides draw the remaining $\frac{1}{3}$ of the time. That information is sufficient to calculate each side's expected territorial share from war. In particular, each side simply receives the weighted average of each outcome. Thus, D's expected share equals:

$$\underbrace{\left(\frac{1}{2}\right)(1)}_{\text{D Wins}} + \underbrace{\left(\frac{1}{3}\right)\left(\frac{1}{2}\right)}_{\text{Stalemate}} + \underbrace{\left(\frac{1}{6}\right)(0)}_{\text{R Wins}} = \frac{2}{3}$$

---

[12] In practice, states sometimes do not consume all of the pie freely available to them (Spaniel and Bils 2018; Bils and Spaniel 2018). But as the stalemate case helps demonstrate, the key results would not change if a state made such a decision.

And R's expected share equals:

$$\underbrace{\left(\frac{1}{2}\right)(0)}_{\text{D Wins}} + \underbrace{\left(\frac{1}{3}\right)\left(\frac{1}{2}\right)}_{\text{Stalemate}} + \underbrace{\left(\frac{1}{6}\right)(1)}_{\text{R Wins}} = \frac{1}{3}$$

So D receives two-thirds of the territory and R receives the remaining one-third on average. But in terms of *expected* outcomes, this is equivalent to saying that D wins the entire war with probability $\frac{2}{3}$ and takes the entire good, while R wins with probability $\frac{1}{3}$ and captures all of the territory.

Now consider a world in which R develops nuclear weapons. Consistent with research that is skeptical of nuclear weapons' ability to win wars, suppose the probability each side wins or stalemate occurs remains static. However, upon militarily defeating R, D's leadership must decide where to draw the new border. Whereas before D could occupy the territory in its entirety, nuclear weapons complicate the issue by forcing R to limit its war aims. As Schelling (1966, 36) notes, "the difference between the national homeland and everything 'abroad' is the difference between threats that are inherently credible, even if unspoken, and the threats that have to be made credible."[13] In general, credible deterrence at home is easier than credible deterrence abroad.

Along those lines, despite being skeptical of nuclear compellent threats, Sechser and Fuhrmann (2013, 177–178) take a moderate position overall:

[It is not] that nuclear threats can never be credible: a state facing imminent conquest, for example, probably would be willing to pay the [international backlash] costs of inflicting nuclear punishment in order to defend itself. Nuclear deterrent threats therefore may be credible, particularly when one's survival is at risk.

In turn, if D conquered all of R's territory, suppose R could credibly retaliate with a nuclear strike. D would be better off maximizing its territorial gains without exceeding R's level of tolerance.[14] In other words,

---

[13] See also Quester 1989 (63) and Zagare and Kilgour 2000 (305).

[14] An alternative interpretation is that the more D conquers, the higher the chance R will inadvertently launch a nuclear weapon, perhaps because invasion leaves forces in a "now or never" position. In this case, D's maximization problem compares the value of another portion of land relative to the likelihood and cost of suffering nuclear devastation. Even if an accidental strike is very unlikely, the costs to a conquerer would be enormous, especially if the weapon struck its capital city or other highly populated area. This would lead the conquerer to be conservative in its territorial ambitions.

D must limit its war aims, similar to how Egypt limited its aims to the Sinai Peninsula in the Yom Kippur War and in contrast to wars before Israel had developed a nuclear deterrent (Paul 1995, 707; Solingen 2007, 189). Although this level of tolerance could theoretically be anywhere on the interval, suppose for the sake of simplicity that it is at $\frac{1}{2}$, the same division as a stalemate. Now winning the war becomes less valuable for D because it can no longer take the entire interval. Thus, its expected share drops to:

$$\underbrace{\left(\frac{1}{2}\right)\left(\frac{1}{2}\right)}_{\text{D Wins}} + \underbrace{\left(\frac{1}{3}\right)\left(\frac{1}{2}\right)}_{\text{Stalemate}} + \underbrace{\left(\frac{1}{6}\right)(0)}_{\text{R Wins}} = \frac{5}{12}$$

Meanwhile, because R never incurs its worst outcome, R's expected share jumps to:

$$\underbrace{\left(\frac{1}{2}\right)\left(\frac{1}{2}\right)}_{\text{D Wins}} + \underbrace{\left(\frac{1}{3}\right)\left(\frac{1}{2}\right)}_{\text{Stalemate}} + \underbrace{\left(\frac{1}{6}\right)(1)}_{\text{R Wins}} = \frac{7}{12}$$

As such, D now receives five-twelfths of the territory and R receives the remaining seven-twelfths in expectation. Thus, R receives more of the good – with the difference between $\frac{7}{12}$ and $\frac{1}{3}$ representing R's favorable shift in power. But, for risk-neutral states, this is equivalent to saying that D wins and takes the entire good with probability $\frac{5}{12}$ and R wins and takes the entire good with probability $\frac{7}{12}$.

In sum, both assumptions map to the same formalization. For either case, developing a nuclear weapon allows R to capture more through war. How exactly this happens – whether by changing the direct probability of victory or altering the terms of post-war implementations – is an interesting empirical and tactical question. Despite the apparent equivalency, no claim here suggests that researchers ought to stop pursuing these topics. Indeed, firmer answers for the deterrence versus compellence debate is necessary to understand which states would benefit the most from proliferating and what types of crises are most open to nuclear coercion. Other strategic factors may lead to similar connections as well.[15] These are critical questions for both scholars and policymakers alike.

---

[15] For example, Brands and Palkki (2011) argue that Saddam Hussein wanted a nuclear arsenal to cancel out Israeli atomic threats similar to the implementation problem described here.

From a bargaining standpoint, however, all this is irrelevant. Through whatever mechanism, having nuclear weapons means that R needs a larger share of a peaceful settlement to be satisfied. Indeed, there may be other causal pathways that allow a nuclear possessor to capture more of the good in expectation and leave the opponent with less. The bottom line is that the standard crisis bargaining model implicitly covers all types of nuclear coercion of that sort by rethinking the probability of victory as the average share captured through war.[16]

Later chapters therefore adopt the average outcome interpretation, and the next chapter uses these findings to develop a theory of bargaining over nuclear weapons.

---

[16] Because the second interpretation is broader, this chapter indicates it should be the standard interpretation of p. Some researchers already use this convention. See Arena and Wolford 2012, Arena and Bak 2015, and Arena and Hardt 2014.

3

The Theory of Butter-for-Bombs Agreements: How Potential Power Coerces Concessions

This chapter pivots to the book's central question: can negotiated settlements convince potential proliferators to forgo nuclear weapons? Many policymakers and political commentators are skeptical. For example, in a 2010 op-ed for the *Wall Street Journal*, former United Nations Ambassador John Bolton (now National Security Advisor) outlined a bleak forecast for negotiations with Iran: "There are only two options: Iran gets nuclear weapons, or someone uses pre-emptive military force to break Iran's nuclear fuel cycle and paralyze its program, at least temporarily" (Bolton 2010). Conservative commentator Charles Krauthammer offered a blunter assessment: "There is zero chance any such talks will denuclearize Iran" (Krauthammer 2009).

These predictions are understandable. Many seemingly impenetrable barriers stand in the way of a bargained resolution. Iran is an avowed enemy of the United States; the countries do not have common interests or obvious room for agreement. Meanwhile, Iran faces a compliance problem. If the United States provides any sort of concession, little stops Iran from enjoying the benefits while it continues to develop a nuclear weapon. With Washington at Tehran's apparent mercy when it comes to a negotiated settlement, military options seem like they could be the best or only hope.

Fortunately, this chapter finds cause for optimism. The results of the model indicate that, in the context of a bargaining game, the demand for proliferation is rare. Butter-for-bombs settlements can be sustainable in the long term, even if the rising state can freely renege.

Depending on the parameters, the interaction ends in one of three ways. First, if the extent of the power shift is too great, the declining state can credibly threaten preventive war. This in turn makes the rising state's threat to build weapons incredible. Likewise, if the rising state's cost of building is too high, the declining state knows the rising state will never build. In either case, the declining state can offer the rising state no concessions and still induce acceptance. The outcome mirrors a world in which the rising state had no ability to shift power.

Second, if the threat to build is credible but investment costs remain relatively large, the declining state optimally offers immediate concessions to the rising state. The rising state accepts those concessions in the present and continuously in the future. Although the rising state could build and force the declining state to give yet more concessions, those additional benefits do not cover the cost of building. Thus, the rising state extracts concessions using military power it has not actually acquired and maintains the status quo because of the attractiveness of future offers. This in turn allays the fears of the declining state.

Finally, if the threat to build is credible and the cost of shifting power is low, the declining state cannot cheaply buy off the rising state. As a result, the declining state chooses to shortchange the rising state initially, forcing the rising state to shift power. Afterward, the declining state makes great concessions. The declining state could still induce the rising state not to build here, but it simply profits more from stealing as much as it can up front. Put differently, the declining state's opportunism – not the rising state's opportunism – causes the power shift. Unlike the other outcomes, however, this possibility is not robust to alternative modeling assumptions. Indeed, taking the model in other directions – allowing the declining state to retract its offers, giving the rising state to increase its barriers to proliferation – transition these parameters to a negotiated outcome.

This chapter has four additional sections. The next section formally defines the model, describes some key features of the interaction, and derives its solution; in equilibrium, declining states and rising states reach peaceful, stable agreements if the cost to shift power falls within a certain range. The following two sections describe the how the deal works and its implications for arms investment, negotiated agreements, and preventive war. A brief conclusion follows.

3.1 MODELING BUTTER-FOR-BOMBS AGREEMENTS

This section introduces the central bargaining model of the book. First, it describes the strategic interaction. Next, it highlights the key features of the model that depart from previous formal work on shifting power. With that, it then derives the game's equilibria and shows that the declining state sometimes offers immediate concessions to convince the rising state not to build, even when conditions appear ripe for proliferation.

3.1.1 Actions and Transitions

Consider an infinite-horizon game between two actors, D (the declining state) and R (the rising state), as illustrated in Figure 3.1.[1] The states bargain over a good standardized to value 1, which represents everything in conflict between them.[2] There are four possible phases of the game: pre-shift bargaining, post-shift bargaining, pre-shift war, and post-shift war. The last two are game-ending, absorbing phases.

The game begins in the first period in the pre-shift phase, before R develops the weapons technology. D makes a temporary offer $x_t \in [0,1]$ to R, where t denotes the period. R accepts, rejects, or builds in response. Rejecting results in a game-ending war; R receives $p_R \in [0,1)$ in expectation while D receives $1 - p_R$. These payoffs persist through all future periods in this absorbing phase, but the states pay respective costs $c_D, c_R > 0$ in each future period regardless.[3]

If R accepts, the period ends. R receives x_t for the period while D receives $1 - x_t$. The game then repeats this same pre-shift bargaining phase, where D makes another temporary offer x_{t+1}.

If R builds, it pays a cost $k > 0$ to begin constructing the new weapons. This price not only includes the financial costs detailed in Chapter 2 but also any loss incurred from violating nonproliferation norms (Rublee 2009) or issues with international economic integration proliferation may cause (Solingen 2007). D sees the decision and chooses whether to initiate a preventive war or advance to the post-shift phase of the game. Preventive war ends the game and results in the same terminal payoffs as though R had rejected D's offer x_t. If D advances, the period ends, and R receives x_t for the period while D receives $1 - x_t$.

---

[1] These labels are a convention from the literature. In the basic model, the rising state rarely rises and the declining state rarely declines. Proliferation occurs more frequently in the extensions explored in later chapters.

[2] Beyond standard policy and territory issues, the good also covers "prestige" issues (Sagan 1996).

[3] One might conceptualize this as a permanent loss of capital if the states fight. However, the results are the same if costs are only paid in the period of fighting. Moreover, the proof is identical except that c_i' substitutes for c_i, where $c_i' = c_i/(1 - \delta)$.

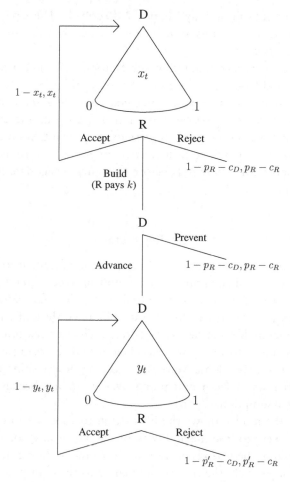

FIGURE 3.1. The Extensive Form of the Baseline Model

If R successfully builds, the game transitions into the post-shift state, and R's outside option of war improves in all future periods. Similar to before, D makes an offer y_{t+1} to R in such a post-shift period. If R accepts, the period ends, R receives y_{t+1} for the period, D receives $1 - y_{t+1}$ for the period; the game then repeats the post-shift bargaining period, where D makes another offer y_{t+2}. If R rejects, a game-ending war results. Here, R takes $p'_R \in (p_R, 1]$ in expectation while D receives $1 - p'_R$. That is, R expects to receive more from war with nuclear weapons than without, whether because those weapons shift the balance of power or limit D's war aims in the way Chapter 2 described.[4] These payoffs again persist through time in this absorbing stage, but the sides still pay their respective costs c_D, c_R.[5]

The states share a common discount factor $\delta \in (0, 1)$. Thus, the states discount period t's share of the good and costs paid by δ^{t-1}. The discount factor reflects two underlying parameters. First, as is standard, greater values place greater weight on future payoffs. Second, and common to models of shifting power, δ also represents the time it takes R to successfully develop its new weapon. Ineffective programs correspond to lower values, as more time must pass before the states renegotiate their terms of settlement.

3.1.2 Key Features

Before solving for the game's equilibria, five important features of the model are worth highlighting. First, following recent trends in power transition research (Jackson and Morelli 2009; Chadefaux 2011; Fearon 2011; Debs and Monteiro 2014), the shift is costly and endogenous. These are minimalist and necessary criteria. The vast majority of major power shifts result from endogenous choices made by rising states (Debs and Monteiro 2014, 4–5). Moreover, keeping power shifts exogenous prohibits the states from bargaining over weapons, because strength appears by assumption.

Second, the model allows the interaction to continue forever. If the rising state were to lose the ability to proliferate at any point, it would have to build in the periods previous to force the declining state to offer concessions. As such, the rising state maintains the ability to proliferate in every pre-shift period. Later chapters will address what happens if the rising state might be unable to proliferate at a future date through endogenous actions.[6]

---

[4] In this manner, R's power shift decision is binary, which is the common treatment in the nuclear proliferation literature. One could alternatively analyze a game in which R's post shift power depends on the quantity of weapons constructed, with k being a strictly increasing function that maps the number of weapons constructed to a cost. The nonproliferation agreements I find below operate similarly in this case, with p'_R and k representing the size of the power shift and the cost associated with R's tradeoff between additional power and utility loss from the investment.

[5] Similar results would obtain if the costs of war changed in the post-shift state.

[6] It is trivial to show that rising states acquire nuclear weapons if proliferation is a now-or-never opportunity, but it is odd to *assume* that a rising state would suddenly lose the

Third, the model only permits one-sided armament. This would appear to stack the deck against nonproliferation agreements. If arms races are a form of a repeated prisoner's dilemma, then an explanation for arms treaties seems to exist already – neither proliferates because the other side will proliferate in response, in a manner similar to grim trigger strategies or tit-for-tat (Axelrod 1984; Downs, Rocke, and Siverson 1986; Ikle 1961, 214–215). Similarly, and in contrast to Kydd (2000), the declining state cannot adjust its military spending to compete with the rising state's armament decision. Thus, any form of nonproliferation agreements must result from a different mechanism.

Fourth, the declining state's transfer must be endogenous. Some past research holds the share of benefits to both parties fixed for nonproliferation outcomes (Coe and Vaynman 2015; Jelnov, Tauman, and Zeckhauser 2017). Such exogenous payoffs can allow for equilibria in which both parties would prefer a change to the status quo distribution of the good, but the game form prevents the states from reaching such an outcome. If the states cannot reach an agreement in this model, it must be either because at least one of them is unwilling to or the parties cannot credibly commit to the terms.

Finally, the model puts the declining state in a strategically vulnerable position – it must offer that transfer to the rising state before the rising state chooses whether to build. Furthermore, the declining state cannot retract that offer should the rising state proliferate.[7] This addresses a major policy concern with Iran. Imagine the United States offered concessions to Iran as a quid pro quo for not developing nuclear weapons. Given concerns regarding anarchy, little would stop Iran from taking those concessions and proliferating anyway. That being the case, Washington ought not to offer concessions, as any hypothetical bribe might not alter Iran's endgame behavior. Ordering the moves in this manner directly addresses the policy concern. Yet, interestingly, removing quid pro quo bargaining in favor of indirect bargaining does not end cooperation.

3.1.3 Equilibrium

Because this is a dynamic game with an infinite number of periods, this section searches for subgame-perfect equilibria (SPE). An SPE is a set

---

ability to proliferate, especially because such an outcome leads to a commitment problem and inefficiency.

[7] This breaks from Chadefaux's (2011) setup, in which concessions and future power levels are quid pro quo.

of strategies that form Nash equilibria in every subgame. This guarantees that players only issue and believe credible threats. Unless otherwise noted, all propositions below describe the unique SPE of their respective parameter ranges.

Before stating the main results, the following lemma will prove useful:

Lemma 3.1. *In every post-shift period, D offers concessions based on R's post-shift level of power (i.e., $y_t = p'_R - c_R$), and R accepts.*

The appendix provides a complete proof of Lemma 3.1. However, the intuition is a straightforward application of Fearon's seminal bargaining game. Because war is inefficient, D can always offer enough to satisfy R. Moreover, the optimal acceptable offer is preferable to war for D. Thus, D offers just enough to induce R to accept, and D keeps the surplus. Peace prevails in the post-shift stages.

Overall, Lemma 3.1 shows that R has great incentive to proliferate – nuclear weapons mean greater coercive power, forcing D to concede more to maintain the peace. Consequently, it is unsurprising that declining states want rising states to commit to nonproliferation agreements. What is surprising is that rising states can credibly abide by such deals. The following theorem summarizes the finding:

Theorem 3.1. *For all parameters, R is willing to accept peaceful, nonproliferation settlements.*

Two factors contribute to R's credible commitment to not build: (1) R's satisfaction with future compensation and (2) R's desire to avoid paying for costly weapons. To understand why nonproliferation commitments are credible, consider two cases. First, suppose that the cost of nuclear weapons exceeds any possible coercive benefits. That is, war without nuclear weapons is more attractive for R than war with nuclear weapons after factoring in the cost to build. Then R has no incentive to build and can trivially commit to nonproliferation.

The second case is more challenging and consequently more surprising. Suppose that the coercive benefits are worth the cost. As Lemma 3.1 shows, D responds to a nuclear R by granting concessions commensurate with R's newfound level of power. This outcome of the post-shift interaction thus sets a cap on the total rewards R can receive by proliferating. Although relatively cheap in this case, the building cost lowers the value of this maximum. Thus, as long as D delivers a stream of concessions in pre-shift periods that is at least as large as that amount, R is willing to accept. That is, R cannot capture more than those offers simply because possession of weapons can only produce a finite amount of benefits. Receiving most of those benefits immediately is preferable because not building saves on the investment cost.

Before moving on to the solution of the game, there are two notes. First, this is a general result. It is *not* dependent on the structure of the bargaining protocol in pre-shift periods, as it simply states that R prefers these outcomes to investment outcomes. Second, the theorem is *not* an equilibrium claim. Rather, it is a "possibility" theorem – it proves that deals are possible provided that D commits to the necessary concessions. Interestingly, this flips the apparent credibility problem of nuclear negotiations. R is always willing to negotiate. The question remains whether D is willing to make serious offers. The propositions below address the issue by solving for the game's equilibria.

The game's outcome depends on how much additional power R would gain if it successfully proliferated (i.e., $p'_R - p_R$). Indeed, equilibrium play splits the power shift into three categories. In the first case, it is "too hot" for D to tolerate, and so it would credibly respond with preventive war. In the second case, the power shift is "too cold" for R to pursue. In the final case, the power shift is seemingly "just right" for proliferation to occur.

I start with the "too hot" case:

Proposition 3.1. *Suppose the potential shift is large relative to the costs of war (i.e., $p'_R - p_R > (c_D + c_R)/\delta$). Then D offers an amount based on R's pre-shift level of power (i.e., $x_t = p_R - c_R$). R accepts these offers and never builds.*

When the potential power shift is sufficiently greater than war's inefficiency, the power shift is "too hot." If R were to build, D would respond with preventive war; fighting is not particularly costly, and D wants to avoid making concessions following a power shift. R internalizes the probability of preventive war and therefore cannot credibly leverage the threat to build; any attempt to do so would only force R to eat its cost of proliferation without obtaining anything in exchange. In turn, D treats the bargaining problem as though R cannot build. Consequently, D offers $x_t = p_R - c_R$ (the amount R would receive in a static-bargaining game), R accepts, and the states avoid war.

Cases of successful deterrence work out extremely well for D. That is, when D can deter R with the "stick" (preventive war), R receives no "carrots" in the form of butter-for-bombs agreements. This is because credible threats are free for D whereas concessions are costly. As such, D has no reason to give R some of the surplus when it can take all of the benefits for itself.

There are a couple of caveats here. One is theoretical. The logic of Proposition 3.1 requires a specific informational structure for the threat of preventive war to deter proliferation. Leveraging preventive war requires D to observe the development of a nuclear program. In contrast, if R could work covertly, then D would not know whether it should prevent come decision time. Meanwhile, even with perfectly observable weapons programs, R must know D's threat to prevent is credible. If not, R may try challenging its opponent by continuing its weapons program. These informational hurdles motivate Chapters 7 and 8.

The second is practical. Regardless of the informational issues, there are many historical cases where declining states were unwilling to use military force to stop an opponent from developing a nuclear weapon. Chapter 6, for example, details how the United States was unwilling to intervene to end the Soviet Union's investment. In short, exhaustion from World War II meant that preventive war would come at a high domestic cost, and poor intelligence would force the United States to fight an far-reaching war to do the job effectively. The incredible threat to intervene only becomes more pronounced when dealing with friendlier countries. For example, following the fall of the Soviet Union, a Russian intervention into Ukraine would set a negative tone for the bilateral relationship for the decades to come.

In short, if the costs of war are sufficiently high, D cannot use the preventive threat to deter R. Thus, for some parameters, D must negotiate with R even if the extent of the power shift is extreme. The remaining cases cover situations when the power shift is not "too hot" in this manner. In fact, the next proposition addresses cases where the power shift is so small that R has no interest in investing:

Proposition 3.2. *Suppose the potential shift is too small relative to cost of investment (i.e., $p'_R - p_R < (1 - \delta)k/\delta$). Then D offers an amount based on R's pre-shift level of power (i.e., $x_t = p_R - c_R$). R accepts these offers and never builds.*

As the explanation for Theorem 3.1 noted, R would never want to build if the investment cost exceeds the coercive benefits of nuclear weapons. Proposition 3.2 covers just this case – the shift is "too cold" from R's perspective. Just as before, R cannot credibly threaten to proliferate under these conditions. In turn, D offers an amount commensurate with R's power as if building were impossible. The outcome is the same as when the power shift is "too hot" despite a distinctly different mechanism causing nonproliferation.

Proposition 3.2 explains why a large chunk of countries have never gone down the nuclear path. The cost of proliferation must be sufficiently low for a country to even think about a program. Technological barriers loom large here. A country like Botswana in the 1960s simply had no plausible path to a nuclear weapon without bankrupting the government. Those countries therefore do not proliferate regardless of what their opponents offer them. Inferring that, those opponents offer no concessions based on the (im)possibility of nuclear weapons.

However, a more subtle interpretation exists as well. The "sufficiently costly" caveat is in reference to the security environment. A country like Iceland may have the financial resources to develop a nuclear weapon. But it lacks any significant coercive bargaining relationships. Put simply, nuclear weapons are not a sensible investment without an adversary to threaten.

Going one step further, a rich and technologically sophisticated country with an intense security relationship may still not want to proliferate if the corresponding power shift is too small. This weighed on Canada's decision to forgo nuclear weapons during the Cold War. Canada is one of the most nuclear-proficient countries to have never developed a bomb, and certainly the Soviet Union's proximity qualified as a legitimate security threat. Yet Ottawa reasoned that any Soviet incursion into Canadian territory would be just as unacceptable to the United States. In turn, a nuclear weapon would not provide Canada with much coercive power it was not already receiving from Washington (Paul 2000, 69–71). The shift in coercive power that nuclear weapons would cause was therefore small, thereby overriding the low price tag.

The high cost of nuclear weapons is a common explanation for nonproliferation in the literature (Jo and Gartzke 2007; Solingen 2007; Rublee 2009). Proposition 3.2 captures the fundamental intuition. However, the nonproliferation explanations that focus purely on economic constraints have a hard time explaining some features of nuclear forbearance. Many studies have noted the use of concessions as an incentive to give up proliferation (Reiss 1988; Reiss 1995; Paul 2000). It would be odd if countries made costly concessions if they were not necessary to end a nuclear program.

Fortunately, the next proposition provides an explanation for this behavior. The remaining cases cover when the shift in power

$(p'_R - p_R)$ does not fall into the previously discussed cases.[8] According to the standard security explanations for proliferation, nuclear investment occurs when a country has the safety to develop (i.e., is not in Proposition 3.1's parameters) and can do so at a reasonable cost (i.e., is not in Proposition 3.2's parameters). Thus, moving outside these cases and into a "Goldilocks" region seemingly leaves the world "just right" for a power shift. Yet the following proposition gives hope. Bargaining can prevail when states reach concessions-for-weapons, or *butter-for-bombs*, agreements:

Proposition 3.3. *Suppose the potential power shift falls in a middle range. If the cost of proliferation is sufficiently large (i.e., $k > \delta(p'_R - c_R)$), D offers concessions to R in every pre-shift period (i.e., $x_t = p'_R - c_R - (1 - \delta)k/\delta$). R accepts and never builds.*

To induce R to accept a nonproliferation agreement, D must develop an offer strategy that makes building a nuclear weapon no better than maintaining the balance of power. A closer examination of the equilibrium offer $x_t = p'_R - c_R - (1 - \delta)k/\delta$ helps explain how D accomplishes that goal. Recall that R receives concessions commensurate with its additional strength if it were to successfully proliferate. In fact, the post-shift offer size from Lemma 3.1 $(p'_R - c_R)$ appears in the nonproliferation agreement here as well. This is not a coincidence – D factors in the concessions it would have to yield at a later date into the offer it gives today.

However, D does not offer that full amount. Indeed, it reduces those concessions by the time-equivalent value of the investment cost $((1 - \delta)k/\delta)$. That investment cost cuts into R's bargaining leverage, as higher costs make R less willing to pursue a nuclear weapon. Thus, as the cost increases, D can reduce its offer and still induce nonproliferation. This has an important second-order effect. Because D keeps the remainder of the offer, higher weapons cost for R yield a greater utility for D.

In that light, it is no wonder that the United States has invested so heavily in the nonproliferation regime. Rublee (2009) argues that the construction of the regime has created a norm against nuclear

---

[8] I also assume that

$$k \in \left(\frac{\delta(p'_R - p_R - c_D - c_R)}{(1 - \delta)^2}, \frac{\delta p'_R - p_R}{1 - \delta} + c_R \right)$$

for the remaining cases. The minimum value constraint for k implies D earns more from engaging in a butter-for-bombs settlement than it does from earning its war payoff in the pre-shift stage. The maximum value constraint ensures that R never prefers rejecting to having a successful power shift transpire, even if D offers R nothing during the pre-shift periods. These cases do not provide further theoretical insight to the analysis.

development. Insofar as states internalize that norm, the model generates two implications. If breaking the norm is costly both domestically and within the world community, the value of k increases. This makes more states likely to fall under the "too cold" parameters of Proposition 3.2. Failing that, D's optimal offer decreases in k for Proposition 3.3. Thus, nonproliferation leaders benefit from the norm because it requires having to hand out fewer concessions to maintain compliance.

Substantively, what do such butter-for-bombs deals look like? Take the grand bargain that Egypt and Israel struck with the Camp David Accords, which I discuss in greater detail in Chapter 5. Israel had captured the Sinai Peninsula during the 1967 Six-Day War. In standard crisis-bargaining models, negotiated settlements are supposed to reflect the balance of power between the states. Given the results of the war, that clearly meant that the Sinai should fall into Israel's column in any agreement. Yet Israel gave it back to Egypt in 1979. Doing so gives Egypt little incentive to proliferate – the share of benefits more closely matched the *potential* power that Egypt could obtain. This is the exact goal of a butter-for-bombs agreement.

More generally, the equilibrium values give straightforward guidelines for policymakers. During crisis negotiations, for the most part, opponents should behave as though credible proliferators already have nuclear weapons. This gives a credible proliferator no incentive to develop a nuclear weapon and revisit the topic at a later date. But these opponents can make such deals more palatable to themselves by slightly reducing the quantity of concessions. They can get away with this because the rising state does not pay the investment cost when it forgoes nuclear weapons. As those costs increase, the offer correspondingly decreases.

One might initially suspect that these deals incentivize investment in nuclear programs. After all, if a potential proliferator reduces its cost of nuclear weapons, D increases its equilibrium offer. However, this is not the case. When D calculates the offer size, it specifically chooses the amount that disincentivizes *any* development at all. Indeed, the offer exactly offsets whatever additional concessions a proliferator could gain by making minor investments in its program.[9] D chooses such an amount

---

[9] This also dispels concerns that engaging in such negotiations with one country may encourage others to increase their latent nuclear capacity if D wants to use concessions to stop proliferation. Imagine that D played this game with a succession of rising states. A butter-for-bombs offer leaves any rising state with a payoff equivalent to what it would earn if it were to proliferate. Thus, if D's threat to intervene is not credible, each state must receive at least that amount in the overall game. Given that, there is no incentive for D to deny concessions to the first party, as each subsequent state is

because any investment in weapons results in inefficiency. If D wants to make a deal, it would rather pick an offer that allows it to consume that surplus.[10]

On that note, what remains unanswered is whether D actually prefers inducing compliance. It may be surprising that D would not want to reach a settlement, but credible nonproliferation requires giving potentially considerable concessions to R. Alternatively, D could impatiently take all of the good today and deal with the consequences of a nuclear R tomorrow. The second condition in Proposition 3.3 addresses when D prefers the settlement. Specifically, the cost of proliferation must be sufficiently high. This is because, as that investment cost grows, D can offer less and still appease R. In turn, D's share of the nonproliferation settlement grows, and so it is more inclined to strike the deal.[11]

This leaves the final proposition:

Proposition 3.4. *Suppose the potential power shift falls in a middle range. If the cost of proliferation is sufficiently small (i.e., $k < \delta(p'_R - c_R)$), D offers nothing ($x_t = 0$) in every pre-shift period. R builds immediately and D does not prevent.*

The logic follows the discussion of Proposition 3.3. There are two perspectives on what causes bargaining to break down here. D deserves part of the responsibility. Theorem 3.1 shows that R can always credibly commit to accepting a stream of offers. As such, D can always bargain away the problem if it wants to. The issue here is that D prefers taking as much as it can up front and suffering the consequences later on.

still going to proliferate down the line in the absence of concessions, and D loses out on capturing the surplus each time. In contrast, Chapter 8 develops a model in which R is uncertain whether D's threat to prevent is credible. There, D has an incentive to acquire a reputation for toughness by denying concessions and intervening in the event an opponent attempts to proliferate.

10 This result does not claim that negotiations following some level of investment ought never occur. Empirically, this is in fact common (Rabinowitz 2014; Rabinowitz and Miller 2015). Rather, it suggests a puzzle as to why any investment occurs at all.

11 Proposition 3.3 describes the unique efficient stationary SPE. A "no deal" type of equilibrium exists as well for these parameters that matches the strategies of Proposition 3.4. In essence, D offers $x_t = 0$ in every pre-shift period and R builds regardless of the offer. Neither side can profitably deviate because each player's strategy is not conditional on the other's. Such "no deal" equilibria are common in games that require mutual compliance to achieve a cooperative outcome. However, no one wins in this equilibrium – *both* are better off in the efficient equilibrium where bargaining succeeds. It is thus natural to focus on Proposition 3.3's equilibrium. The presence of a "no deal" equilibrium also means that other efficient equilibria exist that divide the surplus between the players.

Given that D is unwilling to buy off R, a commitment problem exacerbates the dilemma. Because R builds, the outcome is inherently inefficient. Both parties would be better off if they reached a nonproliferation agreement that splits the surplus between them. However, all such mutually preferable offers are small, and thus R's best response to any such offer is to build. Anticipating this, D minimizes its initial offer and accepts the inefficient outcome.

Although Proposition 3.4 gives a theoretical explanation for proliferation, it may not generate much empirical leverage for four reasons. First, the parameters do not seem to match the historical record. Proliferation occurs in equilibrium here because the opponent is unwilling to buy the potential nuclear state's compliance. In fact, it basically suspends negotiations and holds onto the whole pie for as long as it can.

Historically, however, proliferation opponents seem eager to negotiate an agreement. The United States commonly takes the initiative in engaging potential proliferators. Indeed, Washington's effort spanned the Cold War and persisted following the dissolution of the Soviet Union and the formation of Ukraine, Kazakhstan, and Belarus. In more recent years, it has continued with the Joint Comprehensive Plan of Action with Iran and the failed Agreed Framework with North Korea.

On a macro level, the nonproliferation regime has such proactive offers built into the system. The grand bargain dates back to Dwight D. Eisenhower's "Atoms for Peace" speech in the United Nations. To entice countries to forgo atomic weapons, states would receive assistance with nuclear technology from proficient states. The Non-Proliferation Treaty would later formalize the deal, and the International Atomic Energy Agency now provides member states with services ranging from fuel cycle assistance to irradiating screwworms.[12]

This should not be surprising. Chapter 2 detailed the full expense of nuclear weapons. By reaching an agreement, the opponent can capture the surplus created through deferred investment. Yet Proposition 3.4 requires the cost of nuclear weapons to be small for agreements to fail. If proliferating is generally expensive as Chapter 2's discussion suggests, then few cases would fit the scope conditions.

Second, states often fear the negative externalities from nuclear weapons. The model measures the direct dyadic security effect of

---

[12] This is a pest control measure. The IAEA introduces irradiated male screwworms to wild populations. Mating kills female screwworms. Thus, the IAEA can quickly eradicate the entire population by flooding the habitat with infertile males that kill their partners and crowd out the fertile males (ElBaradei 2011, 76).

proliferation through the shift in power. Beyond that, an additional state with nuclear weapons increases the probability of an accidental detonation, inadvertent nuclear war, and nuclear material falling into the hands of rogue parties. One could add this to the analysis by subtracting that externality from D's payoff for any outcome in which R proliferated. This has two effects on the equilibrium parameter spaces. To begin, D's credible threat to launch preventive war expands, as suffering the costs of conflict looks more attractive when fighting eliminates the externality. In addition, in cases where D cannot credibly threaten preventive war, the region in which D strikes butter-for-bombs agreements increases in size. The logic is similar here: taking all of the good in the short-term looks less attractive when doing so also means suffering the externality.

Third, the proliferation outcome is not robust to an alternative model specification. The game presented here is a worst-case scenario in one regard: if R builds, D cannot retract *any* of its offer. One could imagine a best-case scenario where the agreement is quid pro quo, and R only receives the pre-shift concessions if it does not proliferate. Proliferation never occurs in this setup (Spaniel 2015). Alternatively, one could imagine a blend between these two structures in which D gets a partial refund of the inducements it gave. As the size of that refund increases, Proposition 3.3's analogous parameter space expands. In fact, as long as that refund is sufficiently large, Proposition 3.3 covers the entire range. This suggests one motivation for the creation of the IAEA. A primary task of that organization is to monitor compliance to nonproliferation agreements. This allows opponents to retract offers more quickly, reducing the number of cases that may otherwise fall into a proliferation parameter space.

Such pullbacks occur empirically. Take the 1994 Agreed Framework between North Korea and an American-led international coalition for example. Under the terms, North Korea would have ended its nuclear program and allowed for international inspections in exchange for a diplomatic thaw and energy subsidies. Within four years, the United States knew that Pyongyang had been enriching uranium in violation of the agreement (Kessler 2015); within nine, the agreement had broken down entirely, well before the date that North Korea had a deliverable nuclear weapon.[13] Despite the observational challenges, the United States spent little on wasted concessions. North Korea received oil shipments

---

[13] North Korea's first test – only a partial success – occurred in 2006. Its first fully successful test occurred in 2009.

in the interim, but work on a US-sponsored nuclear power plant went almost nowhere, and the sanctions regime remained constant.

Finally, and counterintuitively, the potential proliferator can *increase* its payoff by artificially enlarging k. To understand why, recall that bargaining is constant-sum. When D forces R to build, D does so because it earns more through bargaining via the inefficient route. However, R receives the remainder of the bargain *and* pays the investment cost. That inefficiency loss comes out of R's payoff. As such, R can improve its payoff by shifting to the efficient outcome.

This helps explain why some states have joined nonproliferation institutions even though it seems to reduce the credibility of going nuclear. If a state found itself thinking that nuclear weapons were extremely cheap, it could improve its welfare by taking measures to make proliferation more expensive. Such contracting appeared critical to resolving the Brazil–Argentina nuclear dilemma. Both of these South American countries explored a nuclear deterrent in the 1980s under military rule and continued the programs as fledgling democracies. They also had the technological sophistication to proliferate. But despite the potential for a fight over regional hegemony, neither side found nuclear weapons particularly compelling. As such, each sought to convince the other to sit down at the bargaining table through bilateral confidence-building.[14]

The process began with the Declaration of Iguazu (Reiss 1995, 55–58). Beyond pledged commitments to peaceful use of nuclear technology, the Declaration also set up a bilateral commission to inspect potential proliferation sites; IAEA inspections followed in the early 1990s. The presidents then began scheduling annual diplomatic visits and consistently reaffirmed their commitments to nonproliferation. Warm relations soon led to increased economic interdependence; reverting to the original nuclear posture would put these mutual gains at risk. With those assurances in mind, Brazil explicitly disallowed non-peaceful nuclear use in its 1988 constitution (Paul 2000, 109). The period of diplomacy culminated in both parties' fulfilling the Treaty of Tlatelolco, which established a nuclear-weapons-free zone in Latin America.[15] Argentina then ratified

---

[14] Of course, there was pressure on the international level as well. The United States, for example, likely tied Argentinean reticence to debt refinancing from the World Bank and International Monetary Fund (Levite 2003, 78).

[15] Argentina and Brazil had signed the treaty in 1967, but neither fully complied. Argentina outright refused to ratify it. Brazil, meanwhile, ratified it in 1968 but claimed to maintain the right to "peaceful" nuclear explosions (Reiss 1995, 64–65).

the Nuclear Non-Proliferation Treaty in 1995, and Brazil followed three years later.

Interestingly, nothing binds Argentina and Brazil to these agreements. The nuclear technology is still there; at any moment, either side could break from their commitments and pursue a nuclear weapon once again. However, such concerns ignore both sides' incentives. Increasing the burden of proliferation is not meant to make proliferation impossible. Rather, the goal is to make it less desirable and harder to overcome domestic opposition, which in turn makes the other side more willing to negotiate a deal. These institutional provisions accomplish this precise goal.

Previous research has observed such divestments and argued that they serve as costly signals of a state's intentions (Volpe 2017). However, no signaling occurs here; both states have complete and perfect information. Rather, the goal is to make the rival find a deal more attractive than offering nothing and forcing the potential proliferator to nuclearize. The divestment decision is more akin to a nuclear "bridge burning" – by removing its atomic infrastructure, a state cannot easily walk back down the path to proliferation. Both burned bridges and nuclear technology can be rebuilt, of course, but doing so is expensive. Thus, on the whole, the process disincentivizes proliferation.

In sum, Proposition 3.4 is not robust. Consequently, later chapters develop alternative explanations for failed nuclear negotiations.

3.2 UNDERSTANDING THE DEAL

The butter-for-bombs equilibrium highlights the importance of *potential* power for the stability of settlements. A sizeable literature in international relations debates whether systems with states of relatively equal power are more stable than systems where one state has a preponderance of power.[16] The bargaining literature critiques these theories by noting that the difference between relative power and relative benefits underlies incentives for war (Powell 1996; Reed et al. 2008). The model adds an additional caveat: for a system to be stable, the benefits must also correspond to the states' *potential* power.

Figure 3.2 illustrates D's equilibrium offer in pre-shift stages as a function of p'_R, R's power if it proliferates. When p'_R is small, R cannot recoup

---

[16] Although the literature goes far beyond these two works, see Morgenthau (1960) for the balance of power argument and Blainey (1988) for the preponderance of power argument.

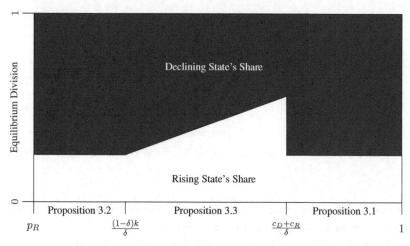

FIGURE 3.2. Division of the Bargain by Size of Power Shift

its building cost. D therefore treats the bargaining problem as though power were static and offers R its pre-shift reservation value for war, which R accepts. When p'_R falls in a middle range, R can credibly threaten to build. D utilizes the butter-for-bombs bargaining tactic, which induces R to accept the immediate concessions and not build. Finally, when p'_R is great, R cannot credibly threaten to build, as D responds to attempted proliferation with preventive war. Consequently, D stands firm and still induces R to accept.

Further, Figure 3.2 illustrates R's non-monotonic preferences over future power. If the power shift is very small, the ability to build does not affect R's payoff at all. In the middle range, R can successfully threaten to shift power, which in turn causes D to make concessions. Moreover, these concessions are increasing in the extent of the power shift. However, the power shift eventually becomes too great. R then cannot build without inducing D to intervene. Thus, R's payoff drops precipitously, as though R does not have the ability to shift power at all.

Beyond that, Figure 3.3 shows the set of stable outcomes for situations of static and dynamic power. If R cannot build additional weapons, then any settlement between $p_R - c_R$ and $p_R + c_D$ is mutually preferable to war. If the rising state has access to weapons, then the range of settlements mutually preferable to power shifts and war falls between $p'_R - c_R - (1-\delta)$ k/δ and $p_R + c_D$. Note that this is a subset of the settlement set in the static world. Thus, for example, to sustain the status quo with Iran, the United

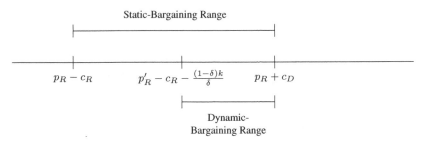

FIGURE 3.3. Set of Efficient Settlements With and Without Nuclear Weapons

States needs to be more conciliatory on average to keep leadership in Tehran from wanting to develop a weapon.

Framed in this way, Figure 3.3 indicates that not all countries require specific concessions to convince them to not proliferate. Before a country obtains the necessary nuclear proficiency to build a bomb, suppose that the division of goods was already favorable to it – in other words, the status quo fell toward the right of the static-bargaining range. After it becomes nuclear proficient, that country is still satisfied with the status quo. It has no desire to proliferate because its share of benefits naturally falls into the dynamic-bargaining range.

Closer inspection reveals that as k increases and p'_R decreases, the overlap between the static- and dynamic-bargaining ranges increases. This provides a simple explanation for why most of the nuclear-capable countries in Table 1.2 have not actually pursued nuclear weapons. Consider three points. First, even for proficient countries, nuclear weapons are very expensive (Schwartz 1998). Second, the coercive effects of nuclear weapons may be limited (Sechser and Fuhrmann 2017). And third, states with favorable positions in the geopolitical order offer blanket benefits to nonproliferators through the Non-Proliferation Treaty. Even if these benefits are not substantial, the high costs of weapons and their limited benefits make it easy for the status quo to naturally fall in a location acceptable to a potential rising state. Thus, though bargaining may prove pivotal in the remaining cases, nuclear-specific concessions may often be unnecessary for inducing cooperative behavior from potential proliferators.

One key way the status quo may not fall into the dynamic-bargaining range is if the state has a long-running dispute over a significant issue. Because the model standardizes the dispute at a value of 1, k incorporates the severity of the stakes, with lower values corresponding to more important affairs. Unsurprisingly, the countries that have pursued nuclear weapons in Table 1.2 tend to be countries with such security threats (e.g., Israel, South Korea, and Iraq). Many countries that have never faced such security concerns during their nuclear-capable eras (e.g., Mexico, Peru, and the Czech Republic).[17] Correspondingly, they never began a program. Taking stock, this logic suggests that the cases in need of further examination are the overlap between capable states and those with major security threats.

Meanwhile, Figure 3.3 has empirical implications regarding the measurement of power. Dyadic shares of power underly many bargaining theories of conflict. Correspondingly, empirical work predicting the outcomes of crises routinely use proxies for the distribution of military capabilities.[18] CINC scores, which incorporate national population, military strength, and industrial capability, are the industry standard (Singer, Bremer, and Stuckey 1972). These components are useful for understanding where the static-bargaining range falls – it centers around p_R, the share of power a country can marshal in the event of a conflict *today*.

However, the dynamic-bargaining range is a subset of static-bargaining ranges. This can lead to a number of issues. As a pure forecasting tool, power proxies that do not incorporate latent nuclear capability under-predict the potential proliferator's average outcome. Put simply, excluding potential nuclear weapons from the analysis leads to an unnecessarily weak prediction. It also complicates statistical inference. Ignoring how nuclear potential creates a second data-generating process leads to noisier estimates. Meanwhile, if the researcher is interested in whether certain variables predict outcomes, the presence of dynamic-bargaining ranges suggests the possibility of omitted variable bias. The takeaway here is that nuclear capability is a predictor of success in military confrontations, and I find statistical evidence for this in the next chapter.

Figure 3.3's visual allusion to Fearon 1995 also helps build the broader agenda for this book's later chapters. Fearon establishes that any division between $p_R - c_R$ and $p_R + c_D$ is mutually preferable to war. This creates a research question known as *war's inefficiency puzzle*: if agreements exist that both parties prefer to conflict, why do wars occur at all? Put differently, establishing the possibility of peaceful settlements does not imply the inevitability of peace. Recognizing that, Fearon

---

[17] Yet others were closely aligned with the United States and Soviet Union and chose instead to free ride on their nuclear patron.
[18] See Carroll and Kenkel 2018 for a list of recent works.

relaxes the assumptions of the baseline model and allows for asymmetric information and commitment problems. If these issues are sufficiently severe, then war may occur. Despite the continued existence of mutually preferable settlements, the parties cannot locate such a settlement or abide by its terms.

The dynamic-bargaining range in Figure 3.3 poses a similar research question. If agreements exist that both parties prefer to proliferation, why do states build nuclear weapons at all? Put differently, establishing the possibility of nonproliferation agreements does not imply the inevitably of nuclear restraint. Recognizing that, the later chapters relax some of the assumptions of this chapter's baseline model, focusing mainly on the interplay between preventive war and negotiated agreements. Chapter 6 relaxes the assumption that D's cost of preventive war remains static over time; this can stop D from credibly committing to concessions over the long term, which causes R to proliferate in the present. Chapter 7 relaxes the assumption that D can observe R's decision to build; this can cause D to abandon negotiations and lead R to proliferate. Chapter 8 relaxes the assumption that R knows D's cost of preventive war; this can cause weaker types of D to feign strength by offering no concessions and forces R to sometimes call D's bluff.

These later extensions do not undermine the general theory that this chapter brings forth for two reasons. First, obstacles to negotiated settlements are more prominent in some cases and less prominent than others. By looking at bargaining in a vacuum, this chapter establishes a fundamental requirement for explaining proliferation by any means. For example, suppose that D's cost of preventive war changes over time. Chapter 6 shows that this can lead to proliferation. But without this chapter's baseline result, it is unclear whether proliferation is an inevitable feature of nuclear negotiations or that the changing cost of preventive war causes this. Proposition 3.3 says that it is the latter.

More generally, it is insufficient to say that a country built a nuclear weapon simply because it wanted to, had the means available, and no other country intervened. Instead, something else must interfere in the bargaining process to explain the inefficient investment. This point about the inefficiency puzzle is critical for future research. Other types of explanations undoubtedly exist for nuclear proliferation. Declining states may not know their rising states' true time horizon to nuclear weapons (Montgomery and Mount 2014) or their cost. There may also be non-unitary actor or non-bilateral benefits to proliferation (Lake 2010). These are worthy topics for future research. But my baseline model still provides value here: those results are more surprising and more valuable because this chapter shows that circumstances generally favor agreements.

The second reason the extensions do not undermine the general theory is that the main results here are robust to those alternative specifications as long as the additional problems are not too severe. For example, if R does not know whether D's cost of preventive war is extremely high or slightly smaller than extremely high, preventive war is incredible in either case. In turn, the outcome is identical to the main model. As such, the knowledge built here carries over to those games and therefore sets scope conditions for when the other bargaining problems matter. I will make note of these as the book progresses.

3.3 IMPLICATIONS OF BUTTER-FOR-BOMBS AGREEMENTS

During his third presidential debate, John F. Kennedy warned of a world of up to twenty nuclear states before his first term ended.[19] But by the end of 1964, only five states (the United States, the Soviet Union, the United Kingdom, France, and China) held nuclear arsenals. Continuing that theme, since the Nuclear Non-Proliferation Treaty's creation in 1968, 190 countries have signed the treaty, and only North Korea has ever withdrawn. Meanwhile, Israel, South Africa, India, and Pakistan are the only other countries to have constructed a nuclear bomb.[20] So, at least thus far, the world has not reached the nuclear tipping point that Kennedy feared.

Yet nuclear weapons provide inherent security and allow states to coerce their rivals during times of crisis. In light of this, why haven't more states followed in North Korea's footsteps by withdrawing from the NPT and joining the nuclear club?

The model provides an explanation: nuclear weapons are simply not in high demand in the context of a bargaining game. Bargaining is constant-sum; if nuclear weapons provide benefits to their possessors, then they must also harm others. Consequently, those fearing proliferation have incentive to offer attractive deals to shut down the nuclear contagion. Meanwhile, the potential proliferator has incentive to listen. After all, nuclear weapons are far from free. Those states would happily accept most of what they hope to gain from proliferating without investing in an actual nuclear test.

---

[19] www.jfklibrary.org/research/research-aids/jfk-speeches/3rd-Nixon-Kennedy-Debate_19 601013.aspx
[20] Of these, South Africa dismantled its weapons at the end of Apartheid.

Figure 3.4 shows why demand is so low. When nuclear weapons cause too great of a power shift relative to the declining state's costs of intervention, the rising state passes on proliferation so as to avoid preventive war. Here, the declining state need not offer any carrots to induce compliance, as its stick is a sufficient threat to stop the rising state. Moreover, deterrence gives the declining state its best possible outcome, as it does not actually initiate a war. Consequently, a state seeking a nuclear arsenal must first seek protection from an alliance partner (Debs and Monteiro 2017) or shore up its conventional deterrent, otherwise proliferation is not a strategically viable option.[21]

But even if the potential proliferator can defend itself from an invasion, it still might not want to seek nuclear weapons. After all, bombs are an investment in the future. Such an investment is only sensible if it yields sufficient returns. Thus, states will not proliferate if the financial cost of nuclear weapons is too great. Similarly, states need to have a contentious security issue for proliferation to make sense.

Nuclear weapons remain unrealized even as the attractiveness of the investment increases. At this point, the potential rising state is

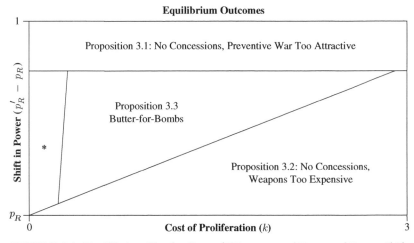

FIGURE 3.4. Equilibrium Plot by Cost of Weapons and Extent of Power Shift

---

[21] Iran has correspondingly placed many of its nuclear facilities underground. This location limits the damage from a possible aerial strike, reducing the Israeli or American ability to effectively intervene.

conditionally willing to shift power. But it is in the declining state's best interest to bribe the would-be nuclear state and avoid facing the consequences of a much stronger rival. The states resolve the crisis without proliferation, as the immediate concessions ensure that building a bomb will not lead to a better outcome. The only parameters where proliferation occurs are marked with the asterisk.

The model also reveals that bargaining over nuclear weapons does not require a rising state to commit to the incredible. In negotiating over nuclear-weapons programs, many political commentators (Bolton 2010; Krauthammer 2009; Fly and Kristol 2010) have warned that potential proliferators cannot be bought off. That being the case, declining states should hold their ground, as bribes have no effect on tomorrow's power politics.

Yet the model shows that such a strategy creates a self-fulfilling prophecy. Consider what occurs off the equilibrium path if the declining state stands firm and offers no concessions to the rising state in pre-shift periods. The rising state does not view the status quo as favorable. Because the declining state is not offering favorable terms up front, the rising state's only alternative is to build today and force the declining state to give concessions later. Thus, if the declining state were to delay those concessions, it would create the exact nuclear problem it wishes to avoid. This counterfactual thinking leads the declining state to offer a deal in equilibrium.

As a final note, these findings instruct us to take a holistic approach to understanding nuclear proliferation. Quantitative studies frequently attempt to understand proliferation behavior by analyzing "supply side" components of nuclear weapons (Jo and Gartzke 2007); states with limited nuclear capacities are unlikely to develop nuclear bombs. Although the model (via Proposition 3.2) confirms the value of supply side explanations, nuclear capacity is not the sole explanatory variable. Indeed, Figure 3.4 shows that supply side arguments explain outcomes in the bottom right portion of the parameter space only; preventive war and bargaining determine the remaining outcomes.

Ignoring these other factors leads to strange interpretations of the data. Sagan (2011, 229–230) notes that, according to the Jo and Gartzke (2007) estimates, Trinidad and Tobago had "a higher degree of nuclear-weapons latency in 2001" than North Korea, despite the latter being "only five years away from detonating its first nuclear weapon." But latent capacity does not become active capacity without the will of the state. Trinidad and Tobago has no significant coercive bargaining relationship and maintains an active military force in the thousands. Meanwhile, North Korea has technically been at war since the 1950s and has more than a million active-duty soldiers. Thus, latency measures require context. Bargaining relationships explain why states choose to develop nuclear capacity.

3.4 CONCLUSION

This chapter formally investigated the credibility of butter-for-bombs settlements. Although international-relations scholars traditionally emphasize how realized power extracts concessions, the model demonstrated that *potential* power is sufficient. Declining states have incentive to proactively bargain with rising states, so as to ensure that nonproliferation remains the status quo. Rising states have incentive to welcome the offers, as they can obtain most of their goals without paying development costs. Credible nonproliferation agreements result.

The model contributes to our understanding of costly weapons production. At present, explanations for non-armament focus on the threat of preventive war and excessively costly investments; many models do not explain how carrots convince states to forgo weapons programs. The butter-for-bombs model fills the gap, showing how states can manipulate their rivals' opportunity cost and thereby avoid nuclear proliferation.

While the model reveals the absence of commitment problems and the existence of a bargaining space, it fails to show how states reach butter-for-bombs deals in practice. Consequently, the next chapters investigate potential nuclear capacity. I begin with a large-n statistical analysis, which shows that opponents of nuclear-proficient states are less likely to reciprocate during crises. Afterward, I use case studies to corroborate the usefulness of the model. Later chapters follow up by adding bargaining frictions – shifting resolve, imperfect information, and incomplete information – to study whether butter-for-bombs agreements result in these contexts.

3.5 APPENDIX

This appendix covers the proofs of the lemmas and propositions from this chapter. For parsimony, I assume that R accepts when indifferent. As is standard with ultimatum games, relaxing this assumption does not yield any additional equilibria. I also limit the discussion to stationary strategies unless otherwise noted. To simplify notation, I scale all payoffs by $1 - \delta$.

3.5.1 Proof of Lemma 3.1

The strategies that induce the result in Lemma 3.1 are D offering $y_t = p'_R - c_R$ and R accepting $y_t \geq p'_R - c_R$ for all t.

First, in every equilibrium for every history of the game, R's continuation value is at least $p'_R - c_R$.[22] This is because R can reject in any period and secure that amount.

Second, R must accept $y_t > p'_R - c_R$ in every equilibrium for every history of the game. Recall R earns $p'_R - c_R$ if it rejects in any period. In contrast, if R receives an offer of $y_t > p'_R - c_R$, accepting generates a payoff of $(1 - \delta)y_t + \delta V_R$, where V_R is R's continuation value. The previous paragraph ensures that $V_R \geq p'_R - c_R$. Using $V_R = p'_R - c_R$ as a lower bound, accepting is strictly better than rejecting if:

$$(1 - \delta)y_t + \delta(p'_R - c_R) > p'_R - c_R$$

$$y_t > p'_R - c_R$$

This holds. So R must accept $y_t > p'_R - c_R$.

Third, D never offers $y_t > p'_R - c_R$ in every equilibrium for every history of the game. Using the one-shot deviation principle, D could instead offer the midpoint between that y_t and $p'_R - c_R$. This amount is still strictly greater than $p'_R - c_R$, so R still accepts. In turn, D receives strictly more for the period and the identical amount in all future periods, so this is a profitable deviation.

Fourth, R rejects $y_t < p'_R - c_R$ in every equilibrium for every history of the game. The first and third steps of this proof imply that R's continuation value is no greater than $p'_R - c_R$. Thus, if R accepts $y_t < p'_R - c_R$, it receives strictly less than than $p'_R - c_R$ for the game. Consequently, rejecting and earning $p'_R - c_R$ is a profitable deviation.

Fifth, since R's continuation value must be no greater than $p'_R - c_R$ and no less than $p'_R - c_R$, it must be exactly equal to $p'_R - c_R$. Given the previous results on R's accept or reject decision, the only way this is possible is if D offers $y_t = p'_R - c_R$ in every period. R cannot profitably deviate because it receives $p'_R - c_R$ by fighting in any period, which is identical to

---

[22] Because I scale all payoffs by $1 - \delta$, the direct meaning of a continuation value is the per-period average of remaining periods. This is mathematically equivalent because all utilities are identical across positive affine transformations.

its payoff for accepting. D cannot profitably deviate because demanding more results in rejection (paying $1 - p'_R - c_D$) while demanding less is a needless concession.   □

3.5.2 Proof of Theorem 3.1

The proof is trivial. By Lemma 3.1, R accepts offers of $p'_R - c_R$ in all future periods. Building in a period costs $(1 - \delta)k$ and allows R to capture $(1 - \delta)x_t$ for the period. Accepting in each period yields the sum of all offers for all periods. Let j be a generic period. Therefore, R can credibly accept a series of offers from a given period forward if

$$\sum_{t=j}^{\infty}(1 - \delta)\delta^t x_t \geq (1 - \delta)x_j + \delta(p_R - c_R) - (1 - \delta)k$$

for all j greater than or equal to the current period. Infinitely many series of offers satisfy this. For example – and this will be critical later – setting all x equal to $p'_R - c_R - (1 - \delta)k/\delta$ makes this hold with equality for all periods.   □

3.5.3 Proof of Proposition 3.1

The strategies that induce the result in Proposition 3.1 are D offering $x_t = p_R - c_R$ and R accepting $x_t \geq p_R - c_R$ for all t.

First, in every equilibrium for every history of the game, R's continuation value V_R for any pre-shift period must be at least $p_R - c_R$. The proof is identical to the analogous claim in the proof for Lemma 3.1, swapping y_t for x_t and p_R for p'_R.

Second, R must accept $x_t > p_R - c_R$ in every equilibrium for every history of the game. R cannot reject in such circumstances due to the analogous proof in Lemma 3.1. R's only other alternative is to build. However, by backward induction, D prevents if:

$$1 - p_R - c_D > (1 - x_t)(1 - \delta) + \delta(1 - p'_R + c_R).$$

Note that because $x_t \geq p_R - c_R$ in this case, $(1 - p_R + c_R)(1 - \delta) + \delta(1 - p'_R + c_R) \geq (1 - x_t)(1 - \delta) + \delta(1 - p'_R + c_R)$. Therefore, to show that preventing is optimal for D, consider instead the following inequality:

$$1 - p_R - c_D > (1 - p_R + c_R)(1 - \delta) + \delta(1 - p'_R + c_R)$$

$$p'_R - p_R > \frac{c_D + c_R}{\delta}.$$

This is the cut-point for Proposition 3.1. Because R earns $p_R - c_R - (1 - \delta)k$ if D prevents, R must accept $x_t > p_R - c_R$.

Third, in every equilibrium for every history of the game, D never offers $x_t > p_R - c_R$. The proof is identical to the analogous claim in the proof for Lemma 3.1.

Fourth, D never offers $x_t < p_R - c_R$ in every equilibrium for every history of the game. If it did, one of three things could happen in response. First, R could reject. D earns $1 - p_R - c_D$ for this outcome. D could make a one-shot profitable deviation to $x_t = p_R$ in period t. Per above, R accepts. D receives $1 - p_R$ for the period and must earn at least $1 - p_R$ for the rest of time for the same reason, which is greater than $1 - p_R - c_D$. Alternatively, R could build. This is only optimal for R if D does not prevent, as R earns $p_R - c_R - (1 - \delta)k$ in that case, which is less than what it earns for rejecting. So R must earn at least $p_R - c_R$ for this outcome. In turn, D earns *no more* than $1 - p_R + c_R - (1 - \delta)k$, after factoring out R's cost to build. But D could make a one-shot profitable deviation to $p_R - c_R + (1 - \delta)k/2$. Per above, R must accept. This gives D the remainder for the period, and D must receive at least that much in every equilibrium in remaining periods. This generates a greater payoff for D than offering an amount less than $p_R - c_R$ and inducing R to build. Third, R could accept. But since the rest of this paragraph and the first and third claims ensure that R's continuation value must be less than or equal to $p_R - c_R$, R could profitably deviate to rejecting. In turn, D would have a profitable deviation to offering $x_t = p_R$ for the same reasons as before.

Fifth, since $V_R \leq p_R - c_R$ and $V_R \geq p_R - c_R$, V_R must be exactly equal to $p_R - c_R$ in every equilibrium for every history of the game. Given the above equilibrium constraints, the only way this can happen is if D offers $x_t = p_R - c_R$ in every period and R accepts. D has no profitable deviation because offering more is a needless concession while offering less results in war or a power shift that forces D to give up even more concessions. □

3.5.4 Proof of Proposition 3.2

The strategies that induce the result in Proposition 3.2 are D offering $x_t = p_R - c_R$ and R accepting $x_t \geq p_R - c_R$ for all t.

First, in every equilibrium for every history of the game, R's continuation value V_R must be greater than $p_R - c_R$ for all pre-shift periods. The proof is the same as the first part of the proof for Proposition 3.1.

Second, R must accept $x_t > p_R - c_R$ in every equilibrium for every history of the game. R has two alternatives: war and building. War generates a payoff of $p_R - c_R$ forever, while $V_R \geq p_R - c_R$ ensures that accepting $x_t > p_R - c_R$ will give a greater amount than rejecting in period t and at least as much in all future periods. Alternatively, R could build. In R's best case scenario, D does not prevent. Using Lemma 3.1, R earns $p'_R - c_R$ in all future periods. Even so, R strictly prefers accepting if:

$$(1-\delta)x_t + \delta V_R > (1-\delta)x_t + \delta(p_R - c_R) - (1-\delta)k.$$

Using $V_R = p_R - c_R$ as a lower bound, this holds if:

$$(1-\delta)x_t + \delta(p_R - c_R) > (1-\delta)x_t + \delta(p_R - c_R) - (1-\delta)k$$

$$p'_R - p_R < \frac{(1-\delta)k}{\delta}.$$

This is the cut-point given in Proposition 3.2.

Third, in every equilibrium for every history of the game, D never offers $x_t > p_R - c_R$. The proof is the same as the third part of the proof for Proposition 3.1.

Fourth, D never offers $x_t < p_R - c_R$ in every equilibrium for every history of the game. The second claim ensures that R will not respond by building. That, combined with the fact that the first and third claims ensure that $V_R \leq p_R - c_R$, imply that R must reject. But D could make a one-shot profitable deviation to $x_t = p_R$. R will accept. That gives D at least as much for the period and at least as much in all future periods. This is greater than earning its war payoff of $1 - p_R - c_D$.

The fifth and final step is identical to the fifth step from the proof for Proposition 3.1. □

3.5.5 Proof of Propositions 3.3 and 3.4

The strategies that induce the result in Proposition 3.3 are D offering $x_t = p'_R - c_R - (1-\delta)k/\delta$ and R accepting $x_t \geq p'_R - c_R - (1-\delta)k/\delta$; the strategies that induce the result for Proposition 3.4 are D offering $x_t = 0$ and R building regardless of x_t for all t.

All stationary equilibria have an equilibrium value x_t^* offered in each period. Note that if R builds and D does not prevent, R earns $(1-\delta)x_t + \delta(p'_R - c_R) - (1-\delta)k$. By the condition that $k < (\delta p'_R - p_R)/(1-\delta) + c_R$, R prefers receiving nothing in the first period and successfully shifting power to fighting a war in the first period. Let V_R be R's continuation value for accepting. Under such conditions, R prefers accepting to building (and therefore also rejecting) if:

$$(1-\delta)x_t + \delta V_R \geq (1-\delta)x_t + \delta(p'_R - c_R) - (1-\delta)k$$

$$V_R \geq p'_R - c_R - \frac{(1-\delta)k}{\delta}.$$

In particular, R's decision does *not* depend on the offer x_t; this is a direct consequence of the bargaining environment without quid pro quo offers. What matters is the continuation value. Note that R can always accept in any equilibrium. If $x_t^* \geq p'_R - c_R - (1-\delta)k/\delta$, R's continuation value must be at least $p'_R - c_R - (1-\delta)k/\delta$. So R can accept. If $x_t^* < p'_R - c_R - (1-\delta)k/\delta$, R's only other recourse is to initiate war. But that pays $p_R - c_R$, which is less than R's value for receiving nothing in the current period and building in this parameter space. So R prefers building and successfully shifting power to accepting.

Now consider D's optimal offer sizes. Offering $x_t > p'_R - c_R - (1-\delta)k/\delta$ cannot be optimal. R would not build under such circumstances. But D could make a one-shot deviation to offering the midpoint between that x_t and $p'_R - c_R - (1-\delta)k/\delta$. The continuation value remains $p'_R - c_R - (1-\delta)k/\delta$, so R still accepts. However, D receives more of the bargaining good for the period and the same amount in the future, which is a profitable deviation.

Similarly, $x_t \in (0, p'_R - c_R - (1-\delta)k/\delta)$ cannot be optimal either. R must build under such circumstances. But given that R is building, D could make a one-shot deviation to $x_t = 0$. R still builds because D does not prevent.[23] D receives more for the period and the same amount for the remainder of time, which is a profitable deviation.

So x_t^* must equal 0 or $p'_R - c_R - \frac{(1-\delta)k}{\delta}$. In fact, both are supported in equilibrium. Suppose $x_t = p'_R - c_R - (1-\delta)k/\delta$ and R accepts if and only if $x_t \geq p'_R - c_R - (1-\delta)k/\delta$. For the parameters of Proposition 3.3, D cannot make a one-shot profitable deviation in any period. Offering more is an unnecessary concession. Meanwhile, offering less triggers R to build. Given this, D's best offer less than $p'_R - c_R - (1-\delta)k/\delta$ is 0. But

---

[23] D would not prevent under the more difficult circumstance when $x_t = p'_R - c_R - (1-\delta)k/\delta$. That is, D would be more inclined to prevent under these circumstances because it keeps less during the pre-shift stage it does when it offers R nothing. D does not prevent here if $1 - p_R - c_D < (1-\delta)(1 - p'_R + c_R + (1-\delta)k/\delta)$. Rearranging, yields

$$k > \delta(p'_R - p_R + c_D + c_R)/(1-\delta)^2.$$

This is given by one of the conditions of the parameter space.

this generates a strictly lower utility if:

$$1 - p'_R + c_R + \frac{(1-\delta)k}{\delta} > 1 - \delta + \delta(1 - p'_R + c_R)$$

$$k > \delta(p'_R - c_R)$$

This is true for Proposition 3.3.

Now consider Proposition 3.4's parameter space. By analogous argument, D can profitably deviate from $x_t = p'_R - c_R - (1-\delta)k/\delta$ to 0. Thus, Proposition 3.3's strategies are not an equilibrium in this parameter space. The only alternative offer still possible in equilibrium is 0. The final thing to verify is that D would not prevent if R built under these circumstances. As before, I can show this by instead showing that D would not prevent under the more difficult circumstance when $x_t = p'_R - c_R - (1-\delta)k/\delta$. D does not prevent here if $1 - p_R - c_D < (1 - \delta)(1 - p'_R + c_R + (1-\delta)k/\delta)$. Rearranging, yields

$$k > \frac{\delta(p'_R - p_R + c_D + c_R)}{(1-\delta)^2}.$$

This is given by one of the conditions of the parameter space.   □

For completeness, Proposition 3.4's stationary strategies also form an equilibrium in Proposition 3.3's parameter space. D cannot profitably deviate if R builds regardless of the offer, and R cannot profitably deviate from building if D never increases its offer. In turn, the set of subgame-perfect equilibria is large here, as Proposition 3.4's guidelines form a punishment strategy. The folk theorem therefore applies. From there, SPE supports any vector of offers over time so long as each state's utility from each stage forward is at least as large as the utility from the punishment strategies. However, it is important to note that each of these equilibria involve some form of a butter-for-bombs agreement and that they Pareto-dominate the no-deal equilibrium.

4

Does Nuclear Proficiency Induce Compliance?

In an anarchical world system, might is supposed to make right. Yet the previous chapter formally demonstrated that *potential* power – not just fully realized power – can coerce concessions from a competing state. In other words, countries that might make might can also make right. Empirical scholars have uncovered evidence that today's capacity partially determines who prevails in militarized disputes.[1] This chapter now puts potential power to the test: is there evidence that states leverage the threat to proliferate to coerce their opponents?

Despite the logical relationship uncovered in the previous chapter, skeptics may still have reasons for doubt. Perhaps states cannot see far enough into the future to understand how standing firm today may force their opponents to proliferate. Maybe the credibility concerns provide too strong of a narrative to policymakers, who may then overlook how the incentives of potential proliferators permit them to abide by an agreement.[2] Or it could be that opponents of potential proliferators are simply too impatient. Thus, in line with Proposition 3.4, they hastily take as much as they can for as long as they can, knowing that this will backfire in the long term.

With the empirical utility of the result still perhaps in question, I now look for large-n support for the value of potential power. Although states might use implicit threats to proliferate in a variety of contexts, this chapter investigates nuclear proficiency and military coercion.

---

[1] See Carroll and Kenkel 2018 for an overview.
[2] Chapter 6 shows that problems with long-term commitment to the deal by the declining state may also interfere with an agreement. If these concerns happen too often, this would be a rational explanation for why potential power cannot coerce concessions.

Proficiency measures a country's general knowledge of nuclear technology, ranging from scientific illiteracy to nuclear mastery. In theory, states with higher proficiency can develop nuclear weapons more easily and are therefore greater proliferation threats. Consequently, I investigate the effect of nuclear proficiency in a single context in which realized nuclear strength plays a role in determining the outcome: dispute reciprocation (Horowitz 2009).

I find support for the implications drawn from the previous chapter's theoretical model. When an average country with low nuclear proficiency initiates a militarized dispute, I estimate that its target reciprocates in kind roughly 68% of the time. However, a country with high proficiency sees its disputes reciprocated only about 42% of the time. The 26 percentage point decrease is both statistically and substantively significant, thereby providing solid evidence of the model's key implication.

The chapter progresses as follows. To begin, I use the formal propositions from the previous chapter to derive empirically testable hypotheses on how states behave during international crises. I then subject the hypotheses to statistical testing using conflict data from Correlates of War and nuclear proficiency data from Smith and Spaniel (2018). The results in the following section show a clear relationship: high nuclear-proficiency predicts less dispute reciprocation. Afterward, I subject the empirical results to a battery of robustness checks to show that the results hold under a variety of assumptions. I end by discussing the theoretical and practical implications of the findings before moving to the next chapter.

4.1 THEORY AND HYPOTHESES

Last chapter's formal model gives a foundation from which to draw empirical implications. The underlying question is how nuclear proficiency alters the bargaining environment that states face in a crisis. Fortunately, the model provides a clear answer. The accumulated findings of Propositions 3.1, 3.2, and 3.3 show that the amount of concessions a state receives is weakly decreasing in its cost to develop a nuclear weapon within those parameter regions.

For a fuller explanation, recall that the cost of proliferation is irrelevant under the "too hot" parameters of Proposition 3.1. Regardless of how expensive the potential proliferator finds nuclear weapons, it does not build because of its opponent's credible threat to launch preventive war. The deals the opponent provides are consistently small here and not a function of the cost of proliferation k.[3] One can confirm this by inspecting Proposition 3.1's region of Figure 3.4 and noting that shifting left or right on the cost of proliferation keeps the players within that parameter space.

The relationship between weapons costs and concessions is more interesting in the remaining cases. For the "too cold" parameters of Proposition 3.2, concessions remain low. Slight decreases to the cost have no effect, as nuclear development remains too expensive to credibly threaten. However, more substantial decreases eventually shift the parameters to Proposition 3.3's just-right case. The potential proliferator begins receiving additional concessions in exchange for nonproliferation compliance. Moreover, those concessions increase as the cost of weapons declines further.[4] Consequently, decreasing costs weakly increases concessions overall.[5]

Two steps remain in connecting that formal result to quantitative analysis: operationalizing concessions and the costs of nuclear weapons. Weapons cost is the easier problem to solve. All it requires is a proxy for the amount of money and resources a country would have to spend to proliferate. As Jo and Gartzke (2007) show, technological proficiency captures that; more proficient countries have fewer research and design barriers and can more easily divert their industries into nuclear-weapons development.

Operationalizing concessions does not have as forthcoming of an answer. Fully tracking crisis bargaining requires obtaining data on offers made, which is a consistent barrier on investigating empirical implications of bargaining models. As such, I must instead fall back on a cruder empirical strategy. The broad takeaway from Chapter 3 is that potential power matters in negotiations. Thus, as a first pass at the theory, this chapter checks whether states with higher nuclear capacities fare better in disputes.

Even having narrowed the focus to dispute performance, there are still many options to choose from. I focus on reciprocation of Militarized Interstate Disputes (MIDs). Reciprocation rates are a useful starting point of analysis for five reasons. First, states often initiate crises as the

---

[3] Instead, the declining state offers $x = p_R - c_R$, and the rising state accepts.

[4] One can see this by observing that the optimal butter-for-bombs offer, $p'_R - c_R - (1 - \delta)k/\delta$, is strictly decreasing in k.

[5] Given the above discussion and Figure 3.2's illustration, the relationship between concessions and the extent of the power shift is more complicated. Schub 2017 operationalizes expected power shifts, and so extending that work may be a fruitful line of future research.

initial step in extracting concessions out of a rival (Leeds and Johnson 2017). Second, reciprocation provides a relatively clear interpretation of the outcome of a crisis. Although a number of escalatory stages exist between reciprocation, fatalities, and war, failure to reciprocate sends the researcher a strong signal that the target state is unwilling to resist the opponent's aggression. Third, given the rich academic and historical emphasis on nuclear deterrence, reciprocation provides a straightforward method to analyze whether such threats – implicit or explicit – can alter an opponent's behavior. Fourth, reciprocation does not require a mapping of the status quo or state preferences related to that status quo. This removes a troublesome coding step from interfering with the statistical results.

Finally, reciprocation lacks the problems a relevant alternative dependent variable faces. In particular, one might be tempted to investigate the correlates of nuclear proficiency and dispute targeting. As I detail below, the model's main takeaway is that the ability to threaten proliferation yields coercive benefits. One possible benefit is that opponents would be less likely to initiate a crisis out of fear that a potential proliferator would build nuclear weapons and revisit the conflict under more favorable circumstances.

However, there is a cross-cutting effect here too. States that cannot plausibly develop nuclear weapons never face preventive war. The same is not true for legitimate potential proliferators.[6] As a result, nuclear proficiency cuts both ways: it may reduce conflict against countries that do not wish to take preventive action, but it has the exact opposite effect for countries that do. In turn, the expected correlation between nuclear proficiency and dispute-targeting is indeterminant. Unless opponents use a potential proliferator's initiation of a crisis as a convenient excuse to take preventive action, reciprocation does not have that barrier to inference.

Combining everything together generates the following hypothesis:

Hypothesis 4.1. *As a state's unrealized nuclear capability increases, the probability its opponents reciprocate militarized disputes decreases.*

Two issues stack the deck against making an inference about Hypothesis 4.1. First, note that the fact that concessions remain constant in the cost of proliferation for Proposition 3.1's "too hot" region. Thus,

---

[6] Although preventive war does not occur in the equilibrium of the main model, it can happen the extensions I develop later. As argued here, those preventive conflicts begin more often against low-cost proliferators.

without a way to exclude those cases, regressions mix disputes where the cost of nuclear weapons matters and cases where it does not. Second, as an empirical question, it is unclear what level of proficiency delineates the capability to credibly threaten to proliferate due to low costs of nuclear weapons. Thus, once more, regressions will mix disputes where the cost matters and cases where it does not. That being the case, it will be all the more surprising if a regression finds support for Hypothesis 4.1.

Moving on, a careful reader may wonder whether the last chapter's model implied a more complicated relationship between capacity and dispute reciprocation. Recall Proposition 3.4: if the cost of nuclear weapons is sufficiently small, the declining state withholds all concessions and forces the rising state to proliferate. Proposition 3.4 therefore suggests that a potential proliferator will stand firm and reciprocate the crisis. This contrasts with the implication of Propositions 3.2 and 3.3 and instead indicates a non-monotonic relationship. The following hypothesis formalizes this:

Hypothesis 4.2. *The probability of dispute reciprocation is non-monotonic in a state's unrealized nuclear capability. As a state's unrealized nuclear capability increases initially, the probability of reciprocation decreases. However, further increases to nuclear capability eventually increase the probability of reciprocation.*

Nevertheless, the previous chapter gave plenty of theoretical reasons why Proposition 3.4 may not have much empirical leverage. Opponents of potential proliferators generally seem eager to reach an agreement; the cost of nuclear weapons is high regardless of technological capacity; adding negative externalities for the opponent adds to the incentive to broker a deal; the ability to retract offers causes Proposition 3.4's parameter space to disappear; and if the potential proliferator ever found itself in such a situation, it would have incentive to artificially increase its cost.

Due to that doubt, it is worth discussing how adding a squared term to nuclear capacity would affect inferences about Hypothesis 4.1 given the logic of Propositions 3.2 and 3.3. Under the "too cold" parameters, small increases to nuclear capacity have no effect on concession rates.[7] When that capability increases high enough, the potential proliferator's threat to develop a weapon becomes credible. The declining state in turn begins factoring in the rising state's proliferation cost into its offer calculation.

---

[7] Formally, the declining state offers $x = p_R - c_R$, which is not a function of the rising state's cost to proliferate k.

A squared term would allow for there to be essentially no effect at low levels of capacity, while progressively larger decreases in reciprocation rates appear in higher levels of capacity. I check for this below.

4.2 DATA AND STATISTICAL MODEL

I draw data primarily from two sources. The Correlates of War's Militarized Interstate Disputes (v4.01) database serves as the main source. It compiles a list of crises in which at least one state issued a threat or took military action against another state. I generated these data from EUGene (v3.204). The second major source of data is from Smith and Spaniel's (2018) v-CLEAR scores, which measure nuclear capability. The raw data used to generate v-scores run from 1938 to 2001. This is the binding constraint on the study, so all analysis below comes from that time period.

4.2.1 Dependent Variable

My dependent variable is whether a state reciprocated a militarized interstate dispute; it is a dichotomous variable, where 1 indicates reciprocation. According to Jones, Bremer, and Singer (1996, 186), "a reciprocated dispute is one in which at least one [target] state ... takes a codeable action against one [initiator] state." Perhaps surprisingly, target states respond less than half of the time (46.8%). Each dispute appears once in the dataset and is the unit of analysis for the statistical study. However, because reciprocation requires coding of an initiator and a target, these are directed dyads.

4.2.2 Independent Variables

NUCLEAR PROFICIENCY. My independent variable of interest is the *Nuclear Proficiency* of the dispute initiator, from Smith and Spaniel's (2018) v-scores. Smith and Spaniel estimate these values using a latent-variable model, which accounts for the fact that nuclear proficiency is inherently unobservable but causes states to take observable actions.

Because nuclear proficiency is the key independent variable in this study, it is worth describing the data in greater detail. In short, v-scores aggregate various types of data: Jo and Gartzke's (2007) seven-point latent-nuclear-capacity scale,[8] uranium enrichment and plutonium-

---

[8] Specifically, this includes data on native uranium deposits, metallurgists, chemical engineers, nuclear engineers/physicists/chemists, electronic/explosives specialists, nitric acid capacity, and electricity production capacity (Jo and Gartzke 2007, 173).

reprocessing activities from Fuhrmann and Tkach (2015), nuclear power plants, nuclear submarines, and nuclear-weapons programs. Latent-variable approaches simultaneously account for the fact that some of these activities are more difficult and better discriminate high-capacity versus low-capacity states. It also separates variation in the latent concept from variation from measurement error, which simple indexing approaches cannot (Jackman 2008). This gives v an advantage over other latency measures.[9]

The below statistical analysis uses two forms of v, one that uses all indicators and one that excludes weapons-related indicators. A natural question to ask is whether nuclear-weapons possession predicts dispute reciprocation. Answering that with both an indicator variable for possession and the more inclusive v measurement effectively splits the impact of nuclear weapons. The alternative v solves that problem. The standard v-scores range from -1.12 to 2.58 within the dispute observations; the v-scores without weapons-related indicators range from -1.10 to 2.63. Higher scores indicate greater proficiency.[10] For model-checking for a non-monotonic relationship, I also include a term for Nuclear Proficiency Squared.

With that in mind, one may wonder whether nuclear-weapons possessors will drive the empirical results. This is a legitimate concern – nuclear-weapons states tend to have the highest v scores for both measurements.[11] I address this by running a model that excludes nuclear possessors, as coded by Bleek 2010.

CONTROLS. To isolate the differences between realized and unrealized nuclear capacity on dispute reciprocation, I control for a number variables of that could potentially cloud the relationship. To begin, I include *Capability Ratio*, a measurement that takes the maximum of the states' CINC scores divided by the sum of the dyad's CINC scores; thus, lower values indicate dyadic parity while higher values imply a preponderance of power on one side. *Polity* scores from the POLITY IV dataset factor

---

[9] Estimating latent variables has become more common in international relations, with applications ranging from voting preferences (Bailey, Strezhnev, and Voeten 2017) to geopolitical relevance (Xiang 2010).

[10] The cardinality of these numbers has no inherent meaning. Rather, the v values facilitate comparisons between countries, which is sufficient for regression analysis. Note that these comparisons only work within a single version of v. As such, the fact that the highest scores occur in the measure without weapons-related indicators is meaningless.

[11] However, this relationship is not universally true. For example, many non-nuclear countries have higher v scores than South Africa during its brief nuclear period.

in domestic governance effects; they range from -10 (complete autocracy) to 10 (complete democracy). The *Log Distance* between the states is a key control because closer states are conceivably easier to reciprocate against. *Major Power* status for the initiator parses out the effects of nuclear weapons versus the ability to project power. Meanwhile, major power status for the target accounts for how such states are more likely to have the military resources to reciprocate. I therefore include indicator variables for both. *S-Score (Weighted)* (Signorino and Ritter 1999) controls for foreign policy similarity between states.

A final potential concern is that nuclear capabilities more generally reflect economic capacity. Indeed, within the militarized-interstate-dispute data, Logged Initiator GDP and nuclear capacity have a correlation of 0.52. That being the case, a high v value could yield fewer reciprocated disputes not due to the described mechanism but rather because the opposing state fears the general underlying technological capabilities of its opponent. I therefore include the natural logarithm of the initiator's gross domestic product (*Logged Initiator GDP*) from Singh and Way (2004).

4.2.3 Statistical Model

Below, I implement a logit model to estimate the probability that a target reciprocates a militarized interstate dispute. There are, of course, many other ways to test the effectiveness of nuclear proficiency in this regard, and I consider them in the robustness section later.

4.3 EMPIRICAL EVIDENCE OF THE POWER OF NUCLEAR PROFICIENCY

I begin with logit models that look for a monotonic relationship between proficiency and reciprocation. Broadly, they support Hypothesis 4.1 – higher nuclear proficiency predicts a lower probability of the target reciprocating a crisis. Table 4.1 presents the results from four separate regressions. The first three include all observations. Model 1 is a naïve logit that contains no controls. Model 2 includes all of the controls except for nuclear-weapons possession, while Model 3 explicitly accounts for that predictor and uses the v measurement that excludes nuclear-weapons indicators. To verify that the results are not driven by nuclear-weapons states, Model 4 excludes those initiators altogether. The key takeaway from Table 4.1 is that regardless of the restrictions on initiators and model specification, stronger capabilities are associated

TABLE 4.1. *Regression Table of Dispute Reciprocation*

	Dependent Variable: Dispute Reciprocation			
	All Observations Included			No NWS
	(1)	(2)	(3)	(4)
Nuclear Proficiency	−0.275***	−0.277***	−0.288***	−0.247***
	(0.045)	(0.087)	(0.091)	(0.095)
Nuclear Weapons			−0.074	
			(0.263)	
Initiator Polity		−0.005	−0.004	−0.021**
		(0.010)	(0.010)	(0.010)
Target Polity		−0.023***	−0.022***	−0.013
		(0.008)	(0.008)	(0.009)
Logged Distance		−0.126***	−0.125***	−0.153***
		(0.021)	(0.021)	(0.023)
S-Score (Weighted)		−0.366*	−0.366*	−0.172
		(0.209)	(0.211)	(0.237)
Initiator Major Power		0.614***	0.671**	1.445***
		(0.217)	(0.265)	(0.374)
Target Major Power		0.141	0.136	0.472**
		(0.205)	(0.205)	(0.237)
Capability Ratio		−0.326	−0.364	−0.791
		(0.428)	(0.429)	(0.488)
Logged Initiator GDP		−0.084**	−0.079**	−0.065
		(0.039)	(0.039)	(0.043)
Constant	−0.004	2.298***	2.234***	2.146***
	(0.055)	(0.730)	(0.740)	(0.815)
Observations	1,925	1,248	1,248	1,032
Log Likelihood	−1,306.608	−810.197	−809.696	−658.873
Akaike Inf. Crit.	2,617.216	1,640.394	1,641.392	1,337.747

Note: *p<0.1; **p<0.05; ***p<0.01

with lower probabilities of MID reciprocation. These results fall in line with Hypothesis 4.1.

Due to the link function, directly interpreting the substantive effects of the coefficients is difficult. As such, I turn to Figure 4.1, which illustrates the predicted probabilities from Model 2 of MID reciprocation as

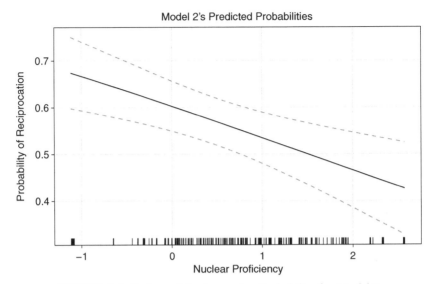

FIGURE 4.1. Estimated Reciprocation Probability for Model 2

a function of Nuclear Proficiency. All other variables are held at their medians, and the dashed lines are the 95% confidence intervals. The model estimates that a country with the technological capacity of Belize in 1990 (that is, none) sees its crises reciprocated about 68% of the time. In contrast, opponents of states with full capacity reciprocate about 42% of the time, a 26 percentage point drop-off and more than 38% less often than their technologically inferior comrades.

Of course, the fully capable states include nuclear powers like the United States, United Kingdom, and France. Perhaps a more informative comparison involves a country like Brazil in 1988. In that year, Brazil possessed light-water civilian nuclear power plants, uranium-enrichment facilities, and plutonium-reprocessing plants. This gives it a v-score of 1.64. Although this is a full point lower than the full-capacity states, a country with that v-score still sees its disputes reciprocated less than half the time. Consequently, going from low to high capacity (but still not having nuclear weapons) results in a substantively significant drop-off in reciprocation.

An overarching theme of this project and the growing nuclear latency literature is that international-relations scholars have placed too much focus on nuclear weapons rather than the ability to build them. Model 3 speaks to this. By disaggregating nuclear proficiency from nuclear-weapons possession, the model can speak to their relative influence in the relationship. Table 4.1 shows that the coefficient for proficiency is almost four times larger than the coefficient for weapons possession. This actually makes proficiency appear less important than it is. Nuclear Weapons is a binary variable; in contrast, recall that the particular Nuclear Proficiency measure for Model 3 ranges from -1.10 to 2.63. Thus, a country does not need to go from no proficiency to full proficiency to shift the prediction by the same amount that nuclear acquisition would.

To illustrate, Romania's v-score in 1989 was 1.28. By comparison, Brazil's v-score in 1994 was 1.55. Model 3 says that Romania would experience a roughly equivalent decrease in reciprocation rates by matching Brazil's proficiency as it would by obtaining a nuclear weapon.

In that light, the differences – or lack thereof – between Model 3 and Models 2 and 4 are particularly interesting. The substantive effect of Nuclear Proficiency is virtually identical in Models 2 and 3 despite the latter containing a control for Nuclear Weapons.[12] Moreover, increasing Nuclear Proficiency leads to a much greater change to the model's prediction compared to possession of nuclear weapons. Comparing Model 2 to Model 4 also illustrates that initiators who possess nuclear weapons are not driving the results; the Nuclear Proficiency remains important and statistically significant.

Before moving on, a closer look at Table 4.1 reveals that nuclear-weapons possession does not have a statistically significant coefficient in Model 3. Some may find this concerning because nuclear proficiency ostensibly extracts concessions because it foreshadows nuclear weapons. However, I caution against overanalyzing the statistical result for two reasons. First, the coefficient is negative, in line with a large literature that connects nuclear weapons to coercive benefits. Second, both nuclear weapons and dispute reciprocation are binary variables. This combination generates a lot of noise, making it difficult to find a result in an analysis with 1,248 observations.

Switching gears, I now look for support for Hypothesis 4.2. Doing this requires an additional regression. However, the appropriate empirical test is not replication of the four models featured in Table 4.1. This is because Proposition 3.4 makes a specific prediction about countries *without* nuclear weapons. Countries with both high capacity scores and nuclear weapons ought to enjoy deterrent benefits. In contrast, if

---

[12] Because these are logit models, this is not apparent from reading the coefficients from Table 4.1. However, inspection of predicted probabilities across models indicates similar substantive effects.

theoretical critiques of Proposition 3.4 are not relevant, countries with high capacity scores but without nuclear weapons ought to have their opponents resist as much as possible. Thus, excluding nuclear-weapons states is the theoretically appropriate test. Table 4.2 reveals the results.

Interpreting coefficient tables for logit models with squared terms is difficult. I instead point to Figure 4.2. Like Figure 4.1, it plots the predicted probabilities of Model 5.[13] Recall that Hypothesis 4.2 predicts that reciprocation rates would minimize for middling proficiency levels. Figure 4.2 offers no support for this hypothesis. Rather, the probability of reciprocation is essentially flat for low proficiency levels before declining at higher proficiency levels.

As previewed earlier, Propositions 3.2 and 3.3 would predict this relationship if they governed the coercive dynamics and Proposition 3.4 wielded no empirical leverage. Indeed, Proposition 3.4 predicts a u-shaped relationship whereas Figure 4.2 illustrates a very weak inverted u-shaped relationship. Moreover, Figure 4.2 suggests that states with v-scores below roughly 0 cannot leverage the threat to build and thus cannot accrue any concessions based on their capability.[14] Higher-capacity states can, and therefore the predicted probability bends downward.[15]

To be clear, these estimates come from models with disputes as the unit of analysis. One may be concerned that selection is a barrier to inference. Two possible data-generating processes are worth exploring in further detail. First, it could be that countries with high nuclear-proficiency levels initiate disputes against weaker targets that are more inclined to quit without any push back. Alternatively, countries with high nuclear-proficiency levels may simply live in areas with fewer serious security concerns, meaning that potential opponents feel less need to reciprocate.

However, these potential selection problems do not mesh with theory and other empirical findings. To begin, countries using nuclear proficiency for coercive gains have no reason to limit themselves to weak targets. Rather, they ought to pressure their existing security

---

13 The domain of Figure 4.2 is smaller on the right side because nuclear powers occupy the highest v values and are excluded from the regression.

14 Zero values for v have no special substantive meaning, so it is purely coincidence that the downward bend in Figure 4.2 does not fully take hold until positive v values.

15 Of course, the predicted probability is not actually flat. In fact, the best-fit line slightly increases for very low proficiency levels. This is inevitable for regressions with squared terms, as they cannot produce truly flat lines. We therefore should not over-interpret the minor curvature of the prediction in this area.

TABLE 4.2. *Regression Table Allowing for a Non-Monotonic Relationship*

	Dependent Variable: Dispute Reciprocation
	(5)
Nuclear Proficiency	−0.176*
	(0.104)
(Nuclear Proficiency)^2	−0.168
	(0.102)
Initiator Polity	−0.021**
	(0.010)
Target Polity	−0.014
	(0.009)
Logged Distance	−0.150***
	(0.023)
S-Score (Weighted)	−0.169
	(0.237)
Initiator Major Power	1.476***
	(0.375)
Target Major Power	0.464*
	(0.237)
Capability Ratio	−0.775
	(0.489)
Logged Initiator GDP	−0.064
	(0.043)
Constant	2.211***
	(0.817)
Observations	1,032
Log Likelihood	−657.534
Akaike Inf. Crit.	1,337.069

Note: *p<0.1; **p<0.05; ***p<0.01

relationships further in accordance with their better threat to proliferate, regardless of how strong those opponents are. In fact, Chapter 2 suggests that the deterrent gains from nuclear weapons are *more* valuable when the opponent is stronger, as the potential nuclear-weapons state needs to force the other side to limit its post-war aims more often. Thus, if

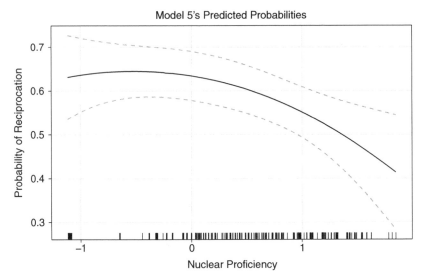

FIGURE 4.2. Estimated Reciprocation Probability for Model 5

anything, states with high levels of proficiency ought to initiate more often against tougher opponents.

In addition, nuclear-proficient states tend not to have easy security relationships (Mehta and Whitlark 2017a). Indeed, Mehta and Whitlark (2017b) show that uranium-enrichment and plutonium-reprocessing technologies are *more* common among countries that have a nuclear-armed rival or share borders with more potential opponents. More intense security relationships would suggest that opponents on average would want to reciprocate more, and yet the empirical results indicate otherwise.

Fortunately, I can also cross-validate these points about the statistical relationship in the case studies that follow. A country like Ukraine worried that it could square off against two different superpowers, which are not the type of pushover countries that would cloud the inference. Meanwhile, Egypt already knew it lived in an intense security relationship and nonetheless received the concessions necessary to render a nuclear program superfluous.

4.4 ROBUSTNESS CHECKS

To investigate whether the negative relationship between nuclear proficiency and dispute reciprocation is an artifact of the specific empirical model, I check a number of other functional forms. Unless otherwise specified, these robustness checks produce statistically and substantively similar results: increasing proficiency decreases the predicted probability of reciprocation.

To begin, it is worth considering alternate operationalizations of nuclear proficiency. The advantage of v is that it estimates the relative importance of various nuclear-related activities. Nevertheless, one robustness check replaces v with the seven-point index from Jo and Gartzke. Another uses Fuhrmann and Tkach's binary measure of whether a state has a uranium-enrichment or plutonium-reprocessing facility, which Mehta and Whitlark (2017a) use as a proxy for the ability to construct a nuclear weapon. The model with Fuhrmann and Tkach's measure does not achieve statistical significance but still estimates a negative relationship. The drop in statistical significance is not surprising given the relatively low number of observations and binary independent and dependent variables. In addition, not all countries that could build enrichment or reprocessing facilities do, making it a noisier variable for what I wish to measure.

The main model does not control for time effects. This could take two forms: years since the previous dispute and the year of the dispute. The latter is particularly concerning because nuclear proficiency scores generally increase over time. In turn, if dispute reciprocation has generally trended downward, proficiency may simply be absorbing the time trend. I therefore run two regressions, one with years since the last dispute with squared and cubic terms and one with the calendar year with squared and cubed terms.

Another time concern is whether the theory only applies to a specific subset of the period. I take two approaches with this. First, I subset the data to just the post–World War II years, as those represent the true nuclear era. Second, I subset the data to just Cold War years (between 1947 and 1991).

This chapter's model originally controlled for power parity versus power preponderance. The last series of major robustness checks replace that with the initiator's capability ratio or separate controls for each state's CINC score. The latter robustness checks ensure that nuclear proficiency's relationship is not simply proxying for the initiator's overall military capacity.

I also run a number of simpler checks. Unlike the other variables, gross domestic product has a lot of missing observations. I therefore omit them and also run two models with proxies for GDP (energy consumption and iron and steel production from Correlates of War) with better coverage. The main model controls for the initiator's and defender's democratic institutions separately. In accordance with the dyadic democratic peace, I replace those with the *lowest* of two Polity scores. Finally, Horowitz (2009) reports differential effects for the United States and Russia. I thus run models that include indicator variables for those countries as initiators and targets of disputes.

4.5 CONCLUSION

This chapter investigated the effectiveness of nuclear proficiency in deterring reciprocation of military threats and coercion – higher capacity states see their disputes reciprocation rates drop by 26 percent. Thus, *unrealized* nuclear capacity surprisingly accounts for substantial deterrent power. Of course, dispute reciprocation is just one way nuclear know-how alters coercive bargaining. Many such environments exist. Future research therefore ought to investigate whether the same unrealized power coerces concessions in these other situations.

Although militarized interstate disputes provide an excellent way to test hypotheses derived from the main formal model, most bargaining over nuclear weapons occurs on an *ad hoc* basis. Due to the secretive nature of international affairs, it is difficult to know what the domain of such cases is, let alone how to code their outcomes. As such, the next chapter switches its methodological approach to qualitative case studies. The process tracing that follows will help illuminate the formal theory and illustrate the causal mechanism that contributes to the empirical results from this chapter.

5

The Diplomacy of Butter-for-Bombs Agreements

The previous chapters have established that conciliatory measures from declining states can induce rising states not to proliferate and that nuclear proficiency influences whether states respond to militarized threats. But how do states reach these butter-for-bombs agreements? And why do states believe they are credible in the long term? This chapter tackles both issues.

On one level, the nonproliferation regime offers blanket benefits to non-nuclear states. Article III of the Nuclear Non-Proliferation Treaty explicitly gives non-nuclear states the right to use nuclear technology for peaceful purposes, such as energy production and chemotherapy. Moreover, on signing the NPT, nuclear powers offered non-nuclear members access to this type of technology (Koremenos, Lipson, and Snidal 2001, 770; Fuhrmann 2012, 6–7). Taiwanese nuclear power plants, for example, generate 20% of the island's electricity but run exclusively on American fuel (Mitchell 2004, 303–306).[1]

However, declining states have worked on an *ad hoc* basis with rivals especially interested in nuclear weapons. Thus, the main reason for the nonproliferation regime's success is not because member states sign a piece of paper – it is because of all the bargaining that takes place prior to member states signing.[2] Each of the case studies in this chapter features a country conditionally willing to proliferate – that is, absent concessions,

[1] Taiwan joined the NPT in 1968 as the Republic of China. Although no longer officially a part of the NPT, Taiwan accedes to IAEA inspections as though it were still signed to the treaty.
[2] To wit, South Korea ratified the NPT while still actively expanding its program to draw out more concessions (Hong 2011, 492).

those countries plausibly preferred developing nuclear weapons so they could coerce some benefits. However, in each case, a second state saved them the trouble by altering the potential proliferator's opportunity cost for investing in arms. With the incentives properly aligned, the potential proliferator became willing to submit to nonproliferation standards.

In particular, this chapter investigates bargaining in the shadow of nuclear proliferation in three situations: the United States and former Cold War foes, Egypt during Arab-Israeli tensions, and the United States and its protection of Cold War allies. These cases show that butter-for-bombs deals have succeeded in a variety of contexts. On one end of the spectrum, Egypt and Israel had one of the most enduring rivalries before resolving their differences at the bargaining table. At the other end, the United States and its Cold War allies were friendly from the beginning; butter-for-bombs bargaining only cemented their relationships. In the middle, the United States and select Soviet successor states lacked a pre-defined relationship; butter-for-bombs bargaining perhaps set the tone for future negotiations.

5.1 A STRATEGY FOR MODELS AND CASE STUDIES

Before addressing these cases, a framework for applying formal results to substantive observations is necessary. Case studies frequently accompany formal models. Sometimes these case studies motivate models as a means of creating theoretical explanations of empirical observations. Others use case studies for illustrative purposes, so as to show how a mechanism works in the real world or to prove the plausibility of parameters required for a particular equilibrium outcome. Yet others use case studies to "test" their models.[3]

Regardless of the motivation for using case studies, researchers must be careful to not select on the dependent variable. Formal models make falling into that trap tempting. Unlike empirical models, which can have multiple competing hypotheses or no prior expectations about the data, formal models with unique equilibria provide precise empirical predictions. Thus, any empirical observation that ends in the predicted and desired result makes an obvious case-study candidate.

However, a proper case study requires a deeper appreciation of the strategic elements at hand. Case studies are always overdetermined. As a result, it is often possible to use first-hand accounts to match an empirical

---

[3] On whether a model can be tested, see Clarke and Primo 2012.

observation to an equilibrium outcome. Yet, because of the large number of possible explanations for any particular observation, matching in this manner fails to discriminate between other explanations and lacks a direct connection from the theory to the empirics.

Formal models provide a partial solution. Game theory develops equations of causation. These equations appear as cut-points – precise combinations of variables that determine whether one outcome occurs as opposed to another. In standard statistical terms, the parameters in these cut-points are the independent variables while the equilibrium is the dependent variable. A good case study therefore maps the independent variables to the dependent variables and ensures that situations with the parameters inside the cut-points correctly predict the corresponding equilibrium outcome (Goemans and Spaniel 2016).

As with statistical analyses, creating variables requires operationalizing the scope conditions of the argument and the theory's outputs. Case studies provide some cross-validation here that statistical analysis alone cannot produce. Some variables are amenable to large-n data collection. For example, last chapter operationalized the cost of nuclear weapons by using nuclear infrastructure; Schub (2017) operationalizes potential shifts in power by looking at existing capabilities. Other variables, like offer sizes compared to the balance of power, are more challenging. This only becomes more daunting in future chapters, where the information that countries possess becomes a critical independent variable. These weaknesses provide an opportunity for case studies to shine by picking up the slack.

Case studies also investigate the soundness of the causal argument. Recall that an argument is *valid* if the premises imply the conclusion. The mathematics behind a model guarantee validity. However, an argument is *sound* if it is valid and its premises are true. Formal theory cannot say anything about the veracity of its assumptions. On the other hand, case studies are well equipped to investigate whether certain assumptions are true – namely, whether the parameters of a particular cut-point (the premises) hold for a given situation.

There are two ways to interpret cut-points to demonstrate that a case plausibly fits the argument. First, one can look at the cut-point holistically. Recall that Proposition 3.2 ("too cold") states that R does not build if $p'_R - p_R < (1 - \delta)k/\delta$. The cut-point could be expressed in a number of different ways, but this manner is particularly illuminating. The left side represents the extent of the power shift; the right side is the per-period costs of building if investment were spread out over infinitely many periods. As such, the cut-point asks a simple question: is building worth the investment? Case study analysis can answer this by investigating a rising state's ability to proliferate and whether it would have invested in a weapons program absent concessions. If so, the inequality holds; if not, it fails.

Second, one can analyze each variable in the cut-point in isolation. Recall that Proposition 3.1 ("too hot") says that D's threat to prevent induces R not to build if $p'_R - p_R > (c_D + c_R)/\delta$. Although there is still an intuitive interpretation to this cut-point – the left side is the extent of the power shift and the right side is the inefficiency of war – sometimes focusing on one particular parameter is illuminating. For instance, imagine war is extremely costly for the rising state, perhaps because fighting will assuredly lead to the rising state's leader being killed or jailed. With rare exception, we usually think of discount factors as quite high. If $\delta = \frac{9}{10}$, then $c_R = \frac{9}{10}$ implies the right side of the inequality is greater than 1.[4] The power shift cannot obtain a value greater than 1. Consequently, by virtue of the large value of c_R alone, we can conclude that Proposition 3.1 does *not* hold.

Isolating variables in this manner often leads to a fallacy, though. One might wish to show that Proposition 3.1's scope conditions hold by focusing on c_D. In particular, the analyst may be focusing on a strategic situation in which a declining state faced especially low costs for war, perhaps arbitrarily close to zero. This is tempting, but it is wrong. Near-zero costs of fighting are insufficient to conclude that the parameters of Proposition 3.1 hold. The term on the right side is $(c_D + c_R)/\delta$. Thus, even if $c_D = 0$, the scope condition still fails if $p'_R - p_R < \frac{c_R}{\delta}$.[5] This can easily hold if c_R is sufficiently large, as might be the case for the reasons above.

However, interpreting cut-points is only the first step. If the mechanism actually caused the observed result, then it must be true that it would *not* have produced that result had the parameters shifted away from that equilibrium outcome space. Put differently, counterfactuals are necessary to increase the degrees of freedom, which is necessary for a causal argument (Fearon 1991). In the context of butter-for-bombs agreements, for example, concessions-for-weapons agreements must take place if the parameters fall in the triangular parameter space of Figure 3.4. However, the declining state must not offer concessions in

---

[4] This is because $c_D > 0$.

[5] This is a subtle part of the logic of preventive war. Even if the declining state can fight for free, it might wish not to – war wastes the rising state's costs, which the declining state could otherwise extract through a peaceful settlement.

the counterfactual case with all other things equal except that the extent of the power shift exceeds Proposition 3.1's cut-point of $(c_D + c_R)/\delta$.

Constructing these counterfactuals can be the most difficult part of case study analysis. The simplest solution is to look for an exogenous shock to the strategic relationship. For instance, China's surge in power in the 1960s led to security fears in Japan and Australia, causing a jump from Proposition 3.2's "too cold" parameter space to Proposition 3.3's butter-for-bombs outcome. This makes the counterfactual easy to construct, because the comparison is a simple before-and-after snapshot of actors' dilemma. Other situations do not have such obvious temporal variations. For those, constructed counterfactuals are necessary.

Following the above theory of case studies, the next three sections trace Chapter 3's causal mechanism by focusing on three critical insights the model elucidated. For butter-for-bombs agreements to hold, three conditions must be true: (1) the rising state must not be concerned about preventive war, (2) the expected costs of a nuclear program must be manageable, and (3) an outside party must proactively engage the potential proliferator in negotiations so as to deter proliferation. As Propositions 3.1 and 3.2 explained, the absence of a preventive war and low investment costs are preconditions for the rising state to credibly threaten nuclear proliferation; if either fails to hold, the declining state has no incentive to buy off the rising state. The final condition, of course, is the actual illustration of a butter-for-bombs agreement.[6]

5.2 SOVIET SUCCESSOR STATES: BELARUS, KAZAKHSTAN, AND UKRAINE

I start with the fall of the Soviet Union, which presented a unique situation in proliferation history. Most states expend significant resources to develop nuclear weapons; Belarus, Kazakhstan, and Ukraine were born with stockpiles on their soil. Ukraine's inherited cache was particularly impressive, ranking third in the world with thousands of tactical and strategic nuclear bombs (Cirincione, Wolfsthal, and Rajkumar 2005, 373).

However, the Soviet successor states did not have operational control over the missiles (Miller 1993, 72). Russia still held the launch codes, and

---

[6] It also rules out the parameters of Proposition 3.4 – if a declining state is willing to bribe a rising state to keep the status quo power distribution, it cannot be the case that $k < \delta(p'_R - c_R)$. This is, in effect, an application of what Fey and Ramsay (2011) describe as "voluntary agreements." In an international system characterized by anarchy, states do not have to consent to an agreement. Thus, if they do, it must be because they believe they will perform better by accepting that deal than by refusing.

Russian-loyal soldiers patrolled the missile facilities. But inherited supplies aside, Belarus, Kazakhstan, and Ukraine held the technological proficiency to develop native nuclear stockpiles. A simple comparison may help illustrate this fact. In 2001, five years before its first partially successful nuclear test, North Korea's v proficiency score (Smith and Spaniel 2018) was 0.741. In 1992, just a year after the dissolution of the Soviet Union and at a politically volatile time in its successor states, Belarus' v-score was 0.812, Kazakhstan's was 1.074, and Ukraine's was 1.075. Moreover, each had nuclear research facilities or research reactors on their soil (Cirincione, Wolfsthal, and Rajkumar 2005, 368–377). Thus, even the successful transfer of existing bombs back to Russia would not guarantee long-term de-proliferation.

Of course, the potential post–Cold War foes resolved the problem. All Soviet nuclear weapons went safely back to Russia. Belarus, Kazakhstan, and Ukraine signed the NPT. The nonproliferation regime reigned supreme and has not shown any signs of faltering in the two decades since.

Again, the question remains why the Soviet successor states sacrificed their nuclear ambitions. Indeed, these states appeared as likely candidates for proliferation, stuck between Western Cold War foes and fears of an imperial Russia. Yet dollar diplomacy won out. The United States and Russia mobilized economic resources, purchased nuclear stability at a reasonable cost, and gave security assurances to promote long-term nuclear stability.

Why buy off the successor states? Moscow and Washington did not have any better options. The situation did not fit the parameters of Proposition 3.2. Each state's know-how and latent nuclear capacity put them in prime position to proliferate. Few research and development costs were necessary; the states would only have to spend on production. And given the questionable security environment at the time, proliferation would have been worth the investment. Consequently, Russia and the United States could not ignore the problem and hope it would go away.

Moscow and Washington could not leverage the threat of preventive war either. On the Russian side, Moscow was focused on domestic turmoil; rallying support for a war to stop a successor state's native nuclear program would have been a tough sell.[7] Meanwhile, the United

---

[7] On the other hand, an attempt to wrest control of existing stockpiles (which would have likely involved shooting Russian soldiers) was much more likely to provoke a bizarre form of preventive war.

States was just beginning its diplomatic introduction to the former Soviet bloc. Threatening preventive war would have set a conflictual tone for decades to come, which left policymakers in Washington to craft a softer game plan.

So the United States turned to butter-for-bombs. Recognizing that the fall of communism represented a unique opportunity in Eastern Europe, Senators Sam Nunn and Richard Lugar sought a proactive approach. Their efforts culminated in 1992's Cooperative Threat Reduction bill, which created funds to purchase and decommission leftover Soviet weaponry. Ultimately, the United States spent $2.6 billion between 1992 and 1997 (Ellis 2001, 9).

The five parties formalized their consensus on denuclearization with the Lisbon Protocol, also signed in 1992. The Protocol amended 1991's Strategic Arms Reduction Treaty (START) and designated Russia as the successor state of the Soviet Union, thus giving Moscow recognized nuclear weapons. Under the agreement, Belarus, Kazakhstan, and Ukraine were to return existing nuclear weapons to Russia (so Moscow could decommission them under the terms of START). The three states also pledged to meet all NPT obligations.

Although the successor states' responses were positive, each took a different final route to agreement as outlined below. The model predicts that the offer a rising state receives decreases as its cost of nuclear weapons increases. Thus, a cheaper path to the bomb means opposing states must concede more to obtain compliance. I find evidence for this below: Belarus had the worst nuclear option and received the least, while Ukraine had the best nuclear option and received the most.

BELARUS. Belarusian acquiescence went over without major incident (Deyermond 2008, 86–92); only a handful of officials advocated a strong, independent Belarus, and they quickly faded from political relevance. Five factors influenced the decision. First, unlike Kazakhstan and Ukraine, Belarus relies on Moscow for conventional military support. Belarus could free-ride on Moscow's power without proliferating. This, compared to Kazakhstan and Ukraine, made the functional extent of the power shift smaller. Thus, denuclearizing was Belarus' path of least resistance.

Second, security guarantees from Moscow were inherently credible. Foreign powers have often used Belarus as an entry point for an invasion of Russia. As such, their interests aligned – so much so that Belrusian military doctrine "assumed that any enemy of Belarus would be an enemy of Russia" (Drezner 1999, 155). Russia happily offered the guarantee as a cheap concession.

Third, the Belarusian energy sector depends on friendly deals with Moscow to keep the country running, receiving 90% of its needs from Russia (Drezner 1999, 156). Russia uses those concessions to buy cooperative behavior. During a brief holdout soon after independence, Russia raised the price of its oil 28-fold. Belarus simply could not afford paying near-market prices for its energy. Moscow returned its subsidies after Minsk fell in line.[8]

Fourth, compared to Kazakhstan and Ukraine, Belarusian nuclear infrastructure was lacking. The Soviet Union never built a nuclear power plant in Belarus, and the republic lacked its own uranium deposits (Paznyak 1995, 165–166). This exacerbated Belarus's energy crisis and meant that Minsk faced a greater-value k to build. In line with Proposition 3.3's butter-for-bombs offer, the technical weakness meant that Moscow and Washington needed to offer fewer concessions to induce Minsk's compliance.

Fifth, the Chernobyl nuclear disaster scarred Belarus. Although the plant sat in Ukraine, it was close to the border. Weather patterns surrounding Chernobyl pushed the most of the fallout into Belarusian territory. Consequently, radiation only contaminated 4% of Ukraine versus 20% of Belarus (Reiss 1995, 130). The economic consequences were equally disastrous, destroying a large segment of Belarus's best agricultural land and costing ten times the size of the government's budget (Paznyak 1995, 166–167). Unsurprisingly, these tolls left Belarus with a natural aversion to nuclear technology – again meaning a greater implicit value for k in terms of the model – and therefore hastened Belarus's acquiescence.

KAZAKHSTAN.   Politicians in Almaty appeared compliant for similar reasons. During the Soviet years, Kazakhstan was the primary nuclear testing location. This status gave president Nursultan Nazarbayev the legal claim that Kazakhstan could join the NPT as a nuclear-weapons state, which he declared was his intent during the first couple years of the transition (Drezner 1999, 160–161). However, the radiological toll gave the newly born Kazakhstan a predisposition against nuclear weapons.[9] Disease, displacement, and 200 million tons of radioactive waste gave

---

[8] The subsidies were larger than a butter-for-bombs agreement would entail alone because Moscow was also renting military bases in Belarus through the below-market price.

[9] To wit, Soviet tests often ignored weather patterns, causing additional radioactive contamination. Soviet scientists later set up medical facilities in the surrounding areas, but their primary purpose was observation, not treatment (Kassenova 2009).

rise to a strong anti-nuclear movement in Kazakhstan, which pressured Nazarbayev to terminate any independent programs (Laumulin 1995, 187–189). In terms of the model, this pushed Kazakhstan's cost for proliferation k higher. Consequently, Kazakhstan required a smaller bribe and made the deal more beneficial to its bargaining partners.

Nevertheless, a few obstacles stood in the way. Kazakhstan has one of the world's largest uranium reserves and stored large quantities of highly enriched uranium. Compared to Belarus, this meant that Almaty faced smaller practical costs to proliferate. But Washington and Moscow also worried about uranium export. Continued American aid dissuaded Kazakhstan from tapping the reserves for its own purposes or to sell to rogue states, while the United States directly purchased the existing highly enriched uranium in 1994 for an unspecified amount between $10 and $30 million (Cirincione, Wolfsthal, and Rajkumar 2005, 371–372; Jones et al. 1998, 80). Meanwhile, the Soviets abandoned an undetonated bomb at one of Kazakhstan's many testing facilities. Unlike the other Soviet weapons, Russia did not have operational control over it. Still, Kazakhstan welcomed Russian officials to remove the bomb and return it to Moscow's control.

One hurdle remained before Kazakhstan would assent to the NPT: China. Unlike Belarus and Ukraine, Kazakhstan shares a large border with China, and its capital at the time was just a few hundred miles from Chinese territory. In a dramatic reminder, having just returned from China, Nazarbayev "reportedly unrolled a map and pointed out to [US Secretary of State Warren] Christopher all of the dangers on Kazakhstan's borders" (Reiss 1995, 148). Washington then tied security assurances to ratification of the NPT. Further security assurances flowed in from China, and Kazakhstan received Russian assurance of protection from China. Combined, these assurances allayed most Kazakh fears. The United States sweetened the deal with an additional $200 million in aid (Reiss 1995, 149), leading the Kazakh parliament to ratify the NPT with a vote of 238–1.

UKRAINE. While Belarus and Kazakhstan quickly accepted American and Russian inducements, negotiations stalled with Ukraine. Two factors were at play: the realization that delay could induce greater concessions and domestic competition within Ukraine between Russian loyalists and Ukrainian nationalists. At first, Ukrainian President Leonid Kravchuk appeared cooperative, privately assuring Moscow and Washington that existing stockpiles would quickly return to Russia and that

Ukraine would sign the NPT (Reiss 1995, 99). However, the Rada, the Ukrainian parliament, played "bad cop" in the rounds of negotiations (Garnett 1995, 137–140). It was reluctant to concede a nuclear deterrent that could counter future Russian aggression, much as the hard realist account would predict (Mearsheimer 1993). Although the Rada ratified START, it in the process rejected the Lisbon Protocol's requirement that Ukraine accede to the NPT (Jones et al. 1998, 26) and stalled implementation of nonproliferation protocols. Support for a nuclear deterrent grew from 18% to 45% from 1992 to 1994 (Riabchuk 2010, 99). Officials realized they could use their international weakness as a form of bargaining strength and began campaigning for a better butter-for-bombs offer (Facon 2012, 161–162).

It should not come as a surprise that Ukraine was the last holdout. Despite the post-collapse economic upheaval, Ukraine held a much larger domestic economy compared to Belarus and Kazakhstan. It was therefore better equipped to endure temporary pain to produce an atomic bomb (Miller 1995, 21). Moreover, Ukrainian nationalists wanted to build the new republic's relationship with the West and secure the country as *Ukrainian*, free from Russian influence.[10] Though nuclear weapons still would not have come cheaply (Reiss 1995, 121), the relative investment cost is lower under these conditions. The model predicts that declining states have to offer more to rising states to ensure the latter's compliance.

This was a delicate balancing act. Washington firmly wanted a Ukraine free from nuclear weapons. Keeping the nuclear program as a bargaining chip risked quashing a nascent friendship with the West, but the stalling tactic worked. The Rada insisted that permanently relinquishing nuclear weapons needed to be conditional on aid and security assurances from both the United States and Russia (Cirincione, Wolfsthal, and Rajkumar 2005, 374–377). The United States correspondingly increased its aid to transfer the existing stockpiles; by the end of the process, Kiev would become one of Washington's greatest aid recipients. Meanwhile, the terms of agreement called for Soviet nuclear weapons in Ukraine to be decommissioned. In return for continued cooperation, Moscow downblended the enriched uranium and shipped it back to Ukraine to fuel nuclear power plants. This trade amounted to a roughly $1 billion concession from Moscow (Drezner 1999, 202).

---

[10] To that end, nationalists in the Rada made Ukrainian the official language in one of their first parliamentary acts (Garnett 1995, 131).

With these inducements in hand, Ukrainian leaders concluded the temporary cost of proliferation would not be worth the eventual payoff. In February, 1993, Russia increased Kiev's energy costs tenfold (Drezner 1999, 199). By the end of the year, the lack of subsidy cost Kiev $5 billion (Reiss 1995, 122).[11] Pressing further meant that Ukraine would have to push through the energy hardship. With the military fearing substantial maintenance costs and the civilian government wanting to jump-start the economy (Paul 2000, 119), Ukrainians reached a consensus and accepted Russian and American inducements. The Budapest Memorandum resulted, with Russia, the United States, and United Kingdom pledging to uphold existing territorial boundaries and terminate economic coercion.

By 1996, Russia had received all leftover Soviet nuclear weapons. The butter-for-bombs agreements had worked. Moreover, the negotiations paved the way for long-term settlement; none of the successor states has reopened its nuclear program in the two decades following the fall of the Soviet Union.

As a post-script, following the 2014 Crimean Crisis, some policymakers in Ukraine expressed regret that Kiev did not pursue nuclear weapons after achieving its independence. In terms of a modeling question, butter-for-bombs agreements are robust to the possibility that there may be some exogenous upheaval provided that the likelihood of a shock to the system is sufficiently low. The only difference is that declining states must overpay on their offers to induce acceptance, effectively compensating for the fact that the potential rising state may lose its benefits in a future period. I return to the subject of what happens in more volatile times in the next chapter.

In terms of an empirical question, it is not clear that the agreement backfired on Ukraine. The counterfactual is not a 2014 crisis with Ukraine holding a nuclear stockpile; it is a counterfactual 2014 crisis with Ukraine holding a nuclear stockpile *and* being substantially poorer due to the sanctions it would have faced and forgone aid. Moreover, in the aftermath of Russia's annexation of Crimea, Ukraine has not made a serious attempt to start a nuclear-weapons program. To the contrary, Ukraine and the United States issued a joint reaffirmation to the principles of the Non-Proliferation Treaty.[12]

---

[11] These subsidies continued over the long haul. Even into the turn of the millennium, Russia supplied a vast majority of Ukraine's gas and oil needs and was the biggest importer of Ukrainian goods (Paul 2000, 118).

[12] https://obamawhitehouse.archives.gov/the-press-office/2014/03/25/joint-statement-unite d-states-and-ukraine

5.3 EGYPT, THE CAMP DAVID ACCORDS, AND EXTERNAL SUBSIDIES

In October, 1974, Egypt declared to the United Nations General Assembly that an arms race in the Middle East would begin if Israel proliferated (Schiff 2001, 280). Of course, Israel had already proliferated in 1967 (Cohen 1998, 273–276). And yet, no arms race occurred. On the contrary, Cairo ratified the NPT in 1981, thirteen years after signing the agreement. Egypt had long warned that its stance against nonproliferation was contingent on Israeli compliance but remained still when it was time to act. Why?

This section argues that inducements from Israel and the United States bought Egyptian compliance. In particular, Israeli's forfeiture of the Sinai Peninsula to Egypt with 1979's Camp David Accords preempted the incentive to nuclearize. Upon receiving the concession and securing other forms of developmental aid, Cairo ended its nuclear aspirations and ratified the NPT.

Egypt's nuclear program went through three distinct phases: conflict, bargaining, and resolution. The conflict phase began immediately following Israeli independence. Egypt lost the 1948 war and spent the next two decades battling Israel, believing it could make up for the initial loss, especially given Israel's delicate geopolitical positioning. During this time, Egypt launched its civilian nuclear program. It militarized the project in 1960 following the discovery of Israel's Dimona facility (Rublee 2009, 109). Cairo turned to Moscow for assistance; the Soviets only replied with security assurances, which Gamal Abdel Nasser believed were insufficient (Bar-Joseph 1982, 206). Given the security environment of the time, this should be unsurprising. The arms race occurred largely due to preemptive concerns (Reiter 1995) and misperceptions on both sides, culminating in two more wars in 1967 and 1973. Under such conditions, nonproliferation agreements ought to fail for the same reason bargaining fails in the shadow of war. A butter-for-bombs deal would have to wait.

Nevertheless, Egypt signed the NPT in 1968. The signing was not a reflection of sincerity or satisfaction with the status quo. Rather, Cairo wished to give Israel a political black eye, as the "rogue" Middle East state with nuclear weapons. The insincerity showed through – Cairo could not verify its compliance with the treaty, opponents suspected it was in violation, and Egypt made no progress in ratifying the treaty. The underlying conflict with Israel persisted.

The bargaining phase followed the conclusion of the 1973 Yom Kippur War and reflected Egypt's realization of its military shortcomings. Egypt had lost the Sinai Peninsula to Israel in 1967 during the Six-Day War and failed to recapture it in this operation six years later. The repeated defeats clarified that Israel was much stronger than Egypt had imagined previously. Cairo subsequently updated its belief that it could defeat Israel in a conventional war. Traditional theories of proliferation (Thayer 1995) would thus predict a surge in Egyptian nuclear capacity, as an atomic threat was perhaps the best way to coerce the Sinai away from Israel. Yet the removal of uncertainty from the bargaining environment led Egypt to start negotiations. After all, the butter-for-bombs logic dictates that states ought not to waste inefficient investment costs in complete information environments.

In relating the post-1973 period to Chapter 3's model, Egypt viewed nuclear weapons as beneficial in the absence of agreement. In other words, the case does not fit the "too cold" parameters of Proposition 3.2. Israel's announcement of its Dimona nuclear reactor spurred the first nuclear discussions (Einhorn 2004, 45). An Egyptian bomb could counter Israel's nuclear deterrent and balance the playing field. In contrast, in terms of benefits, the playing field heavily favored Israel, as three Egyptian–Israeli wars had pushed the status quo heavily in Israel's favor. The loss of the Sinai alone cost Egypt $400 to $500 million annually, largely from profits from the Suez canal (Rublee 2009, 118; Barnett 1992, 111). Combined, these two points indicate that nuclear weapons would have a significant impact on the balance of power (i.e., $p'_R - p_R$ was sizable) and that the value of the return on investment would be high. Put differently, traditional security-based theories do not explain Egypt's decision (Rublee 2009, 136-138).

Meanwhile, cost-wise, Egypt's nuclear proficiency was favorable. Again using North Korea's 2001 v-score of 0.741 as a baseline, Egypt had a 0.971 score in 1963, a 1.084 score in 1979, and a 1.170 score in 1982 after opening a plutonium-reprocessing facility. Although Cairo's nuclear thinking does not have as large of a paper trail as other countries (Rublee 2009, 124–125), Egypt had a long history of funding discretionary projects (Walsh 2001, 215–218). In short, though the program may not have been cheap, Egypt could have sought a bomb if it had the reason to.

Unfortunately, it is unclear whether Israel would have intervened had Egypt come close to proliferating. On one hand, Israeli air strikes in 1981 (Iraq) and 2007 (Syria) indicate that Israel viewed preventive war as a useful foreign policy tool, at least soon after the fact. On the other hand, Israel could have more efficiently continued the 1967 war or 1973 war as a proactive version of preventive war but chose not to. Intervention was a major concern; Israel worried that pushing the fight further into Egyptian territory would have triggered a response from Moscow and strained relations with the United States (Blechman and Hart 1982).[13] Following the war, Israel felt exhaustion from continuous conflict in the Middle East and was searching for a way out. Preventive war would have been a step in the wrong direction. These concerns thus at least give a plausible case that Proposition 3.1's parameters do not fit here. Moreover, Egyptian leadership did not believe the threat of intervention was a concern (Rublee 2009, 137).

Credibility aside, nuclear weapons would not come cheap – economic havoc in the form of food shortages, high inflation, and poor credit distracted Cairo from its military goals (Solingen 2007, 240). But the baseline model from Chapter 3 shows that sizeable costs incentivize rivals to bargain through the dilemma. Cognizant of these issues, Egyptian President Anwar Sadat sought a deal, believing that an arms race would only exacerbate the conflict with Israel (Bar-Joseph 1982, 207). He first looked to the United States to trade aid for his support of NPT ratification. The United States agreed. In 1975, American aid jumped to about $1.3 billion (2011 dollars), up from just $82 million the year previous (Carroll 2013). Receipts in subsequent years hovered around that level, and adding military assistance pushes the figure to $2 billion (Solingen 2007, 241). With such large concessions coming in, Cairo's serious push toward nuclearization ended.

However, this is only half of the bargaining story. The third phase of Egypt's nuclear negotiations centers around ratification of the NPT. Unlike the relatively meaningless signature from 1968, ratification would legally bind Egypt to nonproliferation. Thus, while Sadat's pragmatic approach was a welcome sign, it hardly ended Egypt's nuclear contingency. To rally a broad coalition to ratify the NPT, Cairo required greater concessions. Those concessions came via the Camp David Accords. Although nuclear weapons were not the central focus of the summit, negotiations took place in their shadow. Indeed, Article 2 of Egypt's opening proposal put adherence to the Non-Proliferation Treaty

---

[13] The Soviet Union had previously offered Egypt security assurances if Israel developed nuclear weapons after Moscow denied Cairo's request for nuclear assistance (Aronson 1978, 61).

on the table as a means of furthering guaranteeing security and pros-
perity (Telhami 1990, 214). In conjunction with a comprehensive peace
plan, Israel returned the Sinai to Egypt. The United States, meanwhile,
pledged to continue the lucrative side payments and offered to construct
a nuclear reactor in exchange for ratifying the NPT (Levite 2003, 75).

With that in mind, consider a counterfactual world in which Egypt
obtained nuclear weapons. What more could Egypt coerce out of Israel
and the United States? Israel had previously shown its competence in a
conventional conflict. Given that Egypt lost the Sinai in previous battles,
Cairo could not reasonably expect to extend its territorial gains any further than the Sinai even with the safety net of nuclear-tipped missiles. In
short, a nuclear deterrent could have enhanced Egypt's aggregate level
of power. However, it would not have delivered sufficient concessions
to justify the expense, especially as Egypt became increasingly reliant on
external economic revenue (Bahgat 2007, 10).

Ratification of the NPT finally came in 1981. Previously, opposition
leaders in the People's Assembly insisted on maintaining an ambiguous
course so as to leverage the nuclear threat as a means of driving concessions. But as the 1980s began, Egypt faced a severe energy crisis. With
industrial output dampening, opposition leaders sought nuclear energy
partners. This search had failed over the past couple decades because
partners were not forthcoming in the absence of the NPT's safeguards
(Einhorn 2004, 50–51). Realizing that energy trumped holding out for
a better bargain, opposition leaders dropped their protest, allowing the
People's Assembly to ratify the NPT. Nuclear partners flooded into Egypt
soon thereafter (Rublee 2009, 121).[14]

Sadat was assassinated later that year. His successor, Hosni Mubarak,
maintained the non-nuclear course; international aid had been too much
of a bounty to the Egyptian middle class to be worth sacrificing (Nincic 2012, 133–134). Still, Mubarak was careful to emphasize that NPT
compliance was not a result of Egyptian generosity, warning that Egypt
would not hesitate to proliferate if the circumstances called for it (Levite
2003, 72–73). But with Israel and the United States enjoying the benefits of a bargained resolution, the concessions have persisted over time.
Egypt has correspondingly kept its nuclear ambitions on hold.

---

[14] The nuclear assistance was slow to make real progress (Solingen 2007, 230), as 1986's
Chernobyl disaster generally cooled demand for nuclear power around the world.
Egypt's first reactor came only came online in 1997 with assistance from Argentina
(Einhorn 2004, 52–53; Rublee 2009, 123).

Overall, this case illustrates how bargaining can eliminate the need to proliferate even if the parties do not negotiate over nuclear weapons directly. Forfeiting the Sinai Peninsula maneuvered the share of benefits into both the static-bargaining range and the dynamic-bargaining range, as Figure 3.3 illustrated. In turn, Egypt had no need to explicitly threaten nuclear proliferation, as its share of benefits was already commensurate with its potential level of power.

5.4 COLD WAR ALLIES: SOUTH KOREA, AUSTRALIA, AND JAPAN

The United States faced a recurring problem throughout the Cold War. Many of its friends and allies faced growing security issues as communist rivals expanded regional power. At a time of continued crisis, the deterrent power of nuclear weapons provided an escape. As such, these friends and allies poured money into nuclear programs, hoping for a quick upper hand.

While potential nuclear arsenals posed a threat to the communist opponents, the United States worried its sprawling Cold War alliance would fracture. A nuclear South Korea, for example, could further pressure North Korea. The greater risks could suck the United States into a conflict it would otherwise wish to avoid. As a result, the United States began a trend of negotiating with its allies to keep nuclear weapons out of potential hot zones. The allies would receive financial benefits and security assurances from the United States; in return, the United States would maintain greater control over crisis decisions. This section details three such cases: the aforementioned issue with South Korea, Japan, and Australia.

There are a couple reoccurring themes in these cases. First, because these countries were allies of the United States, their rivals felt the costs of preventive war were too great. Of course, given that these countries were American allies, the United States could not reasonably threaten them with preventive war either. It is not that preventive action was impossible – the United States, in theory, could bomb a South Korean nuclear facility just as it could bomb an adversary's nuclear facility. Doing so incurs a new set of costs, though. Such an action would shatter the bilateral relationship. Given the value of allies, this would be a worse outcome than suffering the consequences of proliferation.

The model incorporates that by setting high values for c_D. In turn, none of these cases fit the parameters of Proposition 3.1. However, unlike the previous case studies, the primary concessions did not come from the rivals. Instead, Washington realized that it could cheaply offer an acceptable deal, thus preempting the need for further nuclear negotiations with the rival countries.[15]

Second, each of these was integrated into the world economy. South Korea, for example, had shunned North Korea's *juche* philosophy of self-reliance and had instead chosen to develop with the help of international trade. Solingen (2007) argues that this acts as a constraining force on nuclear proliferation. Indeed, the model incorporates this factor in the parameter k, which includes opportunity costs such as lost trade that might arise as a consequence of a nuclear program.

The theory of butter-for-bombs makes two predictions about these cases. First, high costs in the form of lost trade does not imply that a country is unwilling to proliferate under all circumstances. Indeed, a large benefit for proliferation can override that disincentive. On the other hand, conditional on requiring concessions to be satisfied, the quantity of concessions decreases in the cost of proliferation. Thus, though these countries may have required concessions, it did not take much to convince them to forgo nuclear weapons.

SOUTH KOREA. The Korean peninsula provides a good starting point. In the 1960s, rivalry with the North pushed South Korea to begin researching nuclear technology. Preventive war could not deter Seoul on this issue. An invasion from the North would prompt American retaliation as a violation of the Korean War's armistice. Consequently, North Korea's cost of preventive war c_D was relatively high. But Proposition 3.1's parameters require $p'_R - p_R > (c_D + c_R)/\delta$; the high value of c_D therefore pushed the Korean issue out of the "too hot" range for the North. Meanwhile, the United States certainly would not have used military might to end South Korea's nuclear ambitions, as doing so would ruin an otherwise mutually beneficial friendship.

Cost issues could not deter Seoul from proliferating either. This is understandable. The Koreas were still technically at war; coercive power remained vital. In times of continued rivalry and crisis, resolve levels run high. As a result, South Korea interpreted the material cost values for k as being small, just as high resolve yields smaller war costs in the standard

---

[15] This may be an avenue for future research. The model predicts that states will reach a deal in bilateral negotiations. When multiple states can all offer sufficient concessions to induce nonproliferation, the model does not make an inherent prediction of which state will step in.

bargaining model of war. Technically speaking, South Korea had a good starting point – its v-score beginning in 1962 exceeded North Korea's from 2001 (Smith and Spaniel 2018). In turn, the Korean case did not fit the parameters of Proposition 3.2, which required that costs be large to reach the region where $p'_R - p_R < (1 - \delta)k/\delta$.

Consequently, an outside party needed to offer inducements to coax South Korea out of its proliferation plans. The United States – not North Korea – fulfilled this role. Indeed, Seoul's pursuit of nuclear weapons began as the United States withdrew aid. South Korea relied on the United States for military aid and support to keep Pyongyang's troops north of the demilitarized zone. President Park Chung Hee worried that South Korea would soon be on its own. In short order, following Richard Nixon's election, the United States implemented the Guam Doctrine, withdrew from Vietnam, and removed 20,000 American troops from Korea (Hong 2011, 487).

Needing a solution, Park turned to the nuclear threat. For the reasons outlined above, the threat was credible. Yet Park perhaps did not see proliferation as his endgame. Rather, he viewed it as necessary to receive firm security assurances from the United States (Kim 2011, 32).[16] As such, Seoul began purchasing nuclear technology from France, Belgium, and Canada and looked to hire ethnically Korean nuclear engineers from the United States and Canada (Oberdorfer 2001, 69). These measures were extremely costly (Ha 1983, 181). Nevertheless, the actions alarmed the United States, which had previously been South Korea's exclusive source of nuclear material and assistance for its only nuclear reactor, the Kori-1.

The gambit worked. While watching the events unfold, the American embassy in Seoul recommended the United States open up negotiations to stop the South Korean program (Hong 2011, 498). Washington heeded the embassy's advice. Seoul won $1.5 billion in military aid (Drezner 1999, 255), received an American nuclear umbrella, and saw a majority of existing American troops stay on its soil.

Seoul settled for such minimal concessions because the country was particularly susceptible to American influence. This was for two reasons. First, pushing Washington risked further American abandonment of peninsula; South Korea could have lost more of the American troops in

---

[16] Skeptics in the United States surmised this was the case (Hong 2011, 499), but Washington nevertheless followed through with the concessions due to South Korea's credible threat to proliferate in the absence of concessions.

the demilitarized zone with the North. And second, South Korea needed American (and Japanese) loans to build its booming economy (Solingen 2007, 90), which accounted for 3.4% of its GNP in 1975 (Drezner 1999, 259–260). Accordingly, Washington threatened sanctions if Seoul continued nuclear development (Mazarr 1995, 25–28). The United States perhaps had even greater leverage in the nuclear-energy sector, as South Korean industrialization led to reliance on imported energy (Lanoszka 2013). Indeed, Washington swore to withdraw roughly $300 million in financial aid for South Korea's civilian nuclear program if it continued toward proliferation. This risked disrupting the development of Kori-2, South Korea's scheduled second nuclear power plant (Drezner 1999, 260–261; Pollack and Reiss 2004, 262–263).

In this situation, Washington manipulated Seoul's opportunity cost. To be willing to build, the South's nuclear-weapons program would have had to extract additional concessions or further assurances. It is difficult to conceive of an issue that would justify the development cost, especially with the threat to withhold aid. It is also hard to imagine that South Korea could have earned considerably more concessions from its rivals or varied its policy substantially from the American ideal point with its own arsenal. As such, despite ratifying the NPT in 1975, Park only paused the program for a few years. His successors finally put it to rest in 1980 (Hayes 1991, 205), opting to free-ride on the American deterrent. Still, in line with Park's policy of contingent nonproliferation (Hong 2011, 506–507), Seoul tied the decision to security concession; if the United States ever lifted it, South Korea would restart the program.[17]

JAPAN. Two factors spurred Japan's flirtation with nuclear weapons: China's successful nuclear test in 1964 and the Vietnam War (Paul 2000, 48). The growing communist threats led Tokyo to reconsider the credibility of the United States's security guarantees. Prime Minister Eisaku Sato thus pressed for atomic development.

Japan's threat to build appeared credible. For similar reasons as South Korea, preventive war was not an effective counter-proliferation measure against Japan. Many regional rivals – China, the Soviet Union, and North Korea – worried that a powerful Japan could regain its World War II era territorial ambitions. Japan's constitutionally limited military did not

---

[17] For its part, the United States also tied the umbrella to adherence to the agreement; in 1976, Secretary of Defense Donald Rumsfeld warned that the United States would "review the entire spectrum of its relations with the ROK" if Seoul were to test the arrangement (Oberdorfer 2001, 72).

alleviate this concern. However, the United States' security commitment to Japan at the time deterred each of those rivals, pushing their costs of war high and outside of Proposition 3.1's parameters.

For a long time, Japan fit the "too cold" parameters of Proposition 3.2. To this day, Japan remains the only victim of offensive nuclear detonations. The scars of Hiroshima and Nagasaki have weighed on Japanese politicians ever since; Chapter 2, Article 9 of the Japanese constitution, which forever renounces war as a tool for the country, reflects this. Meanwhile, 1955's Atomic Energy Basic Law explicitly limited Japan's nuclear programs to peaceful research.

Although technical issues were not a significant barrier, tactical problems led to budget concerns for Tokyo.[18] Being such a small country, land-based nuclear missiles were an easy target for a counterforce attack.[19] Equally problematic was a lack of proximate Soviet targets that Japan could hit. Few Soviet cities were near the Pacific. Without long-range missiles, Japan could only force a million casualties (Paul 2000, 55). Even then, Japan would have to worry about radioactive fallout drifting from bombed Russian cities back to the Japanese islands.

All told, these obstacles meant any nuclear-weapons program would require a submarine-launched ballistic-missile program as well. The material costs of nuclear weapons would have been significant (Endicott 1975, 231) at a time when military spending was not a priority. Japan had been demolished during World War II. Any money invested in nuclear research was money not invested in a more efficient path to economic recovery. As a result, the United States did not need to offer further inducements to keep Japan free of nuclear weapons at first.

However, the situation changed in the 1960s for two reasons. To begin, Japan's economy had fully recovered and was then one of the strongest in the world. And second, China tested its first nuclear bomb in 1964 and followed with improvements to missile-delivery systems. Conservatives within the Japanese government correspondingly pushed for a Japanese deterrent despite the recent security guarantees from the United States (Holmes and Yoshihara 2012, 116–117; Akiyama 2003, 81–82). The newfound wealth and newfound fears changed Japan's calculus. Suddenly the investment cost k seemed lower, enough to push Japan out of the "too cold" range of Proposition 3.2 and into the butter-for-bombs

---

[18] Japan's ν-score exceeded North Korea's 2001 proficiency beginning in 1959 (Smith and Spaniel 2018).

[19] Japan was also weak against a countervalue attack – 400 nuclear missiles could wipe out half the Japanese population (Akiyama 2003, 82).

region of Proposition 3.3. Future prime minister and then director of Japan's defense agency Yasuhiro Nakasone commissioned a white paper on the constitutionality of nuclear weapons (Campbell and Sunohara 2004, 222). What was once untouchable now seemed possible.

Nevertheless, Prime Minister Eisaku Sato saw his country's weakness as a source of strength in negotiations with the United States. Security assurances were insufficient, especially as nationalists felt that the Treaty of Mutual Cooperation and Security between the United States and Japan was already incredible (Akiyama 2003, 86). In talks with the Johnson administration, Sato asked for the return of Okinawa (Endicott 1975, 25-27; Campbell and Sunohara 2004, 222–224). The deal would stall until the Nixon administration; Japan worried that Nixon's policy on allies' self-reliance weakened the United States' security assurances, especially as the 1960 American–Japanese security pact was set to expire in 1970 (Schoff 2012, 104–105). Needing to compensate, Nixon agreed to return Okinawa. Japan signed the NPT in 1970, received Okinawa in 1972, and ratified the NPT in 1976. In addition, Sato created a new nonproliferation doctrine with the "three non-nuclear principles" (non-possession, non-production, and non-introduction into Japanese territory) and the "four-pillars nuclear policy" (promote peaceful nuclear power, lobby for global nuclear disarmament, rely on American security assurances, and follow the three principles). Sato won the Nobel Peace Prize in 1974 for his efforts.

Of course, Japan could not push its demands much further. The aforementioned legal and strategic issues meant that initiating a nuclear-weapons program would be both politically and economically costly. As a result, a large domestic faction would have naturally resisted a departure from nonproliferation norms (Rublee 2009, 34–62). In turn, and in line with the model's prediction that butter-for-bombs offers decrease in k, Japan had to take what it was offered.

That said, Japan's non-nuclear policy continued to be contingent on American concessions. To wit, Morihiro Hosokawa, Prime Minister from 1993 to 1994, warned that "[i]t is in the interest of the United States, so long as it does not wish to see Japan withdraw from the NPT and develop its own nuclear deterrent, to maintain its alliance with Japan and continue to provide a nuclear umbrella" (Levite 2003, 71). Japan's entry into the NPT thus reflects satisfaction with its concessions package, not necessarily an underlying commitment to nonproliferation.

AUSTRALIA. During the early portion of the Cold War, Australia outsourced much of its national security to the United States and the United

Kingdom. However, the nuclear question emerged following London's decision to end its military presence in the Suez. Officials in Canberra worried the departure signaled that the United Kingdom would not honor weak security commitments abroad. Meanwhile, although Canberra believed the United States would have defended Australia in the event of a nuclear attack, the same intervention was questionable in case of a conventional strike (Quester 1973, 163–164). Domestic instability in Indonesia at the time made this second point particularly concerning. The tension only grew with the 1964 Chinese test (Paul 2000, 75).

The conditions for proliferation were favorable at the time. Australia did not need to worry about preventive war. Its geographic isolation made it a difficult invasion target – and high war costs for declining states correspond to Proposition 3.1's "too hot" parameters. A preventive nuclear strike on Australia could have been effective. But given Australia's defensive mindset, the functional power shift would have been minimal enough to make such a massive strike unnecessary, especially with uncertainty surrounding how the United States would respond. Again, this conforms to Proposition 3.1's parameters.

The costs of the program were manageable as well. Australia is blessed with one of the world's largest uranium reserves and hosted multiple British tests in the 1950s and 1960s. Put simply, Australia had both the raw materials and know-how. A 1968 report estimated that Australia could have a nuclear device within ten years at a modest upfront investment (Reynolds 2000, 195). The real cost would be in developing delivery mechanisms – the same factors that made Australia an unlikely target for preventive war also made it substantially more difficult to lob a nuclear missile at an enemy. Still, leaders were optimistic about creative solutions. Politically, the scientific bureaucracy in Australia favored further nuclear research and held enough domestic power to veto adherence to the Non-Proliferation Treaty (Quester 1973, 162). These circumstances situate Australia's position outside of the "too cold" parameters of Proposition 3.2. Consequently, absent concessions, Canberra might have pursued its own deterrent.

However, Australia's strategic concerns had evolved in the interim. Originally preparing for total war, Australia slowly shifted its attention to limited war (Reynolds 2000, 185). Nuclear weapons would not help here, which led Australia to deactivate its program in 1970. At that point, the United States was eager to gather support for the NPT. To elicit Australia's cooperation, United States Secretary of State Dean Rusk visited Canberra. He argued that a nuclear war could not be localized, and therefore the American nuclear umbrella would cover Australia (Reynolds 2000, 195–196). Tangibly, the United States extended scientific nuclear knowledge and permitted Australia to freely explore nuclear technology short of weaponization.

Electoral politics also played a role here worth mentioning. Hymans (2006, 114–140) notes that Australia's path toward proliferation peaked during Prime Minister John Gorton's administration and concluded once the Labor Party rose to power. Further, he argues that Gorton was a "oppositional nationalist" and leadership from Labor was not, corresponding with his theory that oppositional nationalism prompts proliferation.

A second interpretation – and one that fits the bargaining mechanism from Chapter 3 – is that Australia's electorate simply voted their preferences. During this period, Gorton's Liberal Party branded itself as hawkish, far eclipsing the resolve of Australia's median voter. Gorton himself won his job as prime minister after his predecessor's entanglement in the Vietnam War became too unpopular (Edwards 1997), largely due to the need to draft soldiers despite growing likelihood of defeat. Yet Gorton kept the troops in Vietnam and pushed for technological nuclear progress at home, publicly under the guise of peaceful research. These factors proved pivotal in ending the 23-year Liberal reign in the 1972 election. New Labor Prime Minister Gough Whitlam – a dove whose visit to China shortly predated Nixon's – followed his mandate, accepted the concessions, and ended Australia's nuclear bid.

As a final note, it is worth highlighting that concessions to Australia were significantly smaller than concessions to South Korea or Japan. In fact, Leah (2016) argues that security guarantees played much less of a role in Australia's nonproliferation decision than the evolution of geopolitical concerns – though Australia's stance would change if the United States began pulling itself from the region. This is consistent with Chapter 3's butter-for-bombs theory – the more valuable nuclear weapons are, the more potential proliferators need to be appeased. Australia's security environment was significantly less hostile than South Korea's or Japan's, and thus Australia received fewer concessions.

5.5 CONCLUSION

This chapter explored seven empirical cases of potential proliferation. Recognizing the impending efficiency loss, other countries stepped in to negotiate a deal instead. Consequently, at times when proliferation appeared likely, the states in question instead chose a non-nuclear path. Bargaining simply quashes proliferation's desirability.

There is evidence that the theory applies to more than the cases analyzed here. In brief, West Germany found little use for nuclear weapons when it could leverage Washington and Paris for the coercive assistance it required (Paul 2000, 38–47; Chafetz 1993, 135–139). Concessions from the United States and Soviet Union altered nuclear preferences in Yugoslavia as well (Hymans 2012, 157–202). And all of these cases fail to consider "the dog that didn't bark." For example, Canada has never mounted a serious nuclear-weapons program outside of World War II, but it is reasonable to imagine that circumstances would have been different if Canada could not free-ride off of the American deterrent.

However, not all bargains are easy to reach. In particular, bargaining between allies requires substantially fewer costly concessions from opposing states to induce potential proliferators to accept. For the Cold War cases, this was because the relative cost to the United States (security guarantees and troop commitment) was substantially smaller than the power gains American allies received by engaging in the deal. These cases suggest that nuclear proliferation among select states can *reduce* further proliferation by incentivizing allies to bandwagon. In contrast, states without nuclear-armed ideological friends can only receive more expensive concessions from rivals, which in turn makes those rivals find bargaining less appealing. While case studies of Egypt and the Soviet successor states show that such agreements are still possible, this makes negotiation less likely to succeed in other environments with other bargaining problems.

The remainder of this book investigates those bargaining problems. Notably, this chapter only investigated when butter-for-bombs treaties succeed. In contrast, the next set of chapters indicate that commitment problems and information problems lead to bargaining breakdown.

6

Arms Treaties and the Changing Credibility
of Preventive War

The previous chapters established an inefficiency puzzle regarding nuclear weapons. Namely, a range of nuclear-free settlements exist that both sides prefer to proliferation, and those settlements are sustainable over time. Why, then, do states sometimes fail to locate such agreement and share the surplus?

This chapter explores the robustness of that result under a more dynamic setting. Suppose, for the moment, that the rising state will suddenly lose the ability to proliferate tomorrow. A bargaining tension arises. If the rising state does not proliferate today, the declining state can offer the rising state's reservation value for war *without* nuclear weapons for the rest of time. The rising state accepts these offers because its only alternative (war) is not any more attractive. So the rising state must have nuclear weapons tomorrow to secure any concessions in the future.

Moving back a step, the rising state must proliferate today. The declining state would like to buy off the rising state immediately and in the future, but the rising state knows that the promise of later concessions is inherently incredible. Thus, a commitment problem induces the rising state to invest in nuclear weapons.

The above intuition explains why bargaining might break down, but it does so in a trivial manner. A rising state's ability to proliferate does not exogenously vanish from one day to the next. A non-trivial explanation for proliferation would *endogenously* explain why the rising state will be unable to proliferate in the future. In other words, the rising state's limitations must form due to actions the states take within the context of their strategic environment.

This chapter provides such a causal mechanism, focusing on situations in which the declining state's desire to prevent varies over time. If this desire fluctuates greatly, the states find themselves in the aforementioned commitment problem. When the declining state is weak, it wishes it could promise continued concessions into the future. But the moment the declining state's appetite for war returns, it will inevitably cut off concessions. Anticipating this, the rising state ignores the declining state's promises and proliferates while its rival is vulnerable. The result is inefficient but unavoidable.

Putting the theory into context, consider the Soviet Union's dilemma following World War II. At the time, Washington would have liked to buy off Moscow and avoid a nuclear-powered Eastern Bloc. However, the American public was eager to scale back the war machine, having just spent the previous years mobilizing to destroy Nazi Germany and Imperial Japan. As time passed, though, this war exhaustion would inevitably wear off. At that point, Moscow would lose out on whatever concessions it would have hypothetically received. Thus, the credible threat of preventive war in the future compelled the Soviet Union to join the nuclear club in 1949 while the United States was still weak.

This chapter has five additional sections. I begin by describing war exhaustion and how it might impact coercive capabilities. The chapter then modifies Chapter 3's model to include dynamic costs of preventive war; if those costs decrease enough, the rising state proliferates due to the commitment problem. The following section fleshes out the details of the United States/Soviet Union case previously outlined. The chapter then highlights important theoretical issues that affect the results but are common to this type of model and finishes with a conclusion.

6.1 WHAT IS WAR EXHAUSTION?

Political science research into war exhaustion dates back to at least Richardson (1960, 232), who wrote that "a long and severe bout of fighting confers immunity on most of those who have experienced it; so that they no longer join in fights." The idea is straightforward: war is costly, and every incremental unit of effort a state pours into conflict is increasingly costly.[1] Thus, a long and costly fight makes a state warier of joining another fight soon thereafter.[2]

---

[1] That is, in formal language, the first and second derivatives of the function that maps war effort into costs are strictly positive.

[2] Organski and Kugler (1977) describe a similar phenomenon known as the "phoenix factor" in which losers of major conflicts generally rehabilitate their power within 15 to

Empirical research on war exhaustion fails to demonstrate consistent effects either on the system level or national level. In particular, Levy and Morgan (1986) and Garnham (1986) fail to reject the null hypothesis that a recent war makes a state less likely to go to war in the near future. Pickering (2002), controlling for a state's performance in the previous conflicts, finds a non-linear relationship. Meanwhile, Ostrom and Job (1986) see a decrease in the likelihood of militarized interstate disputes following prior conflict, while Feaver and Gelpi (2004, 77–85) note that longer wars further temper military action. Lian and Oneal (1993) find evidence that US public opinion plays a strong factor here, as presidents receive weaker "rally round the flag" bonuses during periods of exhaustion.

However, in his empirical analysis, Garnham is careful not to equate large-n aggregate results with individual-level behavior. He cites aversion to conflict in France post–World War I and in the United States post–Korean War; neither country wished to immediately reenter a state of war due to the toll of fighting. In fact, theories of war exhaustion say nothing about the overall expectation about the likelihood of future conflict. Rather, exhaustion says that, *ceteris paribus*, the costliness of continuous war ought to eventually force a state into submission.

Applying the theory empirically is difficult due to the *ceteris paribus* qualifier. Other effects could conspire to make war more likely and cancel out exhaustion's effect in practice. For example, increased industrial investment for war could make future wars *less* expensive if the state suffered few casualties in the original conflict. Careful empirical methods can resolve these issues by including control variables or factoring in selection effects. But theoretical work in non-dyadic bargaining theory remains under explored, so how one should create such controls is unclear.[3]

A second approach deemphasizes the resolve aspects of fighting multiple wars and instead looks at the practical issues. Treisman (2004)

20 years. War exhaustion is a more general concept because it can afflict both winners and losers of war.

[3] One might wonder why a state would allow itself to grow war-exhausted in the first place if it leads to unfortunate consequences. As the phrase implies, one must have been at war – and for a significant amount of time – to suffer from war exhaustion. However, war exhaustion is consistent with preexisting dyadic models of war. In the next section's model, war exhaustion creates a commitment problem that leads to a loss in utility for the declining state. But this is equivalent to saying that the original war is costly. Whereas we traditionally understand the cost of war as the loss of life and destruction of property, this expanded interpretation allows the cost to also incorporate the second-order costs of war. Thus, conflict can remain optimal despite the possibility of war exhaustion.

notes that when negotiating with two parties over separate issues, fighting over the less important issue leaves the state with fewer military resources to combat the more important issue. So a state may appease the less important rival to prepare for conflict with the more important rival. This chapter picks up the analysis after that conflict has occurred. Although war consumes resources in the short term, a state can reinvest in its military capacity and improve its posture in the coercive-bargaining relationship over the less important issue.

As such, the next section works around the complexities of all geopolitical post-war shocks found in the empirical literature by isolating the effects of war exhaustion on arms agreements. If the declining state cannot deter the rising state today but will deter the rising state tomorrow, a commitment problem results. The rising state jumps at the opportunity to proliferate during the declining state's moment of vulnerability despite the inefficient result.

6.2 MODELING WAR EXHAUSTION

The interaction maintains the same overall framework as Chapter 3's baseline model. The game begins with R not having developed the weapon. In such a pre-shift period, D begins by making an offer $x_t \in [0, 1]$ for period t. R can accept, reject, or build in response. Accepting ends the period, and R and D receive x_t and $1 - x_t$ respectively for t. Rejecting leads to pre-shift war, which ends the game. R receives $p_R - c_R$ for the rest of time, while D receives $1 - p_R - c_D(t)$ for the rest of time, where $c_D(t) > 0$ for all t. Note that D's war payoff is different from the original model, as the cost is a function of the period.

If R builds, it pays a cost k. D observes R's decision and chooses whether to prevent or advance to the next period. Preventing leads to the same game-ending pre-shift war; advancing locks in the offered division for the period and transitions the game into post-shift periods.

Post-shift periods are likewise nearly identical to the original model. Here, D offers $y_t \in [0, 1]$. R now just accepts or rejects. Accepting locks in the payoff pair y_t and $1 - y_t$ for the period and repeats the post-shift interaction in the next period. Rejecting leads to a game-ending post-shift war; R earns $p'_R - c_R$ and D earns $1 - p'_R - c_D(t)$, where $c_D(t)$ is the same cost function as the pre-shift state of the world.

To analyze the subject of interest, I restrict attention to parameter spaces in which $c_D(t) > c_D(t+1)$ for all $t = 1, ..., \bar{t}+1$ and equal to some strictly positive constant for all $t > \bar{t}$.[4] Intuitively, this means that D's costs decrease through the first $\bar{t}$ periods and then stays stable from $\bar{t} + 1$ and forward. In turn, war becomes increasingly attractive for D as time progresses up until a particular point. Interpreting this in terms of war exhaustion, D starts at a most exhausted state, and that exhaustion slowly fades away. At period $\bar{t} + 1$, D's exhaustion disappears entirely.

I now turn to the equilibria. Because this is a dynamic game of complete information, subgame-perfect equilibria remains the appropriate solution concept. Finding optimal strategies in pre-shift states of the world requires first knowing how the states will behave in post-shift states. As Lemma 6.1 asserts, play is identical here despite the introduction of changing costs:

Lemma 6.1. *Regardless of D's changing costs, if R builds and D does not prevent, D offers $y_t = p'_R - c_R$ in every post-shift period and R accepts in every SPE.*

This chapter's appendix contains the proof. Intuitively, due to war's inefficiency, D prefers making an acceptable offer. The offer ensures that D receives the entire surplus regardless of its current cost of war.

Now for the pre-shift stage. Chapter 3 noted that the extensions to the model do not impact the outcome of the game unless the new mechanics have sufficient impact. The following condition defines how much D's cost of war must shift for the war exhaustion mechanism to take hold:

Condition 6.1. *(Changing Credibility of Preventive War) A period $t^* \geq 2$ exists such that $p'_R - p_R > (c_D(t) + c_R)/\delta$ for all $t \geq t^*$ and $p'_R - p_R < (c_D(t) + c_R)/\delta$ for all $t < t^*$.*

Loosely, Condition 6.1 says that at the beginning of the interaction, D's cost of war is large enough that the parameters are below the horizontal line separating Proposition 3.1 from Proposition 3.3 in Figure 3.4. However, at some point later in time, D's cost of war is small enough that the parameters pop above that line. Thus, although a state's cost of war may naturally make minor adjustments over time, Condition 6.1 states that it must be rather large to impact the fundamental bargaining incentives.

The rationale is that all other cases are uninteresting, follow straight from propositions found previously, and render D's changing war tolerance inconsequential. If no such critical period existed, then either D's threat to prevent would remain credible throughout the interaction

---

[4] The results presented would be similar if war exhaustion wore off non-deterministically.

(because the costs of war remain high throughout) or D's threat to prevent would be incredible throughout the interaction (because the costs of war were low to begin with). In the first case, Proposition 3.1 states the equilibrium strategies; D's threat to intervene compels R not to build. Intuitively, if D is willing to prevent, then decreasing the cost of preventive war only reinforces its threat to prevent. In the second case, the remainder of previous propositions contain the solution; R receives a butter-for-bombs offer if its cost to build is low.[5] Intuitively, if D is very unwilling to prevent, then any minor change to the cost of war will have no effect on the incredibility of prevention. Either way, war reluctance has no substantive impact on the game's outcomes. Thus, this section restricts the discussion to the middle cases the condition describes.

There is also a second condition required for the mechanism:

Condition 6.2. *(Rapid Changes to Costs) In period* $t^* - 1$, *preventive war is sufficiently attractive; that is,* $c_D(t^* - 1) > 1 - p_R - \delta(1 - p'_R + c_R)$.

This assumption is critical to generating the results below. If costs fade slowly, it becomes possible for D to credibly buy off R during the waning days of its changing costs by offering so much that R would have to accept under the threat of preventive war. Under these conditions, the flow of goods can satisfy D because it allows D to steal the surplus from R not building.

In interpreting the substantive meaning, the assumption is analogous to known results about preventive war: large, rapid, exogenous shifts in power create a commitment problem (Powell 1999, 115–148; Powell 2006). The difference here is that this is not a model of preventive war. Rather, the rapid shift in D's cost of preventive war causes inefficient arms construction to occur.

Now to the propositions:

Proposition 6.1. *Suppose the potential shift in power is small relative to the cost of proliferation (i.e.,* $p'_R - p_R < (1 - \delta)k/\delta$). *Then D offers* $x_t = p_R - c_R$ *in every pre-shift period. R accepts these offers and never builds.*

Despite the addition of changing costs of preventive war, the substantive result remains the same when the cost of weapons is too great. This should be unsurprising. Proposition 3.2's underlying logic was that R considered the extent of the power shift to be "too cold" to be

---

[5] Proposition 3.4 – and the theoretical and substantive critiques against it – also apply.

worthwhile. In turn, R could not credibly threaten to build and thus could not extract concessions from D. Note that R's preference here is independent of D's decision to prevent. Indeed, regardless of whether D responds with preventive war, R would still rather accept no concessions. The formal proof is nearly identical and thus omitted.

However, the commitment problem enters when the costs are lower:[6]

Proposition 6.2. *Suppose the extent of the power shift is large in comparison to the cost of proliferation (i.e., $p'_R - p_R > (1 - \delta)k/\delta$) and Conditions 6.1 and 6.2 hold. Then R builds and D does not prevent in some period t in every SPE regardless of the value of t^*.*

The intuition reflects the credible commitment problem described in this chapter's introduction. At a critical period, R understands that it will not receive concessions in the future if it does not build and it will receive great concessions if it does. Because the power shift is large here, the difference in payoffs makes the investment worthwhile. D cannot credibly commit to buy off R in future periods. Knowing this – and knowing that any deal made in that period will only last for that period – R builds.

Before moving on, a couple remarks about the model are in order. First, D cannot buy off R at period t^*. To see why, note that when R chooses whether to build, the size of today's offer is irrelevant – R will earn that amount for the period regardless of its decision to shift power.[7] As a result, R must base its investment decision purely on difference in payoffs in future periods. Thus, if the future gains from bargaining more than cover the cost, R must invest. If not, R is in the parameters for Proposition 6.1 and therefore would not have built even in original model from Chapter 3.

Second, note that this prevents D from buying R's compliance forever by offering deep concessions up front, because both sides can look down the game tree and see that bargaining will eventually break down. Thus,

---

[6] From this point forward, the results make the same additional restrictions from Chapter 3 to focus on substantively interesting cases. First, suppose $k > \delta(p'_R - c_R)$. In words, D prefers engaging in butter-for-bombs agreements to taking as much as it can up front. Second, suppose

$$k \in \left(\frac{\delta(p'_R - p_R - c_D - c_R)}{(1-\delta)^2}, \frac{\delta p'_R - p_R}{1-\delta} + c_R \right);$$

in words, R prefers accepting 0 and successfully building to war in any pre-shift period and D prefers making minimalist butter-for-bombs offers during the pre-shift periods to fighting a war at any of those points.

[7] This assumes that D will not prevent if R builds, which indeed must true on the equilibrium path of play.

the inevitability of the closing window prohibits efficient outcomes, even if t^* is quite large. Indeed, the value of t^* is irrelevant to whether proliferation occurs in equilibrium. In this light, t^* merely indicates when the commitment problem comes into focus.

6.3 ILLUSTRATING THE MECHANISM: THE ORIGINS OF THE COLD WAR

To illustrate how the changing costs of preventive war sabotages butter-for-bombs bargains, this section looks at the Soviet Union's decision to proliferate in the immediate aftermath of World War II. Following Chapter 5's case-study philosophy, this section broadly focuses on whether three conditions hold. First, the declining state must prefer buying off the rising state to allowing the rising state to proliferate; this avoids the nonproliferation outcome of Proposition 3.4. Second, the declining state's cost of preventive war must sufficiently decrease as a function of time; this ensures that Conditions 6.1 and 6.2 hold. And third, the rising state must believe it will receive fewer concessions at a later date without nuclear weapons; this means the rising state fears the commitment problem the model traced. The model indicates that these conditions lead to proliferation.

THE PUZZLE. The Soviet Union became the second member of the world's nuclear club on August 29, 1949. Why Moscow viewed proliferation as attractive is evident. The United States and Soviet Union were becoming cold warriors, and the race for geopolitical supremacy was on. Nuclear weapons stabilized the communists' grasp over Eastern Europe. Although nuclear technology was far more expensive back then, the investment was reasonable given the issues at stake.

Existing work on the origins of the Cold War focus primarily on whether the United States or Soviet Union actually had reason to be antagonists. Researchers have not arrived at a consensus (Kydd 2005, 80–83). However, the existence of mutually preferable agreements per the baseline model means that this distrust alone cannot outright explain why the Soviet Union proliferated in 1949. This is in contrast to the conventional wisdom on nuclear weapons, which largely argues that states proliferate when the additional security is worth the cost of construction (Sagan 1996, 54–55) and that "security is the only necessary and sufficient cause of nuclear proliferation" (Thayer 1995, 486).

Consequently, research on the Soviet decision to proliferate focuses on the United States' choice not to launch preventive war; the United States held a nuclear monopoly at the time and perhaps could have forcibly ended the Cold War before the Soviet Union obtained a nuclear deterrent. Still, the general consensus is that war would have been too costly and ineffective to be worthwhile (Sagan and Waltz 2003, 56–59; Gaddis 1982, 149). Thus, the United States stood pat and allowed the nuclear monopoly to become a nuclear duopoly.

Meanwhile, existing formal models of nuclear proliferation tend to focus on the credible threat of preventive war as the chief deterrent to potential proliferators (Debs and Monteiro 2014; Bas and Coe 2016; Bas and Coe 2017). As I demonstrate below, the case of the Soviet Union does not fall under those models' scope conditions. Thinking about Chapter 3's cut-points provides some structure to the discussion. That preventive war was too costly to be worthwhile says that the interaction does not fit the "too hot" parameters of Proposition 3.1; that the weapons were worth the investment merely says that the interaction does not fit the "too cold" parameters of Proposition 3.2. Debs and Monteiro (2017, 116–130) argue that this explains Joseph Stalin's decision. However, even casting aside the theoretical reservations regarding Proposition 3.4's proliferation outcome, Chapter 3's results indicate that proliferation is only a sensible outcome if the cost of development is very small. Yet the United States surely would have preferred offering a settlement instead of forcing the Soviets to proliferate; nuclear weapons were still enormously expensive at the time, leaving plenty of surplus for the United States to capture if negotiations succeeded.[8]

Taking stock, the situation seemed ripe for an agreement: preventive war would not deter the Soviet Union, Stalin believed that the program's cost was worthwhile, and the United States was eager to cut a deal. Why, then, did the Soviet Union instead acquire a bomb?

This section argues that two complementary factors led to the breakdown of bargaining. Both fit the causal mechanism this chapter's model illustrates. First, American and British war exhaustion made preventive war against the Soviet Union an impossibility in the short term but not the long term; American restraint during the Berlin Blockade but acceptance of war during the Cuban Missile Crisis illustrate the United

---

[8] To wit, American proliferation just a few years earlier required 130,000 workers (the size of America's automobile industry at the time) to construct the first nuclear weapon (Hughes 2002, 9). Although secrets stolen from the Manhattan Project eased the Soviet effort, the Soviet Union lagged behind the United States due to an inferior industrial base. This meant that the Soviet Union had to pay a greater cost in diverting industrial resources to the Soviet bomb project.

States' evolving willingness to fight. Second, as Western intelligence infiltrated the previously undisturbed the Soviet Union, the material cost of preventive war diminished over time. Combined, these factors kept the United States from credibly committing to concessions over the long term, which in turn forced the Soviet Union to proliferate while the opportunity remained open.

RISING TENSIONS: CONFLICT IN GERMANY.   Some historical background is in order, beginning with the breakdown in cooperation between the United States and the Soviet Union at the end of World War II. During the war, Washington worked to build ties with Moscow. Indeed, the Soviet Union received the second-most aid from the Lend-Lease Program after the United Kingdom, and the United States offered the Soviets a disproportionately large voting share in the International Monetary Fund and World Bank during the Bretton Woods conference (Mikesell 1994, 22–23; Stone 2011, 54–56).

Although tensions between the allies remained below the surface in the immediate aftermath of the war, the conflict became evident in the next couple years. Moscow pressed for war reparations from Germany and began dismantling East German factories to ship useful parts back to the Soviet Union (Naimark 1995, 141–204). At the time, Joseph Stalin was uncertain whether the Soviet Union could hold onto its territorial gains; reparations ensured at least some long-lasting benefit from the post-war advantage (Stone 1996, 27–28). This presented a problem for Washington, which wanted to return its troops home as soon as possible. Doing that would require rebuilding the German economy to self-sufficiency; reparations had the opposite effect. Lucius Clay, governor of American-occupied Germany, halted payments from the Western allies' sectors in May, 1946 (Reynolds 2006, 276). But this had a spiral effect, causing Stalin to further distrust the Americans. From here, it became clear that the period of cooperation was over.

However, the bargaining logic dictates that even the most antagonistic of states have incentive to negotiate with one another. Without bargaining frictions, states ought to resolve the conflict and avoid the inefficiency of nuclear weapons. So even if American–Soviet tensions began as a matter of distrust (Kydd 2005), that does not explain why the Cold War powers could not develop some sort of resolution.

WAR EXHAUSTION AND DOMESTIC POLITICAL RESISTANCE.   What else explains the lack of agreement? One critical factor was American war exhaustion immediately following World War II, which rendered preventive war incredible over the short term as Condition 6.1 requires. The rush to send troops home created a manpower problem. Some divisions lost all their soldiers with specialized training (Quester 2000, 74); needless to say, tanks without any tank drivers are not useful. This left the United States in a moment of strategic vulnerability. The Soviet Union held a substantial tactical advantage on the ground at the time, outnumbering allied soldiers in Berlin 18,000 to 6,500 with an additional 300,000 in near proximity (Tusa and Tusa 1988, 173). Thus, even if the West could successfully open a front in the Soviet Union, it would have faced an uphill battle in Europe.

To some extent, the discrepancy was a residual from World War II. Whereas the Red Army had fought mostly against Nazi Germany, the United States fought a two-theater war. This meant that Soviet soldiers had a natural numbers advantage in Europe. The Truman administration tried but failed to keep the United States armed and proactive after the war ended; the domestic political situation in the United States simply was not conducive to this policy (Friedberg 2000, 98–107). Wartime price controls and shortages persisted into peace time (Hartmann 1971, 4–5). Republicans accordingly took control of the House and Senate in the 1946 midterm elections on a platform of demobilization and lower taxes, at the expense of military preparedness. Following the electoral defeat, President Truman gave in, allowed the military balance in Europe to decay, and reduced defense expenditures.

Similar electoral problems meant that the United States could not expect help from the United Kingdom. Winston Churchill, British political hero of World War II, expounded the virtues of preventive war against the Soviet Union (Quester 2000, 47–48; Trachtenberg 1988, 9).[9] However, the Labour party defeated the Conservatives in the 1945 Parliamentary election, after victory in Europe but before victory in Japan. Despite Churchill's successes during the war, British civilians had lost their appetite for conflict and believed Clement Attlee's Labour

---

[9] At the end of the war in Europe, Churchill commissioned a contingency plan, entitled *Operation Unthinkable*, which called for a surprise attack on the Soviets on July 1, 1945. Advisors scrapped the idea as infeasible; the best Britain could hope for was fleeting change in Poland, as an invasion of Russia would have been prohibitively difficult for the reasons outlined below. Still, when collecting German arms, Churchill required British troops organize the weapons in a manner such that they could be easily redistributed to the Germans, in case Britain needed German soldiers for the offensive. See Reynolds 2006 (249–251).

party would better implement domestic reforms (Jenkins 2001, 789–794; Berinsky 2009, 201). Churchill had to settle in as leader of the opposition.

The discrepancy between short-term military realities and long-term inevitabilities compelled the Soviet Union to take on a more aggressive policy. Washington engaged Moscow in good faith following the end of World War II. However, worried that the United States would marginalize the Soviet Union, Moscow pursued an expansionist policy in Eastern Europe. When the United States realized Soviet intentions, Washington began a more antagonistic approach. But without domestic resolve for more conflict abroad, the American response was weak – despite calls for preventive war coming moderate voices and not exclusively the "lunatic fringe" (Trachtenberg 1988, 7–11), Washington adopted a passive stance in the aftermath of World War II.

WAR EXHAUSTION IN BERLIN AND THE REALITIES OF WAR AGAINST THE SOVIET UNION.   The Berlin Blockade and subsequent Berlin Airlift provide a nice illustration of this exhaustion around the time of Soviet proliferation. At the end of war, the allies divided Germany into four occupation zones. Although Berlin fell squarely in the Soviet sector, Western allies shared the western half of the city. West Berlin relied on imports for its basic food and energy needs. Yet, in dividing Germany, Washington failed to secure land access to Berlin through the Soviet zone; the United States would try to rectify this one month after victory in Europe, but the Soviets limited the West to a single rail line (Miller 2000, 6–7). Moscow soon cut that off, too.

With trust breaking down, the West developed a plan to rebuild Germany's economy on its own. However, the Soviets sought substantial war reparations. Currency manipulation was a major issue; unbacked Soviet printings had so completely devalued the Reichsmark that cigarettes became a *de facto* currency (Turner 1987, 24). As such, the Western economic-reconstruction plan began with the introduction of the Deutsche Mark. For Moscow, this amounted to economic warfare (Miller 2000, 31–33). Realizing that East–West cooperation over the German occupation was over, the Soviet Union blockaded West Berlin beginning June 24, 1948. Without shipments of basic necessities from the East or the West, Moscow aimed to starve West Berlin into submission within a matter of weeks.

Decision-makers in Washington lamented the seemingly unwinnable situation. Withdrawal was unacceptable, and the chances of negotiating a solution with Moscow appeared slim. Nonetheless, if ever there was a tactical opportunity to challenge the Soviets militarily over Germany, this was it. The United States held a nuclear monopoly at the time; the first successful Soviet test was still more than a year away. Moscow would have been hard-pressed to push the issue past Berlin given the shadow of the American nuclear arsenal. Moreover, the blockade represented a direct violation of the occupation agreement. A military confrontation was justifiable.

Truman instead ordered a massive airlift, the most conservative option available. Washington did not believe the airlift would have any substantive effect on the political situation; to wit, when a reporter asked Lucius Clay whether an airlift could sustain West Berlin, Clay responded "absolutely not."[10] Rather, the airlift represented a lack of viable alternatives at the time. Simpler options, such as sending convoys on the highway with a military escort, created more risk of Soviet intervention and full-scale war. In the end, Washington did not want to leave anything to chance. Thus, the airlift policy aimed to minimize the possibility of war – accidental or deliberate – at all costs (Tusa and Tusa 1988, 173–174; Harrington 2012, 86). Delivering essential supplies through the air would keep West Berlin running and stall for time while not being as provocative as military convoys.

In hindsight, though, the decision was brilliant. West Berlin survived for more than ten months thanks to the non-stop deliveries. Moscow eventually lifted the blockade on May 12, 1949. The result was a propaganda coup for the United States and a devastating loss for the Soviet Union, as the blockade entrenched West Germans against the communist regime. Nevertheless, at the time, the Airlift was a shot in the dark, a least-bad option given that war exhaustion mandated a peaceful outcome even at the expense of Berlin.[11]

THE INTELLIGENCE GAP. As reluctant as the United States was to engage over the Berlin Blockade, the cost to halt the Soviet nuclear-weapons

---

[10] Quoted in Harrington 2012 (101). See Harrington (2012, 99–118) for an overview of American pessimism.

[11] Throughout the process, it is worth noting that the Soviet Union was exhausted too: it had suffered roughly twenty times more casualties than the United States. Moscow correspondingly had little desire to turn the Berlin Blockade into the Berlin War (Harrington 2012, 77–78) and stopped "buzzing" supply planes flying through the corridor once the West began using military escorts (Schelling 1966, 104; Slantchev 2011, 37–38). However, for the purposes of the commitment problem, Soviet war exhaustion had only had a minor impact on the strategic interaction. Proliferating acts as a *fait accompli* to the opposing state. It is up to the opposing state to launch preventive war to stop it, which Washington was unwilling to do at the time.

program would have been exponentially larger. Poor intelligence was a major factor. Indeed, it is hard to imagine the United States in a worse position than that of 1946. During World War II, the United States focused its intelligence efforts on Nazi Germany and Japan. This in part created the Soviet proliferation problem – American efforts to stop German espionage on the Manhattan Project opened the door to Soviet spying (Gaddis 1997, 93). More importantly, though, it left an embarrassing gap at the end of the war:

[T]he Workers' Paradise was "denied territory" in intelligence parlance: there were *zero* American ground agents in the Soviet Union. In 1949 the CIA began a five-year program to recruit and train former Soviet citizens to be air-dropped back on Soviet territory to serve as informants. Almost all of them were arrested immediately and unceremoniously shot. (Gordin 2009, 82)

Washington thus had to rely mostly on open-source information (Goodman 2007, 8), which hardly helped given the issues at hand.

Making matters worse, US intelligence was undergoing a bureaucratic shuffle. Wartime called for an extremely powerful intelligence organization; peacetime no longer required that necessary evil. As such, the Office of Strategic Services disbanded. But this led to a power vacuum. Competing bureaucratic organizations fought to succeed the OSS, leaving the United States without streamlined intelligence (Ziegler and Jacobson 1995, 14–21). The Central Intelligence Agency would not consolidate bureaucratic power for a few years.

Details on the Soviet nuclear program were correspondingly sparse both in terms of time and location. As policymakers in the United States debated whether to initiate preventive war, estimates of Moscow's nuclear timetable were notoriously vague and pushed the best-guess back to 1953 (Holloway 1994, 220).[12] Even after the Soviets tested their first bomb in 1949, the United States still had yet to develop an effective system to monitor test explosions. Low-level flyovers used against Nazi Germany (Ziegler and Jacobson 1995, 1–10) were not practical against the Soviet landmass. Scientists instead conceived of a seismic detector. Unfortunately, the United States had too few bombs available to

---

[12] This led to a second-order problem. The United States never believed that preventive war was urgent; Washington consistently held the belief that the Soviet Union would need more time to build a bomb. But even in a counterfactual world in which Washington knew about the short timeline, preventive war was still not an option for the reasons outlined here.

accurately test the device (Ziegler and Jacobson 1995, 14) and worried about the environmental externalities.

This secrecy was critical for the Soviet Union's success. Today, would-be nuclear countries can construct small facilities to make progress on nuclear weapons. Due to the small scale, they can fit into geographically protected areas. Iran, for example, built the Fordow Fuel-Enrichment Plant deep inside of a mountain. Rivals know exactly where it is but would have a difficult time destroying it short of a ground invasion. In contrast, given the state of nuclear technology at the time, atomic-weapons programs required enormous workforces. Nuclear locations were not facilities but rather full-fledged towns. Indeed, four "atomgrads" – Sarov, Novouralsk, Ozyorsk, and Lesnoy – became secret cities dedicated to weapons design and fuel development. Like any other city, and unlike a mountain, they were vulnerable to bombs.

But not knowing where these atomgrads were, preventive war against the Soviet Union would have required a full-scale invasion and was thus inconceivable. Americans simply had no desire to engage in a small-scale conflict in Berlin, never mind a land war in Asia. Given these constraints, the United States' remaining option was to drop nuclear bombs on the entire Soviet landmass. But this too was infeasible. Following the end of World War II, the American nuclear program fell in disarray. Many scientists left the project, having decided that "their mission had been accomplished" (Hewlett and Anderson 1962, 625). Those who remained were in the middle of a bureaucratic shuffle between the Manhattan Project and the Atomic Energy Commission. By 1948, the United States only had a minuscule arsenal of thirty nuclear weapons and fifty B-29 bombers to deliver them (Gaddis 1987, 109). Even if the United States could have accelerated nuclear-weapons production, the bombers were slow. Destroying targets deep in Soviet territory would have been impossible (Harrington 2012, 81). In the meantime, due to the conventional imbalance that war exhaustion caused, Soviet forces would have overrun American troops in Europe. Put simply, preventive war was not worth the substantial cost at the time, and those insisting on the hard line quickly found themselves marginalized.[13]

---

[13] American leaders also expressed moral concerns about how such a poorly targeted preventive war would undoubtedly result in a high number of civilian casualties,

TABLE 6.1. *Timeline of Events in US/USSR Nuclear Relations*

Timeline of Important Events in US/USSR Nuclear Relations	
5/8/1945	Allied victory in Europe
7/5/1945	Winston Churchill's Conservative party defeated
9/2/1945	Allied victory in Japan
9/18/1947	Central Intelligence Agency established
6/21/1948	Deutsche Mark introduced
6/24/1948	Berlin Blockade begins
6/28/1948	Berlin Airlift begins
5/12/1949	Berlin Blockade ends
8/29/1949	First successful Soviet atomic test
4/14/1950	NSC-68 issued
6/25/1950	Korean War begins
10/25/1951	Churchill's Conservative party retakes majority
8/1/1955	First U-2 flight
10/1962	The Cuban Missile Crisis

FADING WAR EXHAUSTION AND THE CLOSING COMMITMENT PROBLEM. So preventive war was not an option for the United States in 1949. By itself, this is insufficient to explain the Soviet Union's decision to proliferate given that agreements should resolve the proliferation problem. However, America's reluctance was diminishing over time. Condition 6.1 indicates that appreciating the Soviet decision requires thinking about the counterfactual world of the 1950s and 1960s where Moscow accepted a deal. Growing American acceptance of conflict put the United States in the commitment problem described in the extension of the model, which in turn forced Moscow to proliferate.

First, American exhaustion from World War II declined as the calendar pushed beyond 1945. The Korean War began in 1950. America's intervention sent a mixed message. On one hand, the United States fought a proxy war against a regime that was much weaker than the Soviet Union. On the other, Korea was not an existential threat to the United States and of arguably less value than Berlin. But dollars and votes tell a compelling story. The Korean crisis revitalized America's deflated defense budget, allowing Truman to begin implementing NSC-68's recommended policies (Jervis 1980). Meanwhile, on the domestic political front, former Supreme Allied Commander Dwight

though others thought *not* engaging was immoral (Buhite and Hamel 2005, 375). See Silverstone 2007 (51–75) for an overview of the normative concerns in Washington.

D. Eisenhower won the 1952 US presidential election. Cold War tensions also propelled Churchill back into his seat as Prime Minister, largely due to his foreign-policy credentials.

A counterargument here might be that the West's aggressive rebuttal only occurred because the Soviet Union proliferated. However, the real concern was that the Soviet Union had such expansive aims that American policymakers believed that the United States already needed to operate as though it were at war (Trachtenberg 1988, 13). For non-proliferation agreements to succeed, per the baseline model, Washington would have needed to offer Moscow a division roughly equivalent to the actual status quo during the Cold War. Given Moscow's expansive aims, this would have eventually led to the strong Western response regardless of the Soviet Union's nuclear status. As such, in the counterfactual world in which the Soviet Union did not proliferate, perhaps the United States and United Kingdom were not ready for preventive war in the early 1950s, but they were certainly *more* ready than just five years earlier.[14]

By 1962, however, the United States was certainly prepared to engage the Soviet Union in war. On October 14, 1962, the CIA discovered medium-range ballistic-missile installations in Cuba, beginning the Cuban Missile Crisis. At the time, President John F. Kennedy believed that the missiles were not yet operational and thus a prime target for a preventive strike.[15] Although Kennedy aimed to reduce the probability of war as much as possible and prudently opted to blockade Cuba to buy time to find a diplomatic solution, he believed the probability of war with the Soviet Union ranged from one-in-three to one-in-two (Bundy 1988, 453).[16] Nevertheless, he pressed on. Despite the additional physical costs of war at the time, American disdain for fighting in general had diminished.[17] The United States was now ready to take the risks it

---

[14] To wit, the calls for preventive war continued in Washington even after the Soviet Union started producing nuclear bombs (Buhite and Hamel 1990, 376–381), though the overall consensus was the West was only ready to endure the number of causalities a proxy war could create.

[15] In reality, Soviet commanders had nuclear weapons capable of striking Florida available without needing launch codes from Moscow (Allison 2012, 11). However, as a matter of establishing willingness to fight, Kennedy's beliefs trump strategic realities.

[16] The estimated risk of nuclear war was substantially smaller, though (Gaddis 1997, 269).

[17] One might notice an apparent disconnect between the model and this case study here. The model says that if the costs of war are decreasing over time, a commitment problem can result. However, "costs" in this context refer to a combination of the physical toll and state resolve. Thus, even though war would have been more expensive, American "costs" in the crisis bargaining sense would have decreased due to resolve's interaction.

refused to take thirteen years earlier during the Berlin Blockade.[18] Thus, if the United States was willing to pay such heavy costs in a world with Soviet nuclear weapons, it stands to reason that the United States would have been willing to engage in a large-scale war with a non-nuclear Soviet Union.[19]

Second, the intelligence gap was quickly closing. The CIA firmly established itself within Washington's bureaucracy by the start of Eisenhower's term. Although the first round of Soviet espionage ended in absurd failure, future programs would successfully infiltrate the Soviet military and intelligence service. Meanwhile, the Lockheed U-2 spy plane took first flight on August 1, 1955. By June, 1956, the aircraft was providing reliable aerial surveillance of Cold War foes.

With that in mind, consider the off-the-equilibrium-path world of 1962 in which the Soviet Union had not yet proliferated. The United States would have had crisp intelligence sources informing Washington the location of Soviet nuclear locations. Political will for intervention would have been higher than in the immediate aftermath of World War II. Thus, the Soviet Union would have had to reconsider its proliferation plans in the shadow of possible preventive war. At that point, any concessions the United States might have offered earlier would have vanished from the table. This justifies Moscow's decision to proliferate.

STALIN'S DECISION.   Did the above commitment-problem logic affect the Kremlin's foreign-policy planning at the time? Records of Joseph Stalin's private conversations indicate that the answer is yes. To start, Stalin recognized America's short-term conventional vulnerability at the end of the war (Zubok and Pleshakov 1996, 46). Further, he knew of Washington's struggles to mass-produce nuclear weapons at the time. Combined,

---

[18] Of course, a surgical preventive strike was possible in Cuba because of U-2 aerial photography. The United States did not have this luxury in the late 1940s to stop the Soviet Union from first acquiring nuclear weapons. Still, Kennedy knew that a strike on Cuban soil would inevitably kill Soviet troops and consequently spark a greater conflict with the Soviet Union. He was nonetheless willing to run this risk.

[19] One might then wonder why the United States did not intervene before the People's Republic of China's first test in 1964. Policymakers in Washington briefly considered it a possibility, especially as the Republic of China sought assistance. Compared to the Soviet Union, however, the United States' differences with China were small. Regardless of war exhaustion, this raised the functional cost of intervention to unacceptably high levels; indeed, some in the administration felt that "Chinese nuclear capabilities would not [have posed] a major threat to US interests, much less change the balance of power in East Asia" (Burr and Richelson 2000, 56). As a result, the Washington passed on the conflict and made peace with Beijing almost two decades before making peace with Moscow.

these factors gave Stalin the confidence to work on a nuclear weapon unimpeded, at least for a brief period.

Short-term truces aside, Stalin believed that tensions between the Soviet Union and the United States would eventually flare up again. He was likely aware of the calls in Washington for preventive war even during the time of American war exhaustion (Buhite and Hamel 1990, 369). Undoubtedly, these voices would only grow louder as the United States established better military reach over the Soviet Union. Put differently, he believed Condition 6.1 held.

As the model predicts, this made negotiations with Moscow difficult. Indeed, the United States often made overtures to share nuclear technology with cooperating states through a United Nations regime, beginning with the "Agreed Declaration" and continuing with the Acheson–Lilienthal Report and subsequent Baruch Plan (Meyrowitz 1990). Many policymakers wanted any agreement to allow the United States to maintain its nuclear arsenal, but opponents understood that this was a nonstarter for Stalin.

Prospects for an agreement were worse in Moscow. In Stalin's eyes, reaching any agreement in the aftermath of World War II would have put the Soviet Union in a losing position once the post-war lull ended. Stalin correspondingly wanted nothing short of nuclear equality (Zubok and Pleshakov 1996, 46) to maintain the credibility of any post-war deal, which suggests that this chapter's mechanism specifically drove at least part of his behavior.

Faced with a pressing need for nuclear weapons and a ticking clock, speed was Stalin's top priority (Bundy 1988, 177–178). When he asked Igor Kurchatov, father of the Soviet bomb, why a weapon was not forthcoming, Kurchatov pleaded that the program was under-equipped. Further, he believed that asking for more resources at a time when the "country was on starvation rations" was not wise (Gaddis 1997, 95). Stalin, not known for his generosity, responded by raising key researchers' salaries and giving them their own *dachas* and cars. They were to enjoy a comparatively luxurious lifestyle so that they could remain focused on accelerating the project. The nuclear program became the state's top priority, as though a war were already ongoing. At its peak, the CIA "estimated that between 330,000 and 460,000 people" were working on the program (Holloway 1994, 172).[20] Stalin essentially traded efficiency for speed, needing the weapon before the window closed.

---

[20] With a population of around 140 million at the time, this means that roughly 1 in every 400 Soviets were involved in the project.

All told, Stalin knew that a window existed. Acutely aware of the need for credible commitments in the shadow of Hitler's betrayal, he took the opportunity to proliferate while he had a chance. Although there may have been other contributing factors to Stalin's decision – all case studies are overidentified – the commitment problem presented here is a major consideration.

6.4 EXPLORING THE MECHANISM: DOMESTIC POLITICS AND UNRELIABLE PROLIFERATION PATHS

Although this chapter has explored how fading war exhaustion undermines the credibility of long-term concessions, the model reveals a deeper underlying problem. For the rising state to forgo nuclear weapons in the long-term, it must have an expectation that concessions will continue to flow in. Without that expectation, the rising state must proliferate to secure its share of a deal. Fading war exhaustion indirectly removes that expectation by making preventive war credible. However, this is not the only pathway that can force the rising state's hand. I use the remainder of this chapter to explore a few other possibilities.

CHANGES IN LEADERSHIP.   Thus far, this book has analyzed nuclear proliferation using the unitary-actor assumption. However, the model from this chapter has a straightforward interpretation on how domestic politics can affect international outcomes. The perceived cost of preventive war could vary from individual leader to individual leader. If such variance occurs exogenously, more peaceful leaders find themselves in the commitment problem above – they would like to buy off the potential proliferator, but the inability to ensure that future leaders will continue those concessions leads to nuclear investment.[21]

Such exogenous variation is plausible. Foreign policy rarely determines the outcome of US presidential elections, as economic policy predominates the voters' decision-making process. In the absence of an ideal candidate, voters can rationally accept inferior foreign policy as a trade-off for stronger economic competency.

WAVERING PROLIFERATION ASSISTANCE.   Low costs of preventive war effectively remove proliferation as a viable option due to the credible threat of intervention. But a more direct pathway for a state to lose

---

[21] Wolford (2012) makes a similar argument about the outbreak of war. See also Wolford 2007.

the nuclear option is to simply not have the technological capacity to construct a weapon after a certain date. For the most part, this is not a concern. Technology marches forward; a country capable of building a weapon today is almost certainly capable of developing a weapon tomorrow.

However, not all countries can develop a nuclear weapon by themselves. Indeed, nuclear assistance is commonplace (Kroenig 2009a). If a potential proliferator expects that assistance may come to an abrupt halt – thus ending its only reasonable path to a bomb – then it cannot rest on its mere potential power. This logic suggests that rogue nuclear networks like that of A.Q. Khan are particularly destabilizing.[22] Not only does a black market allow more states into the potential nuclear club, it also forces them to invest in the technology before the nonproliferation regime shuts it down.[23]

CIVIL WAR INTERVENTION. More subtly, the rising state must have the ability to enjoy the benefits of potential power into the future. Whereas before the key issue was whether the proliferation option would disappear later, this point transitions into a more fundamental question of whether the state will still exist. Take the North Korean regime, for example. If a popular uprising began, it would not have been unreasonable for the United States or South Korea to intervene under certain circumstances prior to North Korea's development of a nuclear weapon.[24] Given the massive military disparity, this would have likely ended the North Korean regime. The threat to build nuclear weapons in the future gives North Korea no traction here, as the war itself would ensure that North Korea has no future. In contrast, proliferating gives Pyongyang a nuclear deterrent that would reasonably convince Seoul or Washington to not intervene in circumstances they might otherwise.[25]

---

[22] See Corera 2006 for a background on A.Q. Khan.

[23] This would suggest further instability if North Korea began sharing nuclear secrets with other states, who may feel they have to capitalize on the opportunity given potential instability in Pyongyang.

[24] Even against a North Korean opponent without nuclear weapons, either the United States or South Korea would have had to be sure that their intervention would be pivotal to make it worthwhile; North Korea has a large number of artillery units just north of the 38th parallel pointing toward Seoul. A military victory would come at a high civilian price.

[25] The US-led 2011 intervention in Libya provides a useful illustration of this. It is difficult to imagine western countries banding together to overthrow Muammar Gaddafi if there had been a good chance of losing a Western city to a nuclear detonation.

This would help explain North Korea's intransigence through its path toward a nuclear weapon. The 1994 Agreed Framework would have traded North Korea's nuclear program for normalized relations and light-water nuclear power plants built by a multi-national consortium. Instead, North Korea progressed on uranium enrichment.[26] The Bush Administration terminated what remained of the framework in 2003, pulling American support from the international consortium to build North Korean nuclear power plants. Pyongyang exited the Nuclear Non-Proliferation Treaty in the same year. The "Six-Party Talks" emerged from the remains. Other proposals attempted to replace the Agreed Framework – including a February 29, 2012 food-for-weapons deal – but nothing stuck.

Of course, for bargaining to break down in any of these cases, concessions must not be "sticky" – that is, after an accepted offer, the proposer cannot retract concessions without prying them away militarily. In essence, sticky treaties are robust in the sense that future leaders (or the state itself, in the unitary actor framework) cannot easily break the terms. Under this logic, even though a leader might wish to overturn the treaty, past negotiations tie his or her hands. Thus, the lack of robust treaties in both the war exhaustion model and the above informal extensions is a critical hidden assumption; indeed, Proposition 6.2 fails with such treaties.

Unfortunately, political scientists do not yet fully understand the determinants of stickiness, especially in security matters. In the case of civil war intervention, the value of nuclear weapons is precisely to deter military interference in domestic affairs. Thus, the proliferator's opponent must continuously grant the "concession," making such negotiations inherently unsticky. Outside the case of civil-war intervention, economic and diplomatic concessions also appear remarkably fluid. If the declining state literally buys off the rising state by writing a check every year, it can easily terminate those concessions by simply not transferring the money. Because the concessions are not sticky, the rising state has very little recourse.

In contrast, Fortna (2003) and Mattes (2008) find that careful territorial restrictions insure states against shocks that might otherwise cause

---

[26] An alternative perspective is that Congressional Republicans believed that the United States could obtain North Korean compliance at a lower cost and thus blocked critical funding for the agreement (Martin 2002; Chinoy 2008, 8). Indeed, insufficient funding stalled groundbreaking on the nuclear power plant until late 2002, making the targeted 2003 opening impossible. Under this interpretation, Congress miscalculated North Korean resolve – and Congress broke the agreement first, not Pyongyang.

war. For example, while the declining state is suffering from war exhaustion, it could make a deep territorial concession to the rising state. After war exhaustion wears off, the declining state would have a difficult time reacquiring that land in practice, as it would have to forcibly overturn the peace to retake the area. This is in contrast to the model, which does not allow the rising state to simply ignore an offer and thereby defer the war decision to the declining state.

Taking this logic to the main case study of this chapter, bargaining between the United States and the Soviet Union had a clear territorial component. After all, Washington could have conceded Berlin to Moscow during the Blockade. Even after the exhaustion from World War II wore off, the US could not have feasibly reobtained Berlin without crossing a tripwire into war. Thus, the concession is perhaps sticky.

So why didn't the United States engage in Berlin-for-bombs nonproliferation diplomacy? One possibility is that the United States had two audiences – the Soviet Union and Western Europe – and could not satisfy both simultaneously. To appease the Soviet Union, the United States needed to concede Berlin or other portions of Europe. Yet, in doing so, the United States would send the message to Western Europe that it was an unreliable ally. Western European allies were adamant about staying in Berlin (Harrington 2012, 80–81). If the United States were to back down in this situation, it would signal to the West that portions of Europe were expendable. As a result, Washington could not simultaneously appease Moscow while saving face with its friends. Because nonsticky concessions were insufficient to resolve the commitment problem, the Soviet Union pursued a nuclear arsenal during the period of American weakness.

6.5 CONCLUSION

This chapter analyzed the stability of butter-for-bombs agreements when the declining state's ability to launch preventive war varies over time. Although settlements exist that leave both sides better off than had the rising state proliferated, the declining state cannot credibly commit to continue giving concessions after its war exhaustion wears off. Consequently, the rising state must invest in nuclear weapons during the declining state's moment of vulnerability to enforce future concessions later on.

Substantively, this chapter investigated the usefulness of the commitment problem theory in explaining Soviet nuclear proliferation. Waning war exhaustion (and improving American intelligence) ensured that the

United States would eventually obtain a credible threat to initiate preventive war. As a result, the Soviet Union had to pursue nuclear weapons during this window of American vulnerability to secure its future.

The mechanism also appears to help explain facets of two more recent cases: Iran and North Korea. After the Iraqi insurgency began toward the end of 2003, the United States faced a window of vulnerability due to war exhaustion. Iran became intransigent on the nuclear issue, violating terms of the 2003 Paris Agreement shortly after consenting to it.[27] Meanwhile, North Korea accelerated its nuclear program in the years after, with its first test in 2006. Even if the United States and South Korea could have resolved their credible-commitment problem with non-intervention, the war-exhaustion problem may have led North Korea to pursue nuclear weapons anyway.

Unfortunately, evidence that the mechanism was responsible for the Iranian and North Korean decisions are merely circumstantial at this point. Their behaviors are certainly consistent with the theory of war exhaustion. What is missing for now is primary-source information that traces the decision-makers' thought processes in each of these countries. Unlike the Soviet Union, not enough time has passed for that to be available.

In any case, this chapter concludes the discussion of declining states' inability to credibly promise future rewards. The remainder of this book looks into information-based explanations for proliferation. The next chapter begins with imperfect information while the following chapter investigates incomplete information.

6.6 APPENDIX

The appendix covers two proofs: Lemma 6.1 and Proposition 6.2.

6.6.1 Proof of Lemma 6.1

Consider equilibrium play beginning in period $\bar{t} + 1$. From this period forward, D's cost of war $c_D(t)$ is equal to some strictly positive constant. Each of these periods is therefore identical. Consequently, Lemma 3.1

---

[27] This is more surprising given Iran's alleged diplomatic overture earlier in the year. Three days after President George W. Bush declared "mission accomplished" in Iraq, the Swiss ambassador to Iran arrived in Washington. There, he handed American officials with an Ayatollah-approved "roadmap" for normalizing relations (Parsi 2012, 1–5). Although it remains unclear whether the document was authentic (Kessler 2007), such an overture is consistent with the model's overall logic. At that time the United States was at the height of its geopolitical power, and Iran would want to scramble to obtain any concessions whatsoever if the American threat to launch preventive war was credible.

applies, because this interaction after $\bar{t}$ is identical to the model from Chapter 3. So D offers $x_t = p'_R - c_R$ and R accepts in the unique SPE.

Every post-shift period before $\bar{t} + 1$ has a unique cost value, so consider proof by induction for the remaining periods. Take optimal play in period $\bar{t}$ as the base step. R's continuation value for accepting an offer equals $p'_R - c_R$. D's continuation value for having an offer accepted is $1 - p'_R + c_R$. Thus, R accepts if:[28]

$$(1 - \delta)x_t + \delta(p'_R - c_R) \geq p'_R - c_R$$

$$x_t \geq p'_R - c_R.$$

Note that D's payoff is decreasing in x_t if R accepts, so its optimal acceptable offer equals $p'_R - c_R$. D earns $1 - p'_R + c_R$ for this action. If D makes an unacceptable offer, R rejects and D earns less than $1 - p'_R$, a strictly smaller amount. Therefore, in equilibrium, D offers $p'_R - c_R$ and R accepts.

For the induction step, consider an arbitrary period before $\bar{t} + 1$. Suppose R's continuation value for accepting an offer equals $p'_R - c_R$ and D's continuation value for having an offer accepted is $1 - p'_R + c_R$. The following is the unique equilibrium strategies for each such period: D offers $x_t = p'_r - c_R$ and R accepts $x_t \geq p'_r - c_R$ and rejects $x_t < p'_r - c_R$. The proof follows identically from the base case. □

6.6.2 Proof of Proposition 6.2

Three lemmas together imply Proposition 6.2.

Lemma 6.2. *Suppose the states enter period t^* before a power shift has occurred. Then D offers $x_t = p_R - c_R$ in all future periods and R accepts.*

Proof: Suppose the states enter period $\bar{t} + 1$ prior to a power shift. Then Proposition 3.1 holds.[29] D's value for the remainder of the game equals $1 - p_R + c_R$ while R's is $p_R - c_R$.

If $t^* = \bar{t} + 1$, the proof is done. If not, consider proof by induction. Take the base step of period $\bar{t} + 1$. Following Proposition 3.1, consider R's optimal response to some offer $x_{\bar{t}+1}$. R earns $p_R - c_R$ if it rejects. If it accepts, it earns $(1 - \delta)x_{\bar{t}+1} + \delta(p_R - c_R)$. If R builds, because $\bar{t} + 1 > t^*$,

---

[28] Per usual, assume R accepts when indifferent for the purposes of this proof. However, this is a result, not an assumption.

[29] This subgame is the same game as the model from Chapter 3.

D prevents, and R earns $p_R - c_R - (1 - \delta)k$. This is strictly worse than rejecting. Thus, R accepts if:

$$(1 - \delta)x_{\bar{i}+1} + \delta(p_R - c_R) \geq p_R - c_R$$

$$x_{\bar{i}+1} \geq p_R - c_R.$$

So, in equilibrium, R accepts if $x_{\bar{i}+1} \geq p_R - c_R$ and rejects if $x_{\bar{i}+1} < p_R - c_R$.

Now consider D's offer decision. Because D's payoff is strictly decreasing in $x_{\bar{i}+1}$ if R accepts, D's optimal acceptable offer equals $p_R - c_R$. D earns $1 - p_R + c_R$ for this choice. In contrast, it earns less than $1 - p_R$ for making an unacceptable offer, which is strictly less. So D offers $x_{\bar{i}+1} = p_R - c_R$, and R accepts.

For the induction step, suppose R's continuation value equals $p_R - c_R$ and D's continuation value equals $1 - p_R + c_R$. Then the task is to show that in period $t \leq t^*$ D offers $x_t = p_R - c_R$ and R accepts. But showing this is identical to showing the base step, so this holds. ☐

Lemma 6.3. *Suppose the states enter period $t^* - 1$ prior to a power shift. Then R builds and D does not prevent.*

Consider R's response to x_{t^*-1}. Note that by Condition 6.1, D will not prevent in period $t^* - 1$. If R builds, it therefore earns $(1-\delta)x_{t^*-1} + \delta(p'_R - c_R) - (1 - \delta)k$. If R accepts, by Lemma 6.2 it earns $(1 - \delta)x_{t^*-1} + \delta(p_R - c_R)$. Proposition 6.1 covered the instance where accepting is greater than building here, so R prefers building. The remaining option is to reject, which yields R $p_R - c_R$. But, again, the parameter space ensures that R prefers building to receiving its war payoff.

Now consider D's options. No matter the offer, R builds and D does not prevent. Because D's payoff is strictly decreasing in x_{t^*-1}, its optimal offer is therefore $x_{t^*-1} = 0$. So D offers 0, R builds, and D does not prevent. ☐

Lemma 6.4. *War does not occur in pre-shift periods $t = 1, ..., t^* - 1$.*

There are only two ways war can occur in a pre-shift period: R rejects D's offer or D prevents. Condition 6.1 shows that if $c_D(t) > 1 - p_R - \delta(1 - p'_R + c_R)$, then D prefers advancing to preventing in period t. But note that Condition 6.1 also gives that $c_D(t^* - 1) > 1 - p_R - \delta(1 - p'_R + c_R)$. Given that $c_D(t)$ is strictly decreasing from periods 1 to $\bar{t} - 1$, it must be the case that $c_D(t) > 1 - p_R - \delta(1 - p'_R + c_R)$ holds for all $t < t^*$. Thus, D can never prevent in equilibrium during these periods, as advancing is a profitable deviation.

All that is left to show is that R never rejects on the equilibrium path. The restriction that $k < (\delta p'_R - p_R)/(1 - \delta) + c_R$ implies that R earns more from a successful power transition than from rejecting D's offer. From the above, D will not prevent if R builds. Thus, R can profitably deviate from rejecting to building. □

Thus, in any equilibrium, R must build before period t^*. All that remains is to verify that an equilibrium exists. However, this is trivial – the existence of a unique equilibrium outcome after period t^* ensures that the game before that point is functionally a game with t^* periods. So an equilibrium exists, and investment must occur in it. □

7

You Get What You Give: Endogenous Nuclear Reversal

Scholars of international relations see verification as a major hurdle to reaching arms agreements.[1] Judging by verification's centrality in various treaties, the policymaking community agrees. For example, the Joint Comprehensive Plan of Action (JCPOA, or "Iran Deal") has many provisions designed to increase the Iranian nuclear program's transparency. This includes adherence to the Nuclear Non-Proliferation Treaty's Additional Protocol – itself a key information-providing treaty – a list of existing nuclear sites, International Atomic Energy Agency inspection of those sites, a three-fold increase in the number of inspectors in the country, and round-the-clock monitoring of specific nuclear materials.

However, questions of compliance remain. Opponents cannot observe everything that occurs inside a target state. Thus, even if they know that potential proliferators are not using declared sites to build a bomb, they must still worry that *unknown* sites exist that are dedicated to that task. These fears prompted the 2003 Iraq War (Debs and Monteiro 2014) and also contributed to a breakdown of the Agreed Framework between North Korea and the United States in the early 2000s (Beal 2005, 121). In the extreme, pessimists might wonder why states bother with weapons inspections at all.

That said, at the very least, weapons inspections act as a nuisance, forcing potential proliferators to develop their weapons less efficiently by having to play cat-and-mouse games with inspectors or by using secondary locations. Such inconvenience provisions are common in weapons agreements. For instance, the JCPOA requires Iran to divest

---

[1] See Krass 1985, Adelman 1990; Dunn 1990; Gallagher 2003.

its nuclear infrastructure in part by relinquishing control over many of its centrifuges. Steps like this do not make it impossible for potential proliferators to resurrect their programs. They do, however, increase the cost of reactivation.

It is puzzling that states would willingly reverse course like this. After all, devaluing an outside option in this manner can only hurt a state's outcome should it ultimately proliferate. Meanwhile, rivals would seem to have less incentive to offer generous deals if the potential proliferator seeks to strike a bargain instead. And even if an agreement is possible in theory, rivals appear to face a commitment problem in that they could decrease concessions immediately following the reversal.

Thus far, this book's models of bargaining over proliferation have ignored these issues. Rather, if the rising state decides to build a weapon, this has always been perfectly observed, and the declining state could make its preventive war decision based on that information. One may wonder then whether those bargained agreements break down in the presence of imperfect information. Surprisingly, the answer to that question explains why potential proliferators agree to the aforementioned inspection provisions.

This chapter argues additional burdens to proliferation – whether caused by weapons inspections or divestment – allow the parties to reach agreements that would have been impossible otherwise. This is because opponents, in the absence of a deal and unable to effectively monitor the proliferation process, must waste resources on the "stick" of preventive war. Oftentimes, such wars are mistakes because the potential proliferator opted not to develop the weapons at all. Other times, the declining state mistakenly chooses not to prevent while the rising state builds. Alternatively, an agreement with the potential proliferator requires giving concessions commensurate with the quality of its nuclear option. Intuitively, rivals pay the "carrots" when these concessions are cheaper than using the stick. One determinant of the optimal choice is the cost to proliferate; the higher it is, the more likely the rival is to offer concessions.

What remains unclear is whether the rising state finds the declining state's minimally acceptable nonproliferation agreement more favorable then the "no deal" outcome in which the rising state proliferates with positive probability. One may initially think that the rising state prefers this second outcome, especially because shifting from no agreement to agreement requires increasing the rising state's cost of proliferation. Yet I show that the many inefficiencies of no agreement – namely, the costs of war and weapons programs – ensure that the rising state prefers inducing an agreement even though it must sabotage its outside option to obtain that outcome. Consequently, in equilibrium, the potential proliferator voluntarily undergoes a nuclear reversal.

For clarity, the nuclear reversal in my model – and in most empirical examples – does not terminate the proliferator's ability to build a bomb. Indeed, potential proliferators would never permit such draconian measures, which would lead to bad outcomes for all parties. Instead, the goal is to undergo just enough of a reversal to incentivize negotiations. Although potential proliferators can cheat on these reversals by developing weapons anyway, the negotiated settlements give them incentive not to. Accordingly, as uncomfortable as it may seem, rivals can live with the uncertainty that potential proliferators could secretly nuclearize.

To elucidate the above logic, I modify Chapter 3's model to include clandestine proliferation. The revised model generates four key implications. First, reversals are most likely when the potential proliferator's route to a bomb is cheap and the extent of the possible power shift is large – in other words, the conditions seemingly most likely to result in nuclearization. Second, reversals are intentionally limited because further divestment and more onerous weapons inspections decrease the amount of concessions the opponent needs to offer. Thus, limited reversals are *not* proof that the potential proliferator will secretly nuclearize. Third, as the cost of preventive war decreases, the extent of a nuclear reversal increases. This is because the potential proliferator needs to offer more to entice the opponent to propose a deal. Finally, despite having to avoid preventive war and facing potentially substantial costs to nuclearize, the potential proliferator can capture all of the surplus created by reaching a deal.

This chapter contains four additional sections. The next section gives a richer description of nonproliferation inspection and verification regimes, further motivating the four critical components of the model. The third section then describes the model and solves for its equilibria. The fourth section investigates the empirical implications of the model that were outlined in the previous paragraph. I conclude with some key policy implications.

7.1 MONITORING PROBLEMS AND FEATURES OF INSPECTION REGIMES

A common problem in international relations is the inability to observe past actions of rivals. This can lead to inefficient behaviors in many domains. For example, armies may initiate fighting out of concern that the other will initiate first, even if neither side actually benefits from that fighting. Domestic coalitions cannot always monitor a leader's behavior in crisis diplomacy, allowing the leaders to take actions their supporters would not approve of (Brown and Marcum 2011). And one of the general concerns about cyberwarfare is the difficulty of attributing the attack and therefore not knowing whom to retaliate against (Clark and Landau 2011).

If observation is the problem, accurate monitoring is the solution. Combatants can call in international observers to serve as early-alert warning systems, mitigating first-strike advantages and permitting peace to prevail (Fortna 2004). Competing branches of governments can decrease the barriers to whistleblowing to encourage those with insider information to come forward (Spaniel and Poznansky 2018). And states can reduce their cyber vulnerabilities by increasing their digital-forensics capability.

To date, scholarly research on arms treaties has followed a similar pattern: inability to observe the state in question is the problem, so information acquisition is the solution. Weapons inspections and arms verification have focused on informational aspects. The earliest treatments build on the iterated prisoner's dilemma mechanism (Axelrod 1984; Downs, Rocke, and Siverson 1986; Ikle 1961, 214–215). Arms races often have a payoff structure like a prisoner's dilemma, where each state individually prefers building but both are worse off with that outcome than had no one increased their arms allotments. Using the shadow of the future, trigger strategies that punish deviations to uncooperative actions can facilitate mutual cooperation. However, players must observe their opponents' past actions to effectively implement trigger strategies. This type of information revelation was thus a key part of arms agreements between the United States and the Soviet Union (Dunn 1990; Gallagher 2003).

The iterated prisoner's dilemma mechanism has two major limitations, though. First, the mechanism only applies to situations where both parties might increase armaments. Yet there are many asymmetric examples where one state tries to convince a second not to build weapons. Second, prisoner's dilemmas ignore richer strategic environments that feature both bargaining and the possibility of preventive war.

Pushing forward, Debs and Monteiro (2014) address both these points. Their interaction features a subgame that appears in the model I develop below, so it is worth understanding their underlying mechanism. Suppose (1) a state cannot observe its rival's decision to proliferate, (2) the potential nuclear state finds weapons worth the investment,

	Prevent	∼ Prevent
Build	Preventive War; Wasted Costs	Successful Power Shift
∼ Build	Preventive War	Status Quo

FIGURE 7.1. Simplified Game of Covert Nuclear Proliferation

and (3) the opponent prefers launching preventive war to permitting a successful power shift. Then the states are effectively playing the simultaneous move game substantively described in Figure 7.1.

Debs and Monteiro's key insight is that optimal strategies allow *all* outcomes to occur with positive probability.[2] To see why, note that preventive war and building cannot occur with certainty because the potential proliferator would want to deviate to not building to save on the wasted costs. But a mistaken preventive war cannot occur with certainty either because the rival would want to switch to not preventing. Maintaining the status quo with certainty is equally unsustainable because the potential proliferator could sneak in a successful power shift. And a successful power shift cannot be the guaranteed result because the rival would want to switch back to preventing. Thus, each side must mix to limit exploitation.

However, the result of this mixing is inefficient. After all, mistaken preventive war occurs with positive probability. Debs and Monteiro show that one solution to this problem is to increase the rival's ability to observe the potential proliferator's move – this deters the opponent from building and minimizes the chances of a preventive war in the absence of an actual weapons investment. Some weapons-inspection regimes serve this exact purpose. The Additional Protocol of the Nuclear Non-Proliferation Treaty, for example, requires signatories to give weapons inspectors broader access to nuclear sites with less forewarning.

Unfortunately, though, credible information provision is not always possible. Potential proliferators, it seems, have incentive to continue nuclearizing at undeclared and unknown facilities. Lacking omniscience, rivals simply have to "live with uncertainty" (Dunn 1990). Yet living with uncertainty appears to imply playing Debs and Monteiro's interaction, which still results in mistaken preventive wars some of the time.

---

[2] See Jelnov, Tauman, and Zeckhauser 2017 for a similar setup that produces the same implication.

If information can never be perfect, is there another way to solve the problem? Indeed, there is. In fact, although verification receives most of the attention, many inspection regimes have secondary clauses geared toward the destruction of existing weapons infrastructure. To wit, consider the following features of the JCPOA:

- At the Arak facility, the reactor under construction will be filled with concrete, and the redesigned reactor will not be suitable for weapons-grade plutonium. Excess heavy water supplies will be shipped out of the country. Existing centrifuges will be removed and stored under round-the-clock IAEA supervision at Natanz.
- The Fordow Fuel-Enrichment Plant will be converted to a nuclear, physics, and technology center. Many of its centrifuges will be removed and sent to Natanz under IAEA supervision. Existing cascades will be modified to produce stable isotopes instead of uranium hexafluoride (UF_6). The associated pipework for the enrichment process will also be sent Natanz.
- Remaining operational centrifuges will be the IR-1 design, Iran's least efficient model.
- All enriched UF_6 in excess of 300 kilograms will be downblended to 3.67% or sold on the international market, down from around 12 tons.
- All enriched uranium oxide will be fabricated into fuel plates, sold on the international market, or diluted to 3.67%.

These features are not geared toward providing information. Rather, they dismantle Iran's nuclear infrastructure. Such a nuclear reversal does not make acquiring nuclear weapons impossible, just harder. The skill to produce reactors, centrifuges, heavy water, and enriched uranium does not go away. But replacing all of those materials – a necessary step to proliferate – is immensely costly. Further, Iran would suffer a backlash from interested foreign actors for having reached an agreement only to backtrack at a later date.

Further, these features are not unique to the JCPOA. Disarmament is a primary pillar of the Nuclear Non-Proliferation Treaty, and manufacturing nuclear weapons materials puts signatories in violation of its terms. Meanwhile, other provisions appear on an *ad hoc* basis. Libya shipped large portions of its nuclear infrastructure to the United States in the 2003 agreement (ElBaradei 2011, 157; Corera 2006, 221–222). Kazakhstan and Ukraine sold or shipped off their supplies of highly enriched uranium in return for Russian and American aid following the dissolution of the Soviet Union (Cirincione, Wolfsthal, and Rajkumar 2005, 371–375; Jones et al. 1998, 80; Drezner 1999, 204). START had similar divestment requirements, including the guillotining of hundreds of B-52 Stratofortress bombers. And integration of nuclear scientists into the nonproliferation regime generally creates a brain drain, where technicians immigrate to above-the-board employment opportunities (Hymans 2012).[3]

One might argue that the inspection provisions are more about costly inconvenience and less about information. Even if IAEA weapons inspectors keep close tabs on known sites, Debs and Monteiro's work indicates that rivals must be worried about what they *don't* know. Although the JCPOA contains a provision to address unknown sites, it has no bite if the IAEA never discovers them. Meanwhile, if Iran practices cat-and-mouse games, it could use known facilities as well. In turn, proliferation opponents might not know whether Iran will comply with the inspection regime. Nevertheless, they can be sure that secretly replacing entire facilities will be a massive economic burden, while cat-and-mouse games will slow progress and be decidedly inefficient for a potential nuclear program.

These points lead to two interrelated questions. First, if proliferation opponents can never be certain of a potential nuclear state's actions, will deals ever work? Second, why would a potential nuclear state ever agree to such reversal provisions? Indeed, they only make the proliferation process more expensive. Thus, if the state sought to make a deal, the additional cost would disincentive opponents from offering large concessions; after all, deals reached in coercive bargaining are commensurate with the actors' outside options. Meanwhile, if the state merely wanted to proliferate, it should be making that process as straightforward as possible.

The next section introduces a model that can answer these questions.

7.2 BARGAINING WITH IMPERFECT MONITORING

I now integrate imperfect information into Chapter 3's model. For tractability, because butter-for-bombs agreements are sustainable in the

---

[3] Similar provisions exist in non-nuclear deals as well: Section II of the Washington Naval Treaty includes a long list ships for the signatories to scrap. Also note that while some of these cases featured joint reductions, not all do. Consequently, a quid pro quo argument – as seen in the civil war literature (Fortna 2004; Mattes and Savun 2010) – cannot explain this behavior.

long-term, this section focuses on a two-period interaction.[4] The game begins with a one-time decision from R to pick a cost to proliferate $k \geq \underline{k}$. Substantively, selecting $\underline{k}$ means R will allow itself the cheapest and easiest path possible to a nuclear weapon. Progressively higher values correspond to the adoption of various barriers to proliferation: policies similar to those in the JCPOA, dismantling existing nuclear infrastructure (which would need to be rebuilt to produce a bomb), allowing weapons inspectors to effectively shut off civilian infrastructure from contributing to a weapons program, or permitting nuclear scientists to take positions overseas.[5] Put differently, the greater the level of k, the greater the level of nuclear reversal.[6]

Following that decision, the states play a bargaining game in a pre-shift state of the world. D offers $x \in [0, 1]$. R rejects, accepts, or builds. Rejecting ends the interaction and gives each side its pre-shift war payoff; these payoffs persist over an infinite horizon. Accepting means that R forgoes nuclear weapons if the interaction reaches the post-shift period.[7] Building incurs the cost k but means that R will increase its power in the post-shift period if D does not prevent.

Unlike previous versions, however, D cannot differentiate between R accepting and R building.[8] This is where the setup diverges from Chapter 3's baseline model. At this point, D must prevent or pass *without knowing R's build decision*. Preventing ends the game in pre-shift war as before regardless of R's decision. If R accepted, passing ends the interaction and locks in the offered distribution for the rest of time.

If R built and D passed on preventive war, the game advances to the post-shift phase. D now sees that R built and offers $y \in [0, 1]$.[9] R accepts

---

[4] In this chapter's appendix, I provide a brief discussion explaining why the results extend to an infinite-horizon setup.

[5] The restrictions R imposes on itself are disconnected from the informational structure. If the inspection regime both increased information and the cost to proliferate, it would be difficult to track which mechanism assists in the creation of a deal. Because R cannot manipulate information revelation here, we can attribute the creation of a deal directly to the increased burdens.

[6] Although I focus on technological reversal, any other mechanism that increases the cost of proliferation also fits the theoretical results below. One pertinent alternative is domestic political constraints like the anti-nuclear fatwa Ayatollah Khamenei issued in 2003.

[7] In contrast to Benson and Wen 2011, reaching an agreement does not provide D with additional information. This stacks the deck against a deal.

[8] Thus, unlike Debs and Monteiro's model, this interaction has no noisy signal. This is a "worst-case scenario" analysis – yet, even with *no* information, institutions can lead to Pareto improvement. Achieving an efficient outcome is easier with a noisy signal, though signal improvements shift surplus to D.

[9] Intuitively, this means D cannot see technological progress until R can credibly demonstrate it. For example, upon proliferating, R might publicly test a nuclear weapon to

or rejects. Accepting ends the game with that distribution for the rest of time, while rejecting gives each side its post-shift war payoff.

To recap, the timing is:

1. R selects $k \geq \underline{k}$, its cost to proliferate
2. D makes an offer $x \in [0,1]$; R accepts or rejects
3. If R accepts, simultaneously R and D respectively choose whether to build or not and launch preventive war or not
4. If a power shift occurs, D makes a second offer $y \in [0,1]$; R accepts or rejects

As in the baseline model, D is strategically vulnerable in this setup: R can take D's concessions for the period and proliferate anyway. This addresses an important concern policymakers have about the JCPOA and similar agreements. Iran, for example, could enjoy sanctions relief and an improved stature among both its allies and enemies for the moment, develop nuclear weapons, and gain the security benefits later. Proliferation could be a self-fulfilling prophecy as a result – potential proliferators nuclearize because they are not receiving concessions, and rivals do not offer concessions because the opponent is nuclearizing. If deals are possible despite R's temptation, it would assuage this policy concern.

7.2.1 The Proliferation Decision

Ultimately, we care about R's divestment decision. But the game can unfold in many different ways depending on the value of k that R chooses.[10] Consequently, I begin by covering all of the possible outcomes R can induce by choosing particular values for k. At that point, solving for the divestment decision just requires finding the value of k that leads to the best payoff for R in the subsequent negotiations.

Because this is a sequential game of complete but imperfect information, subgame-perfect equilibrium is the appropriate solution concept.[11] Given that the post-shift state of the world is identical to the game with

show its strength to D, thereby alleviating the information problem. See Meirowitz and Sartori 2008 for a model when this is not the case.

[10] The discussion below investigates when $\underline{k} > \delta(p'_R - c_R)$. The goal here is to understand the origins of proliferation; when $\underline{k}$ falls below that critical value, Chapter 3 already showed that bargaining will fail to yield an agreement and also showed that welfare improving institutions can endogenously inflate k to be that large. Therefore, if a new mechanism causes proliferation to occur here, it must be that $k > \delta(p'_R - c_R)$.

[11] This may seem counterintuitive at first given that the monitoring problem appears to create incomplete information. However, the inability to monitor R simply means that

perfect monitoring, Lemma 3.1 still applies. This is because, though D cannot observe R's build decision, it can observe whether R has nuclear weapons after moving to the next period. Thus, the post-shift period is a game of complete and perfect information without any power shifts beyond what has already happened. As such, in every post-shift period, peace prevails. D offers $y = p'_R - c_R$ and R accepts; D earns $1 - p'_R + c_R$ and R earns $p'_R - c_R$ for the rest of time. This sets the stage for the four subsequent bargaining cases, which I analyze below.

To begin, recall that proliferation is "too cold" when the cost of weapons is too high relative to the extent of the power shift. Under these conditions, D realizes that war strictly dominates building for R, and thus it infers that R will never build. Note that D's ability to monitor R is irrelevant here; D does not need visual confirmation of R's move if it knows that R has no desire to build under any circumstances. Thus, Chapter 3's "too cold" Proposition 3.2 carries over here:

Proposition 7.1. *Suppose the potential shift in power is small relative to the cost of proliferation (i.e., $p'_R - p_R < (1 - \delta)k/\delta$). Then D offers $x = p_R - c_R$ and R accepts.*[12]

Although R successfully avoids preventive war in this case, it also cannot leverage the threat to proliferate to extract concessions when k is so high relative to the power shift. Consequently, R will look to avoid putting itself in this situation when it considers its divestment decision.

For intuition, consider the case of Burkina Faso. Even if the United States or any of its geographic neighbors could not observe Ouagadougou's decision to build a nuclear weapon, there is no need to initiate a preventive war. Burkina Faso has virtually no nuclear infrastructure.[13] Other countries know this and can reason that there are no geopolitical circumstances under which Burkina Faso would proliferate. In turn, fighting a preventive war to stop a nuclear program that other countries can deduce does not exist makes no sense.[14] They therefore

---

D must make its decision to prevent simultaneous to R's decision to build. Thus, the game only has *imperfect* information. Because optimal strategies do not depend on prior beliefs, perfect Bayesian equilibrium is unnecessary.

[12] The equilibria in this chapter are not unique. Off the equilibrium path, the simultaneous move portion of the interaction has multiple equilibria if $x = p_R + c_D$. But because this is off-the-path everywhere but the parameter range for Proposition 7.4, the equilibrium outcomes are unique. See Lemma 7.3 in this chapter's appendix for an explanation.

[13] To wit, it consistently has the lowest values on the v scale, possessing none of the infrastructure components in any year for which data are available.

[14] That is, they know that not building strictly dominates building and apply iterated elimination of strictly dominated strategies. This makes not preventing the obvious optimal choice.

strike an agreement with such countries but do not give additional concessions to incentivize nonproliferation.

Proposition 7.1 should not come as a surprise because similar results existed in previous chapters. But what happens when proliferation is a credible threat? Initially, one might think that all butter-for-bombs agreements from Proposition 3.3's "just right" parameter region will immediately fail as a result of the monitoring problem. After all, D cannot directly observe R's compliance. However, Proposition 7.2 shows that this fear is overstated:

Proposition 7.2. *Suppose the potential power shift falls in the "just right" parameter region and the cost of investment is large (i.e., $p'_R - p_R \in ((1 - \delta)k/\delta, (c_D + c_R)/\delta)$ and $k > \delta(p'_R - p_R - c_D - c_R)/(1 - \delta))$. Then D offers $x = p'_R - c_R - (1 - \delta)k/\delta$ and R accepts in every SPE.*

Note that Proposition 7.2 generates the same result as Proposition 3.3 – that is, butter-for-bombs agreements that exist in a world with perfect monitoring also exist in a world with completely imperfect monitoring.[15]

Why is D's lack of information irrelevant? Consider R's incentives. When it receives the optimal butter-for-bombs agreement, R does not choose to accept out of fear that D will prevent. Rather, R opts against building because D's offer is so attractive that additional weapons are no longer profitable; the size of the offer endogenously manipulates R's opportunity cost to ensure this. As a result, even if D is completely blind to R's actions, it can still rest assured that R will not break the butter-for-bombs agreement.

For example, consider why Japan does not develop nuclear weapons. The imperfect information aspect of nuclear proliferation plays no role. Washington would not launch a military strike against Japanese targets even if Tokyo went down that route. Instead, Japan's relatively advantaged position in the status quo makes nuclear weapons look unprofitable. It therefore stays the non-nuclear course.

Compared to the "too cold" outcome, this "just right" outcome looks more attractive to R – when the cost of weapons is small compared to the power shift, it can exercise a credible threat to proliferate. D provides concessions to avoid this outcome. The question is whether R could do better by choosing an even smaller cost.

---

[15] Chapter 3 did not focus on Proposition 7.2's second condition because it was not pivotal in whether proliferation resulted in equilibrium. As Proposition 7.4 will show, however, it is critical in cases of imperfect monitoring.

	Prevent	$\sim$ Prevent
Build	$p_R - c_R - (1 - \delta)k, 1 - p_R - c_D$	$(1 - \delta)x + \delta(p'_R - c_R) - (1 - \delta)k,$ $(1 - \delta)(1 - x) + \delta(1 - p'_R + c_R)$
$\sim$ Build	$p_R - c_R, 1 - p_R - c_D$	$x, 1 - x$

FIGURE 7.2. Simultaneous Move Subgame for a Generic Offer x

The previous propositions covered the two easy cases – D could avoid a proliferation outcome because the weapons were unreasonably expensive or because it could use tempting carrots to ensure compliance rather than the stick of preventive war. What about situations that fall under Proposition 3.1's "too hot" parameters, where D used the threat of preventive war to convince R to submit?

Such threats are no longer effective in a world of imperfect information. D previously needed to observe building to know to initiate preventive war. Now it can only speculate on R's build choice. This forces D to choose between one of two options. First, it can still provide the optimal butter-for-bombs offer to ensure R's compliance. As Figure 7.2 illustrates, filling in $x = p'_R - c_R - (1 - \delta)k/\delta$ causes not build to dominate build. Using iterated elimination of dominated strategies, D knows to not prevent.

Second, it can choose any amount lower than that.[16] This can lead to the mixing behavior previously discussed. R would build if it knew D was not preventing, as the offer is insufficient. But because the extent of the power shift is high (as compared to the previous case Proposition 7.2 covered), D would prevent if it knew R were building. Meanwhile, R would not build if it knew D were preventing to avoid the wasted cost, and D would not prevent if it knew R were not building, as the costs of war are unnecessary here.

Thus, the question is whether D would want to offer the butter-for-bombs deal and induce compliance or offer a smaller amount and face the consequences of the mixing game. If D chooses the former option, it simply receives the remainder of the offer. This remainder grows as the cost of investment increases, as D can extract that quantity through the agreement. The latter leads to a more complicated set probabilistic outcomes that depend on the precise mixed strategies.[17] However, if the cost of

---

[16] Of course, a third option exists: D could pick $x > p'_R - c_R - (1 - \delta)k/\delta$. But this is a needless concession to R, and thus D never selects such an amount in equilibrium.

[17] Figure 7.2 shows that D receives a fixed value of $1 - p_R - c_D$ if it prevents regardless of R's choice. The indifference conditions of mixed strategy Nash equilibria therefore dictate that D's expected payoff is simply $1 - p_R - c_D$.

investment is sufficiently large, the deal is more profitable than facing that no deal outcome. Put differently, if k is large enough, D prefers buying R's compliance to testing its luck with preventive war. But if k is too small, buying R's compliance is more expensive than simply fighting.

This gives rise to the following two propositions:

Proposition 7.3. *Suppose that both the potential power shift and cost of investment are large (i.e., $p'_R - p_R > (c_D + c_R)/\delta$ and $k > \delta(p'_R - p_R - c_D - c_R)/(1 - \delta)$). Then D makes the butter-for-bombs offer and R accepts.*

Proposition 7.4. *Suppose that the potential power shift is large but the cost of investment is small (i.e., $p'_R - p_R > (c_D + c_R)/\delta$ and $k < \delta(p'_R - p_R - c_D - c_R)/(1 - \delta)$). D does not reach an agreement with R. Multiple equilibria exist under these circumstances. However, in all equilibria, D initiates a preventive war with positive probability and therefore all equilibria are inefficient. In some equilibria, R proliferates with positive probability as well.*

In short, the cut-point on k appearing in Proposition 7.4 implies that if the cost of proliferation is sufficiently low, equilibria exist that exhibit the mixing properties described above. That said, the appendix shows that this parameter space allows for multiple equilibria. As becomes critical later, this is because the mixing equilibrium generates an expected payoff for D equal to its preventive war payoff. In turn, D is indifferent between pursuing the mixing outcome and offering terms so attractive to R that D prefers to immediately fight if accepted. All such equilibria are inefficient, though. How much of that inefficiency results from war between the states versus the cost of proliferation depends on the specific equilibrium. The key takeaway for later, however, is that R's divestment decision manipulates which parameter space the bargaining game falls into: high values for k induce D to prefer striking a deal, whereas low values for k trigger the possibility of war and proliferation.

Figure 7.3 summarizes the four possibilities described above. Note that the bottom half's butter-for-bombs and no-concession regions are similar to the bottom half of Figure 3.4, which mapped the outcomes with perfect information. Thus, monitoring problems are irrelevant when the extent of the power shift is low. This is because D never used its incredible threat of preventive war to alter the bargaining outcome.

The top half shows some drastic differences. Previously, large power shifts meant that D had a credible preventive-war threat and could correctly observe when to exercise that option. Internalizing this, R never

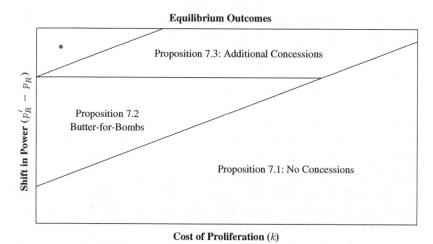

FIGURE 7.3. Equilibrium Plot by Cost of Weapons and Extent of Power Shift

built, and D calculated its offer as though proliferation were impossible for R. None of those results carry over here. In the top-left corner, marked with the asterisk, previously peaceful agreements have devolved to both war and proliferation.

The remainder maintains peace and nonproliferation but for different reasons than before. In particular, D achieves its goals by offering a butter-for-bombs agreement. This concession is commensurate with R's ability to proliferate; D therefore pays R substantially more than in the perfect information case. Moreover, it pays a greater amount than it does in the normal butter-for-bombs region; the optimal offer $x = p'_R - c_R - (1-\delta)k/\delta$ depends on the extent of the power shift, and that power shift is greater in this region than in the lower middle region. Finally, in the top right area, D avoids giving any concessions. But now it is entirely because the weapons are too costly and not a consequence of any threat to prevent.

7.2.2 The Divestment Decision

Given the many different paths the game can take, R has the opportunity to influence the final outcome by shifting its value of k at the beginning. As discussed before, it may seem that R would always want to maintain the status quo cost to proliferate $\underline{k}$, as any increase would only harm its outside option. Let $k^* \equiv \delta(p'_A - p_A - c_D - c_R)/(1-\delta)$, which is the critical cost that separates Proposition 7.3 from Proposition 7.4. The final proposition says that R sometimes prefers k^*, not $\underline{k}$:

Proposition 7.5. *Suppose R's baseline cost to build is sufficiently low (i.e., $\underline{k} < k^*$). Then R inflates its cost to $k = k^*$.*

In words, if R's natural cost of proliferation is low enough that preventive war may occur, it ratchets up its cost to the minimum level necessary to induce D to offer a deal. If D would offer a deal in the absence any divestment, R maintains its minimum cost and does not divest.

This result is counterintuitive and worth further explanation. Recall that the cost of proliferation in part determines whether D is willing to cut a deal with R. If the cost of proliferation is extremely large, D only needs to offer the potential proliferator a minimal amount and would thus prefer taking the remainder to fighting a war. But if the cost of proliferation is extremely cheap – which would be the case if R refused to divest – D prefers its war payoff and is unwilling to make the bribe.

In between these extremes, a particular cost of proliferation makes D indifferent between bribing R and fighting. Thus, at that cost, D is willing to take the efficient route. Here, D still receives its war payoff. Meanwhile, all of the costs that would have otherwise been wasted on war and proliferation can efficiently go to R. This is more than it would receive if k were lower and the parties mixed instead. Thus, *the potential proliferator gains from increasing its cost to build a nuclear weapon.*

Figure 7.4 illustrates both states' payoffs as k increases, holding the other parameters at $p_R = 0.2$, $p'_R = 0.7$, $c_R = 0.1$, $c_D = 0.25$, and $\delta = 0.9$. These parameters put the interaction in the top half of Figure 7.3, which means that preventive war might occur depending on the value of k that R selects.[18] When R chooses a high value for k, this places the interaction in the "too cold" top right of Figure 7.3. D treats the bargaining problem as though power were static and extracts the entire surplus. As Figure 7.4 shows, this results in a great payoff for D and a small payoff for R.

Choosing a medium value for k places the interaction in the "just right" top middle of Figure 7.3. D offers concessions, inducing R not to build. In fact, due to the monitoring problem, D pays a premium to R specifically to convince it not to proliferate. Figure 7.4 shows this leads to a good outcome for R. But note that as k increases in this range, R's

---

[18] This is necessary for divestment to occur. If k were in the bottom half, D is naturally offering an agreement, and so R has no incentive to divest to avoid preventive war.

Welfare as a Function of *k*

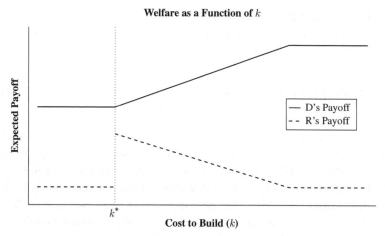

FIGURE 7.4. Payoff as a Function of the Cost to Build

payoff declines. This is because D's offer is a function of *k*, and it can offer less to R when the cost of proliferation is higher.

Finally, choosing a small value for *k* places the interaction in the inefficient top left region of Figure 7.3. War and proliferation can result with positive probability. Figure 7.4 illustrates the inefficiency this causes, with both players receiving lower payoffs.

R's decision effectively boils down to looking at its payoff in Figure 7.4 and choosing the value of *k* that nets its maximum. That optimal value is *k**, which is just enough to induce an agreement. It does not go past that so as to force D to give it the largest offer possible. Divestment allows the parties to escape both war and proliferation.

To be clear, when $\underline{k}$ is less than *k**, divestment is a *prerequisite* for successful negotiations. If R does not raise its price, then D refuses to make the butter-for-bombs offer. Nevertheless, one should not conclude that D can require divestments from R for negotiations to occur generally.[19] Indeed, in the middle range of Figure 7.3, R stands firm on not divesting, instead choosing to keep *k* at $\underline{k}$. D cannot credibly threaten to withhold concessions if R chooses to do this; once R selects $\underline{k}$ in this region, D must offer the butter-for-bombs deal to retain some of the surplus. As such, divestment only occurs when R wants incentivize a deal.

---

[19] Beyond the monitoring mechanism discussed here, R would not want to increase its investment cost in other model setups because the butter-for-bombs offer is decreasing in *k*. This is doubly true in situations where R has to build due to commitment problems like those discussed in Chapter 6, as R must actually pay the cost in those cases.

Note too that R chooses to move to k^* if $k^* > \underline{k}$ no matter how small $\underline{k}$ is. This means that even if nuclear weapons were nearly free, R prefers instead to make them costly.

7.3 UNDERSTANDING WEAPONS INSPECTIONS AND NUCLEAR REVERSALS

How do nuclear reversals, restrictions, and weapons inspections alter the bargaining environment? For weapons inspections in particular, the straightforward interpretation is that they provide information to rivals. Suppose a potential proliferator cannot effectively hide their programs from the prying eyes of inspectors. If rivals would launch preventive war short of a signal not to, a potential proliferator might wish to invite weapons inspectors into its country and allay its opponents' fears. Because refusal to admit inspectors inherently signals violations, the rivals could efficiently sort out the proliferators from the nonproliferators.

However, weapons inspectors are an imperfect solution. Proliferators have a home-field advantage – violations could be anywhere in the country, leaving weapons inspectors with a lot of ground to cover without sufficient manpower. Strong intelligence alleviates some of the problem by giving inspectors likely locations of infractions, but that can be lacking as well given that the absence of a smoking gun is not proof of compliance. In the extreme, cat-and-mouse games with inspectors might prevent inspections from providing any relevant informational content whatsoever.

Fortunately, even such ineffective weapons inspections have a hidden secondary effect that partially solves the proliferation problem. Although intelligence can be imperfect, the most efficient locations to construct weapons are often evident. Weapons inspections effectively shut down these avenues to proliferation because inspectors can investigate known sites and report violations. In turn, proliferating states must seek alternative means to develop their weaponry. But because the weapons inspectors close off the most efficient means, the alternative methods are inherently costlier. Combined with divestment of technology, equipment, and materials, potential proliferators can use these international regimes to transition the bargaining environment to the efficient range.

Consequently, imperfect monitoring – that is, the inability to know with certainty whether a state has invested in nuclear proliferation – is perfectly acceptable. Weapons inspectors do not act in isolation; they are part of a greater negotiation strategy. Although the cost of proliferation might still prove worth the finished product, the additional inefficiency incentivizes the rival to offer a deal, thus eliminating the motivation to proliferate. In turn, potential nuclear states accept inspectors and divest their infrastructure to make their nonproliferation commitments credible.

Indeed, this is a general theme of the "grand bargain" that the nonproliferation regime promotes. The understanding of the Non-Proliferation Treaty is that states trade the legal right to own nuclear weapons for technological assistance from nuclear-proficient countries. In practice, however, the benefits are not equal. Getmansky (2017) finds that states further from the United States' ideal point receive more technical cooperation from the IAEA – but only if they have agreed to the NPT's Additional Protocol, which subjects signatories to stricter inspections.

Both of these points are consistent with the model's general logic. States with greater disagreements have more to gain by acquiring nuclear weapons. In turn, these countries must receive more benefits to make nonproliferation look satisfactory. But when preventive war is cheaper than buying compliance, the United States prefers withholding concessions. The Additional Protocol resolves the problem. Deeper inspections increase the cost of proliferation, which in turn incentivizes the United States to cut a deal.

Perhaps surprisingly, weapons inspections might appear weak under these circumstances. For example, the JCPOA grants Iran some advanced notice before inspectors can visit certain facilities. Although that time cannot mask radioactive signatures, policymakers worry that Iran might instead develop infrastructure that could disappear (Schumer 2015). This makes sense in light of Proposition 7.5. *Some* additional barriers to proliferation increase the potential builder's welfare, but too many are detrimental. In turn, potential proliferators unsurprisingly reject full reversals of their programs.[20] But absence of full reversal is not evidence of intention to proliferate.

This is a point worth emphasizing, as policymakers skeptical of nuclear agreements often point to partial compliance as proof of duplicitous behavior. Nevertheless, it is easy to sympathize with the rising state's dilemma by thinking about the extreme case. If that country truly has no plans to develop a weapon, why doesn't it completely divest of all nuclear technology and allow thousands of weapons inspectors to flood the country? Practical issues aside, the downstream consequences of

---

[20] By the same token, it should not be surprising that opponents push for full nuclear reversals – their payoffs weakly increase in the cost to build.

such a decision are obvious. Potential proliferators may claim sovereign rights or geopolitical dignity, but there is a more basic concern. Without any capability to develop a weapon, the declining state has no reason to offer a butter-for-bombs deal. Instead, the concessions it makes are in line with the "too cold" parameters of Proposition 7.1. The rising state receives an amount equal to its pre-shift value for war and nothing more.

Consequently, the rising state must strike a balance between divesting enough to convince the declining state to offer a deal and not divesting so much that it sabotages itself in negotiations afterward. As Figure 7.4 illustrates, the optimal tradeoff is $k = k^*$. But Figure 7.4 also shows why states get into a war of words over inspection levels. Once the proliferation cost exceeds k^*, bargaining is entirely zero-sum. Whatever the rising state loses by increasing the proliferation cost, the declining state gains an equal amount. Simultaneously, dropping below k^* is catastrophic for both. The declining state therefore has incentive to declare any given intensity of inspections as unacceptable. If believed, the rising state would submit to deeper inspections, which increases the proliferation cost further and decreases its concessions received. Rising states therefore resist stricter inspection regimes so as to capture more of the surplus.

Along those lines, the model does *not* predict that onerous weapons inspections will be welcome under all circumstances. Indeed, as Figure 7.5 illustrates, nuclear restrictions are only mutually agreeable when proliferation and war would otherwise occur in equilibrium; reversal leads to welfare improvement in that case. Consider what happens once the

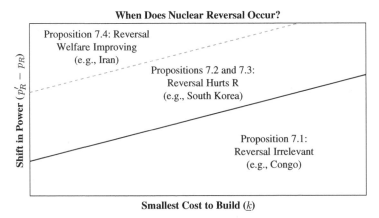

FIGURE 7.5. How Nuclear Reversals Impact the Rising State

parameters reach the regions of Propositions 7.2 and 7.3. Deals naturally occur here without any divestment, and the concessions are commensurate with the rising state's ability to proliferate. Naturally, as Figure 7.4 shows, the value of those concessions decreases in k. States that are in these regions before any divestment consequently maintain the status quo. Once again, lack of divestment does not indicate guilt. Rather, rising states in these cases refuse to divest so as not to sabotage their own bargaining leverage.

One can see how this logic played out in negotiations between the United States and some of its Cold War allies. Recapping Chapter 5's analysis, Australia, Japan, and South Korea each considered developing their own weapon. Meanwhile, the United States sought to curb the spread of nuclear bombs. Given the relatively warm relations between the United States and each of these countries, preventive war was not a credible threat. Such a constraint pushes the allies into Proposition 7.2's parameters. Correspondingly, the United States offered economic and security concessions (Drezner 1999, 255; Campbell and Sunohara 2004, 222–224; Reynolds 2000, 195–196). Critically, though, the allies did *not* adopt reversal measures, just as the model would predict; divestment would only harm their bargaining position.

Of course, stepping outside of the model, countries with no plans to abide by an agreement for another reason would resist inspections and divestment in the same manner.[21] Thus, the point here is not that resistance to inspections implies that a country will abide by nonproliferation norms. Instead, refusal to admit inspectors may or may not be a bad signal for the longevity of a nonproliferation agreement. Declining states would still benefit from intelligence operations to decipher their opponents' true intentions.

In the remaining case, reversal is irrelevant. If the potential proliferator's minimum proliferation cost $\underline{k}$ forces it to choose values exclusively in the range from Proposition 7.1, the exact choice does not matter – it has no desire to build weapons regardless of the specific circumstance. These parameters cover states that would not reasonably build nuclear weapons under any conditions, either because they lack major security threats (e.g., Iceland) or they do not have the economic means (e.g., The Democratic Republic of the Congo).

---

[21] This could be perhaps because of the commitment problem described in the previous chapter, some domestic benefit that overrides the unitary actor inefficiency, or a different bargaining problem.

Figure 7.5 also reveals a counterintuitive empirical implication. From the outset, one might think that reversal is most likely to occur when weapons are most costly and have the least impact on the balance of power – in other words, when nuclear weapons are bad investments. In fact, reversal is irrelevant under those circumstances because the potential proliferator would never want to build. Instead, reversal is most likely to occur under the exact opposite conditions: when weapons are cheap and the extent of the power shift is the greatest. Under such circumstances, it would seem that potential proliferators would be hard-pressed to reverse their programs because nuclear weapons are great investments here. In turn, one might expect these parameters to be the most likely to lead to bargaining breakdown and the corresponding inefficient outcomes. But precisely due to those concerns, the potential proliferator opts for reversal.

Before concluding, a couple of other important empirical implications follow from Proposition 7.5. To begin, not all nuclear reversals are equal:

Corollary 7.1. *Suppose nuclear reversals are welfare-increasing (i.e., $\underline{k} <$ k^*). Then the proliferation cost R chooses is decreasing in D's cost of preventive war.*

Equivalently, the cheaper preventive war is for D, the less nuclear capacity R retains.

The proof is as simple as noting that if the potential proliferator wants to reverse course, the optimal divestment sets k equal to $k^* = \delta(p'_R - p_R - c_R - c_D)/(1 - \delta)$. Thus, increasing c_D decreases that optimal value, meaning R divests less. Intuitively, decreasing the cost of preventive war makes D less willing to cut a deal. Because the consequences of no agreement are disastrous, R must further divest to incentivize a bargain.[22]

Corollary 7.1's prediction matches the United States' experiences in the two most recent nuclear deals. In December, 2003, Libya announced it would terminate its program. At the time, the United States was at the height of its post–September 11 geopolitical strength; Washington had quickly dispatched unfriendly regimes in Afghanistan and Iraq but was not yet experiencing the full force of the insurgencies that would follow. Libya's program was relatively small and therefore an easy target. Combined with the fact that the Bush administration generally had hawkish tendencies, the United States' effective cost of war at the time

---

[22] This effect is local. If c_D increases enough, nuclear reversals are no longer welfare-increasing, and so R maintains the its natural proliferation cost $\underline{k}$.

was low. The model predicts that Libya would choose a high proliferation cost. Correspondingly, Libya dismantled virtually all of its nuclear infrastructure (ElBaradei 2011, 157; Corera 2006, 221–222; Bowen 2006, 72–77).

War against Iran – though perhaps plausible (Kroenig 2012; Moneteiro and Debs 2014, 50–51) – would not be so simple. Although tensions exist between Iranian leadership and its populace, the country is comparatively more united than Libya was prior to the 2011 civil war. Moreover, Iran has invested in fortifying its nuclear sites; a death knell to the program would need significantly greater military effort, likely requiring a ground assault of some kind. Meanwhile, the United States has endured more than a decade of insurgencies and risks further polarizing the Muslim world with another conflict in the region. The model predicts that Iran would choose a more moderate proliferation cost. Correspondingly, the JCPOA leaves Iran with a plausible path to proliferation.

In applying Corollary 7.1's prediction across substantive cases, note that the argument refers to the proliferation cost chosen in equilibrium. This is the end level of nuclear infrastructure, not the amount of divestment a particular country chooses. The actual divestment level is the end value chosen k^* minus its starting point $\underline{k}$. Thus, if a country starts with a very low cost to proliferate, it may simultaneously give up more than another country and yet still finish with a lower proliferation cost.

Taking this to the Iran and Libya cases, Libya arguably divested very little nuclear infrastructure, if only because it had little to begin with. In contrast, the JCPOA forces Iran to part with a lot of access to its nuclear technology. But because Iran had made far more progress than Libya, Tehran can still revert back to proliferating at a lower cost than Muammar Gaddafi could pre–Arab Spring. This is what Corollary 7.1 predicts – because preventive war was a cheaper option versus Libya, Iran's post-divestment proliferation cost would remain relatively low.

Regardless, the winner of divestment may come as a surprise:

Corollary 7.2. *Suppose nuclear reversals are welfare-increasing (i.e., $\underline{k} < k^*$). Then R captures the entire surplus.*

From a game-theoretical perspective, Corollary 7.2 is strange. Normally, in bargaining games in which only one individual has proposal power (e.g., ultimatum games), the proposer captures the entire surplus. Here, the proposer is D. Yet, in equilibrium, R's endogenous nuclear reversal leads to a cost that makes D indifferent between making a deal and going to war. Thus, D's payoff equals $1 - p_R - c_D$; because the result is efficient, this implies that R takes the remainder, or $p_R + c_D$. The surplus goes to the receiver.[23]

From an empirical perspective, from the outset, it would appear that R is the more vulnerable state in this type of interaction. After all, it has not acquired a nuclear weapon yet, doing so is costly, and the opponent can stop that shift with preventive war. This intuition is wrong. R can manipulate D's incentives so that R receives all of the benefits from reaching a deal. Arms treaties therefore primarily benefit potential proliferators, not their opposition.

7.4 THE ROBUSTNESS OF NUCLEAR REVERSALS

As other chapters have noted, the model I develop highlights some strategic concerns at the expense of others. Nevertheless, Corollary 7.2 demonstrates why the model is robust to a number of substantive concerns that might otherwise seem to derail reversal efforts. I detail a few of these concerns below.

First, consider how inspections may cause power shifts. Some potential proliferators might be reluctant to allow reversal regimes into their countries, as information leaks could give rivals tactical advantages. Other states worry that weapons inspectors – in the process of shutting down the most efficient paths to proliferation – will steal trade secrets (Schiff 1983, 94).[24] This is, in part, why rivals delegate weapons inspections to international organization and not bilateral task forces (Schiff 1983, 95). But international organizations are not perfect. To wit, the United Nations Special Commission on Iraq, the regime that monitored Iraqi compliance following the Persian Gulf War, ceased operations in 1999 amid allegations that Western intelligence agencies had infiltrated it (Blix 2004, 36–37; ElBaradei 2011, 32–33).

Fortunately, espionage does not inherently doom inspection regimes. At its core, Proposition 7.5's result stems from the fact that inflating k past k^* yields efficiency gains. As Corollary 7.2 explained and Figure 7.4

---

[23] R does not capture the entire surplus in other parameter spaces. In the butter-for-bombs cases of Propositions 7.2 and 7.3, the natural cost of nuclear weapons is big enough that the remainder of the agreement gives D an amount larger than $1 - p_R - c_D$. Therefore, D improves over its war payoff. R also improves over its pre-shift war payoff because it can use the threat to proliferate as bargaining leverage but does not obtain the full surplus. In the "too cold" case of Proposition 7.1, D offers just enough to convince R not to fight (i.e., $x = p_R - c_R$), and thus D captures the entire surplus.

[24] Accordingly, the JCPOA (via the Additional Protocol) allows Iranian intelligence to deny visas to weapons inspectors of its choosing.

illustrated, these additional benefits flow to the potential proliferator. In fact, the power shift caused by inspector espionage would have to exceed the sum costs of war to make a deal impossible. Given how international regimes work precisely to limit a rival state's role in the process, this necessary condition seems implausible. Consequently, those states would still happily reverse course – the substantial gains more than offset whatever tactical problems come with them.

Second, reversal regimes and their associated weapons inspectors are not free – someone must pay for their employment, administrative support, and logistics. As such, reversal regimes can only lead to welfare improvement if their cost is less than the inefficiency from warfare and weapons construction.[25]

Given how economically disruptive and destructive war is, reversal is easily the cheaper option. The JCPOA, for example, calls for a maximum of 150 weapons inspectors. In Iraq, UNSC Resolution 986 funded weapons inspections with just 0.8% of the revenue brought in from the food-for-oil program. Meanwhile, the total yearly budget for IAEA inspections is about $120 million (ElBaradei 2011, 80). Many states share the cost of this burden, as is standard with information-providing institutions (Keohane 1984). Even in marginal cases, third-party states have incentive to contribute to avoid war's negative externalities. Thus, although these costs add to the difficulty of reaching an agreement, they do not render reversals impossible.

Finally, as stated from the outset, the model looked at the worse-case scenario where D cannot observe R building. As it turns out, relaxing this assumption merely shifts around surplus. A noisy signal revealing that R has built effectively makes nuclear weapons more expensive – some portion of the time, D will see it and declare war, thereby forcing R to pay the cost of proliferation without any benefits. This gives rise to regions analogous to Figure 7.5.[26] If the proliferation cost remains high enough, D is willing to buy off R (at a lower price), and states avoid the inefficient mixing outcome. But when the cost is sufficiently low, the parties still end up mixing.

---

[25] This is essentially a costly peace argument (Powell 2006; Coe 2012).

[26] When the probability of revelation is sufficiently high, R loses its credible threat to build if D's cost of preventive war is low. This is because D observes the decision too often and initiates an intervention, and R prefers maintaining the status quo to wasting its investment cost k a high percentage of the time. Thus, as Chapter 3 suggested, the original results still have theoretical leverage in this extension, provided that D's monitoring problem is not too severe.

Once more, this logic helps explain why potential proliferators demand limits on information revelation to their opponents. With a perfectly informative signal, the credible threat of preventive war eliminates nuclearization as an option entirely, causing the potential proliferator to lose out on all the surplus. But even smaller measures hurt the value of its outside option. In turn, *some* information revelation proves useful if it convinces the rival to cut a deal and preserve the efficient outcome. However, any further information provision can only hurt the potential proliferator. Once again, as a consequence, rivals cannot use refusal to provide information as proof positive that the potential proliferator will nuclearize.

7.5 CONCLUSION

This chapter explored the role of divestment strategies in combatting nuclear arms programs. Whereas research normally focuses on the monitoring and verification clauses of arms agreements, I showed that reversing course can entice opposing states to offer generous terms to terminate nuclear programs. Although refusing to divest may allow the country to develop nuclear weapons unimpeded, war sometimes also might occur; the expected inefficiency outweighs the potential gain from developing nuclear weapons. Consequently, potential proliferators are the primary beneficiaries of divestment despite the apparently precarious nature of such a strategy.

I conclude with three policy implications special to monitoring issues. First, rivals of states with nuclear programs should not treat proposed reversals as obvious traps. Although such agreements might seem too good to be true, potential proliferators have good reason to divest their infrastructure and avoid facing preventive war. Moreover, North Korea notwithstanding, such reversal deals have a good track record. This does not mean that the JCPOA or other future deals are guaranteed to work – other mechanisms may lead to bargaining failure – just that policymakers should not immediately dismiss them as inherently incredible.

Second, however, it is important to note that reversals are mere stepping stones to an agreement. Potential proliferators do not divest out of generosity – they do so because they expect to receive concessions in return. Despite apparent commitment problems, these concessions are credible because potential proliferators maintain some ability to restart their programs. Thus, rivals should not see reversal as a victory in itself – concessions must follow, or the nuclear outcome will result anyway.

Third, the core mechanism likely generalizes to other policy arenas like civil war monitoring, domestic constraints, and cyberwarfare. As described earlier, the common solution to these problems is information accumulation. Just like with nuclear weapons, however, perfect information may be impossible to come by. But the model suggests that states can apply the alternative solution to these domains as well: by increasing the costs of taking private actions, states could potentially avoid the inefficient behaviors.

Unfortunately, the model also hints at a constraint to credible commitment. With nuclear technology, proper divestment does not disrupt its productive purposes. For example, downblended uranium is still suitable for many nuclear reactor designs, and the international community can supply enriched uranium to fuel power plants and offset the lost productivity of centrifuges. Yet resolving monitoring problems in other fields may result in direct costs. Divesting from the cyberspace arena may require eliminating a country's computer network, which is plainly infeasible. Thus, resolving commitment issues requires finding clever solutions that increase the cost of violation *without* requiring extensive upfront costs.

Moving forward, although this chapter has shown that weapons inspectors build trust and lead to cooperation, cases remain where proliferating states forbid inspections and flagrantly violate nonproliferation commitments. Given the benefits of butter-for-bombs treaties and institutionalizing compliance to make such agreements credible, why does this occur? The next chapter introduces incomplete information to the interaction and shows that declining states rationally gamble by acting tough, hoping that the threat of preventive war is sufficient to induce compliance. In turn, the model will help explain the critical problems that the nonproliferation regime encounters that this chapter's model could not adequately address.

7.6 APPENDIX

This appendix covers the proofs missing from the main text of this chapter and details the robustness checks mentioned earlier. As stated before, the proof for Proposition 7.1 follows from the proof for Proposition 3.2 and thus does not appear here. Therefore, this appendix only considers cases in which $p'_R - p_R > (1 - \delta)k/\delta$.

7.6.1 Proof for Proposition 7.2 and Proposition 7.3

Proposition 7.2 and Proposition 7.3 appeared separate for expositional purposes. The proof, however, is identical. From Figure 7.2, note that if $x \geq p'_R - c_R - (1 - \delta)k/\delta$, not building dominates building for R. By iterated elimination of dominated strategies, D does not prevent if $x < p_R + c_D$.[27] R receives x and D receives the remainder. Because D's payoff is strictly decreasing in x, its optimal offer in this range is $x = p'_R - c_R - (1 - \delta)k/\delta$.

If $x > p_R + c_D$, D prevents. If $x = p_R + c_D$, D is indifferent between preventing and not preventing. In either case, D's payoff is less than had it offered the optimal butter-for-bombs amount if:

$$1 - p_R - c_D < 1 - p'_R + c_R + \frac{(1 - \delta)k}{\delta}$$

$$k > \frac{\delta(p'_R - p_R - c_D - c_R)}{1 - \delta}.$$

This is the second condition appearing in the propositions, so it holds there.

Now consider any offer smaller than $p'_R - c_R - (1 - \delta)k/\delta$. This can only be more profitable for D if D does not prevent and R does not build with positive probability. (If D prevents, it receives its war payoff; if D does not prevent and R builds, D receives more from having induced R to accept the optimal butter-for-bombs offer.) Such an outcome cannot occur with certainty, as R could profitably deviate to building. It also cannot be the case that D does not prevent with certainty and R mixes between building and not building because R's indifference condition requires $x = p'_R - c_R - (1 - \delta)k/\delta$. The only remaining possibility is where D mixes between preventing and not preventing. However, the indifference conditions mean that D must earn $1 - p_R - c_D$ in expectation. As shown above, Proposition 7.3's second condition implies that it could profitably deviate to an amount slightly larger than $p'_R - c_R - (1 - \delta)k/\delta$.

Thus, D optimally offers $x = p'_R - c_R - (1 - \delta)k/\delta$.   □

7.6.2 Proof for Proposition 7.4

Reconfiguring a cut-point, Proposition 7.4 states that D receives its war payoff if $p'_R - p_R > c_D + c_R + (1 - \delta)k/\delta$. However, this can occur in many different ways depending on the offer D makes initially. Because there many different possibilities, consider the three cases (in the form of three lemmas) below.

[27] If $x > p_R - c_R - (1 - \delta)k/\delta$, iterated elimination of strictly dominated strategies yields a unique solution. If there is only equality, assume that R accepts with probability 1. This is without loss of generality for the same reasons as in the standard ultimatum game, which has no equilibria in which the receiver rejects with positive probability when indifferent.

Lemma 7.1. *If* $x < p_R + c_D$, *D prevents with probability*

$$\frac{\delta x - \delta(p'_R - c_R) + (1 - \delta)k}{\delta x - \delta(p'_R - c_R)}$$

and R builds with probability

$$\frac{x - p_R - c_D}{\delta(x - p'_R + c_R)}.$$

Proof: If $x < p_R + c_D$, it is trivial to show that no pure-strategy Nash equilibria exist and that the only way one player can be willing to mix is if the other also mixes. Thus, consider mixed-strategy Nash equilibria by deriving the indifference conditions.

To begin, let σ_p be the probability D prevents. Then R's expected utility for building equals:

$$\sigma_p[p_R - c_R - (1 - \delta)k] + (1 - \sigma_p)[(1 - \delta)x + \delta(p'_R - c_R) - (1 - \delta)k]$$

$$\sigma_p[p_R - c_R - (1 - \delta)x - \delta(p'_R - c_R)] + (1 - \delta)x + \delta(p'_R - c_R) - (1 - \delta)k.$$

And R's expected utility for not building equals:

$$\sigma_p(p_R - c_R) + (1 - \sigma_p)x$$

$$\sigma_p(p_R - c_R - x) + x.$$

Setting these two equations equal to each other and solving for σ_p yields:

$$\sigma_p = \frac{\delta x - \delta(p'_R - c_R) + (1 - \delta)k}{\delta x - \delta(p'_R - c_R)}.$$

Now consider D's indifference condition. D's expected utility for preventing is $1 - p_R - c_D$ regardless of R's strategy. Meanwhile, letting σ_b be the probability R builds, D's expected utility for not preventing equals:

$$\sigma_b[(1 - \delta)(1 - x) + \delta(1 - p'_R + c_R)] + (1 - \sigma_b)(1 - x)$$

$$\sigma_b[\delta(x - p'_R + c_R)] + 1 - x.$$

Setting these two values equal to each other and solving for σ_b yields:

$$\sigma_b = \frac{x - p_R - c_D}{\delta(x - p'_R + c_R)}.$$

Note that if D is mixing, it is indifferent between preventing and not preventing. Because preventing yields a flat $1 - p_R - c_D$, D receives its war payoff in this case. □

Lemma 7.2. *If* $x > p_R + c_D$, *D prevents and R does not build.*

Proof: Suppose $x > p_R + c_D$. Iterated elimination of strictly dominated strategies proves the claim. D strictly prefers preventing if R does not build. If R builds, D earns $1 - p_R - c_D$ for preventing and $(1 - \delta)(1 - x) + \delta(1 - p'_R + c_R)$ for not preventing. Using $x = p_R + c_D$ as an upper bound for D's payoff, preventing is strictly better if:

$$1 - p_R - c_D > (1 - \delta)(1 - p_R - c_D) + \delta(1 - p'_R + c_R)$$

$$p'_R - p_R > c_D + c_R.$$

Recall that $p'_R - p_R > c_D + c_R + (1 - \delta)k/\delta$ for this parameter space. So the inequality holds. Therefore, preventing is always strictly better than not preventing for D.

By iterated elimination of strictly dominated strategies, R does not build. This leads to a pure strategy outcome in which D receives $1 - p_R - c_D$. □

Lemma 7.3. *If $x = p_R + c_D$, R does not build and D prevents with probability*

$$\sigma_p \in \left[\frac{\delta(p_R + c_D - p'_R + c_R) + (1 - \delta)k}{\delta(p_R + c_D - p'_R + c_R)}, 1 \right].$$

Preventing now weakly dominates not preventing. Not building is the best response to preventing, so preventing and not building is an equilibrium.

No other pure-strategy Nash equilibria exist. Not preventing and not building is not an equilibrium; R needs at least $p'_R - c_R - (1 - \delta)k/\delta$ to not want to deviate to building, but $p_R + c_D$ is less than that. Building and not preventing is not an equilibrium because D prefers to prevent. Lastly, preventing and building is not an equilibrium because R could deviate to not building and save the investment cost.

Now consider mixed-strategy Nash equilibria. Because preventing weakly dominates not preventing, if R mixes, D must prevent as a pure strategy. But because R strictly prefers not building in this case, R cannot optimally mix.

Thus, the remaining cases to consider require D to mix and R to select a pure strategy. D is indifferent between preventing and not preventing only if R does not build. For R to be willing to not build, Lemma 7.1 shows that

$$\sigma_p \geq \frac{\delta(p_R + c_D - p'_R + c_R) + (1 - \delta)k}{\delta(p_R + c_D - p'_R + c_R)}.$$

Thus, in equilibrium, R does not build and D prevents with probability at least $[\delta(p_R + c_D - p'_R + c_R) + (1-\delta)k]/\delta(p_R + c_D - p'_R + c_R)$. Because D is indifferent between preventing and not preventing in all of these cases, it earns its war payoff. □

To conclude the proof of Proposition 7.4, the final step is to find the value for x that maximizes D's payoff in the subgames the lemmas described. But note that D receives $1 - p_R - c_D$ regardless of its choice. As such, *all* offer sizes are optimal. In turn, for any value for x, a SPE exists. All SPE are inefficient by virtue of the fact that D initiates preventive war with positive probability in all of them. In addition, SPE exist in which proliferation occurs, preventive war occurs, and mistaken preventive war occurs. □

7.6.3 Proof for Proposition 7.5

Recall from Proposition 7.4 that when $p'_R - p_R > c_D + c_R + (1-\delta)k/\delta$, or $k < \delta(p'_R - p_R - c_D - c_R)/(1-\delta)$, multiple equilibria exist. The proof for Proposition 7.4 showed that all equilibria are inefficient and D earns $1 - p_R - c_D$ in all of them. Because the sum value of the game is at most 1, this means that R receives no more than $p_R + c_D$. But all equilibria entail inefficiency, whether through war or investment. Thus, R must receive strictly less than $p_R + c_D$.

The size of the inefficiency could depend on the offer D makes initially, and there are infinitely many such possibilities in equilibrium. Nevertheless, the exact portion is irrelevant to the argument. Instead, quantify the loss as $L > 0$.

In contrast, consider D's payoff for choosing some value $\hat{k}$ such that $\hat{k} \geq \delta(p'_R - p_R - c_D - c_R)/(1-\delta)$. Propositions 7.2 and 7.3 state that D offers $x = p'_R - c_R - (1-\delta)\hat{k}/\delta$ and R accepts. D prefers this outcome to choosing a value of k less than $\delta(p'_R - p_R - c_D - c_R)/(1-\delta)$ (and inducing the inefficient outcome) if:

$$1 - p'_R + c_R + \frac{(1-\delta)\hat{k}}{\delta} > 1 - p_R - c_D$$

$$\hat{k} > \frac{\delta(p'_R - p_R - c_D - c_R)}{1-\delta}.$$

Meanwhile, R prefers the alternative outcome if:

$$p'_R - c_R - \frac{(1-\delta)\hat{k}}{\delta} > p_R + c_D - L$$

$$\hat{k} < \frac{\delta(p'_R - p_R - c_D - c_R + L)}{1-\delta}.$$

Such a mutually preferable alternative investment cost $\hat{k}$ exists if:

$$\frac{\delta(p'_R - p_R - c_D - c_R)}{1 - \delta} < \frac{\delta(p'_R - p_R - c_D - c_R + L)}{1 - \delta}$$

$$L > 0.$$

This holds. Therefore, both parties benefit from increasing the costs of proliferation. The question is which agreement R most prefers. Because R's payoff is strictly decreasing in k, that optimal value for k is k^*.[28]   □

7.6.4 Discussion of an Infinite-Horizon Model

For simplicity, the model analyzed a two-period interaction. However, it is easy to verify that the same welfare-improvement mechanism works if the states bargained repeatedly. The key to seeing this is recognizing that an efficient agreement – without war or proliferation – requires R receive at least $p'_R - c_R - (1 - \delta)k/\delta$ and D receive at least $1 - p_R - c_D$ by accepting a settlement in each period. But choosing a k value less than k^* ensures that the sum of these minimal payoffs exceed 1, making it impossible to reach such a settlement. Inefficient behavior must result.

Further, for the same reason as in the two-period model, D must expect to receive $1 - p_R - c_D$ in the absence of a deal. Due to the inefficiency, R must receive strictly less than $p_R + c_D$.

However, raising k to at least k^* permits D to make acceptable offers. In turn, R can take the surplus. This is preferable to keeping k below k^* and receiving strictly less than the remainder of R's reservation value. Hence reversal would still occur in an infinite-horizon setup.

---

[28] Note that D is indifferent between making an acceptable offer and making an unacceptable offer when $k = k^*$. However, for similar reasons as to why the ultimatum game has a unique equilibrium, D must make the acceptable offer with probability 1 in all subgame-perfect equilibria.

8

Bluffing Preventive War

On June 7, 1981, fourteen of Israel's best fighter pilots gathered at Etzion air base, near Israel's southernmost point. At 3:55 pm local time, the pilots entered their F-15 and F-16 fighter jets and took off. Their target: Osirak, a nuclear facility on the outskirts of Baghdad. Less than an hour later, the fighters destroyed the installation. Israel had successfully executed one of the cleanest acts of preventive war in history.

This book's core theoretical model shows how a credible threat of preventive war shifts bargaining power to the declining state. But thus far, the declining state has used that leverage to achieve better *peaceful* outcomes; the threat alone deterred the rising state. But Israel's 1981 attack, dubbed Operation Opera, demonstrates that rising states do not always internalize a declining state's preventive intentions. Why not?

Operation Opera was neither the first nor last preventive assault.[1] In fact, Operation Opera was the second attack on Osirak in less than a year; during the early stages of the Iran–Iraq War, Tehran saw an opportunity to quash a potential nuclear weapons project in its infancy. However, Operation Scorch Sword caused virtually no damage.[2]

Seventeen years later, Israel executed an assault known as Operation Orchard. This time, Syria was the target. Not much is known about the attack. The IAEA flagged the target site as a possible nuclear-research facility, but Syria claimed it was an ordinary military depot. Either way, the Israeli Air Force leveled it. Israel only admitted culpability in 2018.

---

[1] See Fuhrmann and Kreps 2010 for an exhaustive list of attacks on nuclear facilities.

[2] Iraq also executed similar strikes on Iran's Bushehr reactor. That said, Bushehr was in its earliest stages, and Iran had abandoned the project at the start of the war (Sick 2001, 133).

Preventive attacks on nuclear-related installations are not just a recent phenomenon. Indeed, they are as old as nuclear programs themselves. Norway's Vemork Hydroelectric Plant was one of the earliest facilities capable of producing heavy water. On the eve of Nazi Germany's invasion of Norway, French special forces smuggled the plant's entire supply out of the country. When Nazi officials ordered the Vemork plant to produce more heavy water, Allied forces and Norwegian resistance sabotaged its machinery, dealing a significant blow to Germany's nascent nuclear program.

Although the previous chapter highlighted the role of imperfect information in explaining preventive war, the rising state's nuclear facilities were well known to each of the declining states in these cases. How, then, can we explain such preventive strikes? The Norwegian heavy-water sabotage is intuitive – bargaining had already broken down between the Allies and Nazi Germany, so we should expect military investments and the corresponding countermeasures. Iran was similarly at war with Iraq at the time of Operation Scorch Sword. But Israel was not at war with Iraq or Syria prior to those operations. Why couldn't these states bargain their way out of conflict?

This should be the expectation. With complete and perfect information, the rising state internalizes the declining state's threat. If that threat is credible, the rising state will not pursue an arms program, lest it needlessly pay a cost only to face preventive war. If the threat is not credible, the declining state offers butter-for-bombs concessions, preempting any need for those weapons and stealing the surplus in the process. The result is always efficient. Yet, in practice, states sometimes pursue weapons programs and sometimes their rivals intervene. Why?

So far, this book has not explored the role of incomplete information in the decision to proliferate.[3] Yet the above discussion suggests that a rising state may doubt a declining state's willingness to fight preventive wars. Previously, the rising state has always known whether the declining state would prevent if the rising state built. But as the crisis-bargaining literature has demonstrated, state resolve is not always transparent and can trigger war. Consequently, one may wonder whether butter-for-bombs bargains work when the rising state doubts the declining state's commitment to nonproliferation.

---

[3] An interaction features imperfect information if one or more actors are unaware of previous actions. In contrast, an interaction features incomplete information if one or more actors do not know the preferences of another actor.

To analyze how incomplete information sabotages bargained settlements, this chapter explores a model in which the rising state is unsure whether the declining state is a "strong" or "weak" type. Strong types prefer engaging in preventive war to stop the rising state from proliferating. Weak types find preventive war too costly to engage in. The rising state does not know which type it is facing and must make inferences based on the declining state's actions.

The model has a number of compelling features. First, nonproliferation settlements are readily available for all types. Strong declining states can convince the rising state not to proliferate with mere threat of preventive war. Weaker declining states can bribe the rising state with butter-for-bombs offers to remove any incentive to proliferate. Thus, proliferation is not due to the lack of available settlements.

However, incomplete information builds the perfect storm for conflict. If the rising state cannot directly observe whether the declining state is strong or weak, weak declining states have incentive to bluff. To understand why, suppose the rising state were to believe that the declining state is strong upon receiving no concessions. Then a weak declining state would want to mimic the strong type to convince the rising state not to build. After all, why give costly carrots when the stick is free to leverage? Weak declining states resolve this dilemma by sometimes proposing conciliatory butter-for-bombs settlements and sometimes bluffing as though they were strong. Strong declining states, meanwhile, always offer no concessions.

The bluffing behavior leads the rising state to adopt a dangerous response. When the declining state presents butter-for-bombs settlements, the rising state has no incentive to proliferate and therefore does not invest in nuclear weapons. But when the declining state offers no concessions, the rising state is unsure whether it is facing the weak type or strong type. The rising state resolves this dilemma by sometimes investing and sometimes conceding the issue.

Calling the bluff has explosive consequences. When the rising state attempts to proliferate, it does not know whether the declining state is strong or weak. This turns out well for the rising state in the latter case. But strong declining states respond with preventive war. Thus, by sometimes calling the bluff, the rising state will occasionally regret it in retrospect.

The rising state's response has interesting welfare implications for the weak declining state. Intuitively, one might believe that the weak types would benefit from the uncertainty, as they could free-ride off of the strong type's credible threat. However, this incentive to bluff causes the rising state to act more aggressively to avoid exploitation. The end result is that the weak type ends up no better off than had it conceded the issue up front and offered the necessary butter-for-bombs bribe. On the other hand, the incentive to bluff causes misery for the strong type and the rising state, who both must waste resources to avoid being manipulated.

Empirically, the equilibrium provides an intuitive explanation for preventive nuclear strikes. States can rationally leave nuclear facilities in the open if they believe their rivals are unlikely to attack them. But if the rivals know they have an easy preventive strike available, they execute those strikes.

This chapter has four additional sections. To begin, I briefly discuss the connection between information and war. Next, I formally define the new extension to Chapter 3's baseline model and show the conditions under which the above strategies are optimal. The following section provides a case study of Israel's decision to intervene in Iraq. A brief conclusion ends the chapter.

8.1 INFORMATION AND WAR

Incomplete information as an explanation for war is not new. Fearon (1995) observes that if everyone knew the relative probability of victory and costs of fighting, then states should locate a peaceful division of the stakes that makes both sides better off. Without that information, a state does not know its opponent's bottom line in crisis negotiations. In turn, the optimal bargaining strategy may be to make stringent demands that only weaker, less resolved opponents are willing to accept. Stronger, more resolved opponents respond with war.

Here, however, the source of incomplete information is different. The main question is whether a declining state faces high or low costs as it relates to halting a power shift. As previous chapters have outlined, the literature on shifting power and war is more nuanced. Fearon (1995) also establishes that power shifts allow the rising state to extract more concessions in the future. Working backward, the declining state may prefer a costly but advantageous preventive war today to an efficient but disadvantageous peace tomorrow.

Chadefaux (2011) critiques this by noting that war here is an artifact of the exogenous shift in power. When states negotiate over the balance of power in future stages, they select values to ensure that neither prefers war under today's balance to what deals may come tomorrow. This is because war is inefficient. A state captures more by moving power at an acceptable rate and exploiting its greater leverage later than by attempting a larger shift only for its opponent to strangle the power baby in its cradle.

At a very basic level, this chapter mixes incomplete-information explanations for conflict with commitment-based approaches. This is not a common research strategy but has generated fruitful results before. More specifically, the model asks what happens when the rising state does not know the maximum level of power the declining state is willing to accept in the next period. This contrasts the model I develop from Wolford, Reiter, and Carrubba's (2011), who assume that the declining state does not know the rising state's cost of war.[4] Likewise, it is different from Streich and Levy (2016), who work through the logic of when the declining state is uncertain over the probability of victory today.

Uncertainty over the declining state's cost of war creates a nice parallel. In standard incomplete-information models of war, not knowing the opponent's minimally acceptable policy demands causes states to adopt unacceptable bargaining strategies. War can result, and this is a robust finding across many modeling approaches (Powell 1999, 97–104; Slantchev 2003; Fey and Ramsay 2011). Here, the rising state appears to have a similar incentive to adopt a risky power development strategy. The question is whether this also leads to war.

The answer is not immediately obvious. In this book's framework, the rising state and declining state are not just bargaining over a policy in dispute – they are also implicitly bargaining over the costly weapons themselves. This breaks from Chadefaux 2011, in which the cost of shifting power is not a topic of discussion. Internalizing how a rising state may be tempted to build nuclear weapons, even weak declining states may wish to override that incentive with a butter-for-bombs style agreement. Thus, the central strategic tension may manifest itself at an earlier stage, when weak declining states must decide between conceding the issue and bluffing strength by trying to leverage the (actually incredible) threat of preventive war.

Existing formal work on nuclear negotiations (Debs and Monteiro 2014; Bas and Coe 2016; Bas and Coe 2017) does not address this type of environment. The focus of this literature has been to explain how rising states internalize the credible threat of preventive war and whether

---

[4] There are other differences as well. Wolford, Reiter, and Carrubba have an exogenous shift in power but bargaining-and-learning-while-fighting. I have an endogenous shift and bargaining over weapons.

declining states can actually leverage that threat given monitoring problems. Incomplete information is not a concern.[5] In contrast, the rising state doubts the credibility of the threat in this chapter's model. Thus, a key question is how the declining state's actions – namely, its proposal strategy – signal credibility. I now address that question.

8.2 MODELING THE BLUFF

For the same reasons as last chapter, this chapter focuses on a two-period version of the bargaining problem. In the first period, D offers $x \in [0, 1]$. R sees D's offer and accepts, rejects, or builds. Accepting ends the game and locks in the payoff pair $(x, 1 - x)$ for the rest of time for R and D, respectively. Rejecting leads to pre-shift war. As usual, R prevails with probability p_R and D wins with complementary probability. R still pays c_R for fighting. D, in contrast, is either a *strong* type or a *weak* type. The strong type pays costs c_D while the weak type pays c_D', where $c_D' > c_D$.

Lastly, R can build. If so, it pays a cost k. D sees R's decision and chooses whether to prevent, which leads to the same pre-shift war payoffs as before. If D advances to the post-shift stage, it offers $y \in [0, 1]$. R accepts or rejects that. Accepting locks in the payoff pair $(y, 1 - y)$ for the rest of time. Rejecting begins post-shift war. The payoffs are the same as in the pre-shift war, except R wins with probability $p_R' > p_R$ and D wins with probability $1 - p_R'$.

To incorporate uncertainty, Nature begins the interaction by selecting whether D is strong or weak. Specifically, Nature selects D as strong with probability q and weak with probability $1 - q$. The distribution is common knowledge but only D observes the realized draw. Thus, R must update its beliefs about D throughout the interaction.

Because this is a sequential game of incomplete information, perfect Bayesian equilibrium is the appropriate solution concept. As usual, I begin with the post-shift portion of the interaction:

Lemma 8.1. *Suppose the states reach the post-shift period. Then D offers concessions commensurate with R's new power (i.e., $y = p_R' - c_R$), and R accepts.*

---

[5] Jelnov, Tauman and Zeckhauser 2017 is an exception. However, their source of incomplete information is how costly the rising state finds opening itself up for inspections. As such, their source of uncertainty is on the other player and has no direct effect on the credibility of preventive war.

Essentially, the post-shift period is identical to the post-shift periods in the previous games. Why does the uncertainty not matter here? R's decision rule compares its payoff for war versus its payoff for acceptance. Neither of these depends on D's cost of war. Likewise, D's offer strategy is to give R the minimum amount necessary to induce acceptance. That amount is $p'_R - c_R$, which is also not a function of D's cost of war. As such, D offers that minimal amount, and R accepts.

Thus, uncertainty only has bite in the pre-shift phase. But even then there are some cases when the uncertainty is not important. If D always has a credible threat to intervene (because its costs are either tiny or just very small), R's uncertainty is irrelevant because it knows it should not build in either case. Likewise, if D never has a credible threat to intervene (because its costs are huge or just very large), R's uncertainty is irrelevant because it knows that it can safely build in the absence of an acceptable offer. In turn, the only interesting case is when there is some chance that the threat to prevent is credible and some chance that it is not. Thus, as Chapter 3 suggested, R's information problem must be sufficiently severe to change the theoretical predictions from the baseline model. I formalize this by placing two conditions on the parameter space:

Condition 8.1. *Let the strong type's cost of war be sufficiently small, or* $c_D < \delta p'_R - p_R - \delta c_R$.

Condition 8.2. *Let the weak type's cost of war be sufficiently great, or* $c'_D > p'_R - p_R - c_R - (1-\delta)^2 k/\delta$.

Combined, these conditions ensure that the strong and weak types have sufficiently differing preferences for preventive war. Condition 8.1's value for c_D implies that the strong type has zero tolerance for power shifts and will certainly intervene if R builds. Condition 8.2 requires that the weak type prefers allowing a power transition to preventive war whenever the offer is less than the optimal butter-for-bombs quantity $p'_R - c_R - (1-\delta)k/\delta$.[6]

Thus, with complete information, different outcomes result. R and the weak type of D would negotiate over building weapons out of the shadow of preventive war; the strong type of D would coerce R not to build by the credible threat of preventive war. Making these assumptions generates strategic tension in the interaction: R must decipher whether D is strong or weak and makes its investment plans accordingly.

---

[6] As usual, I also maintain the assumption that $k > \delta(p'_R - c_R)$ to rule out the substantively uninteresting case described in Chapter 3.

Even then, deciphering D's type is irrelevant when the cost of weapons is too high:

Proposition 8.1. *(Analogous to Proposition 3.2.) If the extent of the power shift is small compared to the cost of weapons (i.e., $p'_R - p_R < (1 - \delta)k/\delta$), both types of D pool in all PBE. They offer $x = p_R - c_R$ and R accepts.*

By now, the intuition should be well understood, and the proof follows directly from previous "too cold" scenarios. Here, the shift provides too few benefits to be worth the cost. As a result, independent of D's cost of preventive war, R will not build. In turn, both types of D propose R's minimally acceptable settlement. R accepts and the game ends.[7]

The strategic dilemma is more complex outside of the "too cold" region. Here, strong types prefer to intervene if R invests. Internalizing this, R would not want to invest if it knew D's resolve. Yet the weak type cannot leverage that same threat. Ordinarily, this would mean that the weak type would offer the necessary butter-for-bombs deal to reach an efficient resolution. But with incomplete information, the weak type might want to mimic the strong type's offer and trick R to not build because of the false possibility of preventive war. It is therefore up to R to suss out whether D is weak or strong.

As is typical for this type of bargaining game, perfect Bayesian equilibrium's liberal off-the-path beliefs admit a large number of equilibria. Some of such equilibria require strange off-the-path inferences. For example, D might need to offer great concessions to R to convince R that it is strong, as R could believe (off-the-path) that D is weak if it makes any other offers, even if those offers are stingy. To avoid these situations and maintain tractability, this section searches for equilibria in which the strong type of D offers $x = p_R - c_R$.[8] Note that this is the amount that it would offer in the game with complete information. Thus, equilibria with that quality give the weak type incentive to pretend it is strong by mimicking what the strong type would normally do.[9]

The question remains how the weak type of D acts. There are two plausible courses of action. First, it could mimic the strong type's

---

[7] There are multiple PBE here because R could hold any number of beliefs about off-the-path offers. Regardless of those beliefs, however, it is never in R's interest to build because of the low ratio of return on investment.

[8] Unlike the other equilibria described, the class I detail here survives the D1 refinement.

[9] This offer strategy has empirical plausibility. As the Operation Opera case study later illustrates, Israel stood firm in the lead up to the strike; it did not offer concessions in a bizarre effort to maintain a reputation for strength.

behavior and offer a small amount. If R buys the bluff, this pays handsomely – the weak type secures nonproliferation despite not offering any concessions to achieve that result. But if R calls the bluff, the weak type loses all of the surplus it would have kept had it bought R's compliance by offering a butter-for-bombs deal (i.e., $x = p'_R - c_R - (1 - \delta)k/\delta$).

The second option is to offer that butter-for-bombs deal straightaway. R will certainly accept that amount no matter what it believes about the probability D is strong or weak, as that amount makes developing weapons unprofitable regardless of the threat of preventive war. This guarantees the weak type's share of the surplus. But it also requires paying more than the weak type would have to if its bluff were believed.

Ultimately, the outcome depends on how easily the weak type can get away with that bluff. This in turn depends on whether R believes D is weak or strong. I start with cases when D is likely strong:

Proposition 8.2. *Suppose D is sufficiently likely to be strong (i.e., $q > 1 - (1 - \delta)k/[\delta(p'_R - p_R)]$). Then both types of D offer no additional concessions (i.e., $x = p_R - c_R$). R accepts.*

Imagine that D always offers the small amount regardless of its type. R wants to build against the weak types because it will face no repercussions but wants to not build against the strong types so as to avoid wasting the investment cost k. Thus, when R is virtually certain it is facing the strong type, gambling that D is weak is not worthwhile. Consequently, it accepts the small offer. The weak type can also deduce that R's gamble is not worthwhile, so it can confidently bluff strength and know it will get away with it. Given that this leads the weak type to receive its best payoff within its strategic constraints, the weak type has no reason to behave any differently.

This is exactly what Proposition 8.2 describes. The cut-point on q represents the lowest probability that D is weak under which the gamble is not worthwhile for R.[10] As such, as long as the probability D is strong is greater than that value, the weak type bluffs strength, and R dares not call that potential bluff.

When D is more likely to be the weak type (i.e., when q is low), bluffing in this manner no longer works. Indeed, if the weak type bluffs with certainty, R optimally calls that bluff with certainty. The resulting proliferation outcome leaves the weak type worse off than if it had offered a

---

[10] See the appendix for derivation of the cut-point.

deal in the first place. Therefore, the weak type cannot always bluff as it did when q was high.

However, the weak type cannot always concede its vulnerability by offering a butter-for-bombs deal with certainty. To see why, consider how R responds to such a strategy. The strong and weak types cleanly separate: the weak type makes the butter-for-bombs offer (i.e., $x = p_R' - c_R - (1 - \delta)k/\delta$) and the strong type does not make those additional concessions (i.e., $x = p_R - c_R$). In turn, R knows that it is facing the strong type when it receives the smaller offer. It therefore knows it should accept that small offer, as attempting to build will result in preventive war. But this brings back the weak type's incentive to bluff – it could offer the smaller amount and induce acceptance under the false premise that the small offer only comes from the strong type. As such, the weak type cannot concede its vulnerability with certainty.

To resolve the dilemma, the weak type sometimes bluffs and sometimes reveals its weakness by proposing a butter-for-bombs settlement. This results in some interesting counterplay from R. It accepts the butter-for-bombs deals with certainty. But when it receives no deal, it must sometimes call potential bluffs by attempting to proliferate so as to deter the weak type from offering the stingy amount. In response to building, the strong type exercises its credible threat to launch preventive war. The weak type, meanwhile, concedes defeat and allows the power shift to transpire.

The following proposition summarizes these strategies:

Proposition 8.3. *Suppose D is sufficiently likely to be weak (i.e., $q < 1 - (1 - \delta)k/[\delta(p_R' - p_R)]$). Then the strong type of D offers no concessions (i.e., $x = p_R - c_R$); the weak type sometimes offers no concessions and sometimes offers a butter-for-bombs deal (i.e., it mixes between offering $x = p_R - c_R$ and $x = p_R' - c_R - (1 - \delta)k/\delta$). R accepts the butter-for-bombs deal with certainty but sometimes accepts and sometimes rejects a no-concessions offer.*

Unfortunately, this bluffing behavior leads to inefficiency. With complete information, the strong type offers $x = p_R - c_R$ while the weak type offers $x = p_R' - c_R - (1 - \delta)k/\delta$. In either case, R accepts. Both outcomes are efficient because R never builds and the states never fight a war. On the other hand, in the equilibrium Proposition 8.3 describes, both war and investment occur with positive probability. The outcome is therefore inefficient in expectation.

Worse, the weak type's incentive to bluff does not produce any benefits for it. Although the weak type successfully tricks R into not building with positive probability, R also sometimes calls the bluff. In those cases, the weak type forgoes the chance to capture the surplus created by R not building. This drawback exactly counterbalances the potential benefit from the bluff. The strong type and R instead pay the price for the inefficiency, as their preventive war and building behaviors are costly but necessary to stop the weak type's exploitation.

Before moving on, a remark about the causal mechanism of war is in order. Clearly, preventive motivation underlies the interaction. Treatments of this date back to Thucydides' (1972) *History of the Peloponnesian War*. Levy (1987) summarized the motive as a "better now than later" logic; if war is inevitable, declining states prefer initiating the fight when the military balance is favorable. Fearon (1995) refined this thinking by noting that declining states and rising states have mutual incentive to broker a deal after a power shift has transpired. Thus, declining states fight because they prefer a costly war to an efficient but disadvantageous *peace* later. The mechanism at play here certainly fits this narrative – the strong type interrupts the rising state's investment because it prefers a war to stop the power shift over the deal it must reach with a nuclear opponent.

However, the causal pathway runs deeper than that. Chadefaux (2011) states do not fight wars under normal circumstances when they can bargain over power. This opened up a new research question: can preventive wars still occur with endogenous power shifts? Debs and Monteiro (2014) and the previous chapter have indicated that the answer is yes if the declining state cannot observe the rising state's armament decision, assuming that the rising state cannot credibly take on measures that make arms costlier. Whereas that mechanism is fundamentally about imperfect information, this chapter's mechanism incorporates incomplete information. The declining state cannot credibly communicate whether it finds nuclear proliferation permissable or not. In turn, the rising state sometimes gambles on a weapons program that the declining state will not actually permit.

The common theme in this new, endogenous power shift literature is that preventive wars only occur in the presence of some other bargaining problem. For the model developed here, Chapter 3 shows that complete information allows the parties to reach a settlement. Yet adopting incomplete information creates the perfect storm for conflict. The interaction of the rising state's uncertainty and its own inability to credibly commit to the terms of today's settlement means that war occurs some of the time.

8.3 ILLUSTRATING THE MECHANISM: ISRAEL, IRAQ, AND OPERATION OPERA

Studying preventive war in a nuclear context is difficult. As mentioned earlier, there are only a few known instances of military assaults intended to disrupt a nuclear facility.[11] Of these, two (Israel–Iran and Norway–Germany) came in the context of a greater conflict. This makes the quantitative analysis of nuclear prevention an onerous task, especially because strategic randomization injects noise into the data-generating process. In turn, studying the usefulness of the model requires comparing it to the historical record in relation to Israel–Iraq and Israel–Syria. However, Operation Orchard (the attack on Syria) occurred in 2007; consequently, much of the historical details remain unknown.[12] In turn, this section focuses on the 1981 Israeli attack on Iraq's Osirak reactor as an illustration of the mechanism.

In the process, this section also contributes to the understanding of Iraqi nuclear motivations. The standard explanation for Saddam Hussein's decision making (Brands and Palkki 2011) falls back to the core realist theories of nuclear proliferation. That is, Saddam believed he was in an intense security relationship with Israel and that nuclear weapons would provide coercive leverage. But this does not explain Saddam's actions. Why try building nuclear infrastructure when an opponent was just going to tear it down?

The theory from this chapter provides an explanation: uncertainty over Israel's willingness to intervene. Braut-Hegghammer (2016, 46–70) recognizes Iraq's concern that an Israeli intervention was a possibility, but there was hope that warnings of the consequences would provide sufficient deterrence. I expand on this and trace the causal mechanism from the model. To do so, demonstrating three components is necessary:

---

[11] This does not count instances of conflict motivated partially by preventive concerns. For example, Arab states may have instigated the Six-Day War to fight Israel before the latter had full access to nuclear weapons (Evron 1994; Karl 1996; Ginor and Remez 2006), though this view is controversial (Galon 2008).

[12] The timing is particularly problematic because the model relies on incomplete information to explain preventive war. As such, to adequately assess the usefulness of the model, an inside perspective on what the actors understood at the time of the conflict is necessary. Unfortunately, this type of historical record takes a long time to develop.

(1) Iraqi active development of nuclear technology was common knowledge and indeed a feature of Iraq's path to a weapon, (2) Iraq believed that Israel was not likely to intervene if it built the Osirak reactor, and (3) Israel calculated that a preventive strike was preferable to allowing Iraq to continue progressing on the reactor. The first point confirms that imperfect information was not the causal mechanism. The second verifies the role of incomplete information in the interaction. Finally, the third point follows Chapter 5's call to empirically evaluate a model's critical cut-points.[13]

Analyzing the strategic components of the attack first requires an understanding of the players and the timeline of their actions. Thus, this section begins with a historical overview of Operation Opera, aimed at gathering the facts of the attack.[14]

8.3.1 Overview of the Iraqi Nuclear Program and Operation Opera

Iraq's involvement with nuclear technology began in the mid-1950s under King Faisal II as a part of American President Dwight D. Eisenhower's "Atoms for Peace" plan. However, the July 14 Revolution of 1958 saw a military coup overthrow the monarchy. Without American support or sufficient domestic nuclear know-how, the regime turned to the Soviet Union for assistance and signed an agreement on August 17, 1959. This led to the Soviet installation of an IRT-2000 reactor, which had a limited capacity of a few megawatts and was primarily a research facility (Evron 1994, 25–26).

The Iraq–Soviet Union pact eventually soured. The Ba'ath Party rose to power in 1968. With Saddam Hussein in *de facto* control of the government, Baghdad sought a more powerful reactor. The Soviet Union, worried that this would lead to proliferation, rejected Iraqi advances (McCormack 1996, 47). Iraq turned to France, and the parties agreed to terms in 1974. France then installed an Osiris-class reactor ten miles

---

[13] A fourth relevant question is whether Israel's cost of preventive war was generally decreasing over time, creating the commitment problem Chapter 6 explored. This seems to not be the case, at least not to the extent that Condition 6.1 requires for the decrease to matter. Israel's most recent conflict was the Yom Kippur War of 1973, which was eight years prior to Operation Opera and lasted less than three weeks. Meanwhile, as the case study details below, Osirak's location was an open secret, so there were few intelligence gains to be made. In short, the problems the United States faced following World War II were not present for Israel here.

[14] See Perlmutter, Handel, and Bar-Joseph 2003 (xxix–l) for a more detailed timeline of the events from 1974 to 1981.

outside of Baghdad. The site came to be known as *Osirak*, a portmanteau of Osiris and Iraq. France began construction of the project in 1979. It came online the next year, and Iraq started receiving uranium shipments in July, 1980. Unlike the Soviet IRT-2000 reactor, Osirak had a powerful 40 megawatt capacity and could process more than 150 pounds of uranium, enough for three atomic bombs (Cordesman 1999, 605).

With that in mind, France instituted a number of safety protocols designed to ensure that Iraq could not use it to construct nuclear weapons. First, France hoped to alter the terms of its original agreement and send "caramel" fuel instead. Caramel contains lower concentrations of enriched uranium and is therefore ill-suited for nuclear weapons (Reiter 2005, 359) but still useful for nuclear research. Iraq bluntly rejected the switch. France caved, worried that Iraq would cancel its lucrative contracts and go elsewhere (Nakdimon 1987, 103).

Aware of Iraq's potentially duplicitous intentions, France only resupplied uranium to Iraq after receiving the spent uranium from the previous shipments. This meant if Iraq were to cheat on the deal, its nuclear stockpile would be limited. Moreover, cheating without detection would have proven difficult. Iraq deposited its accession to the NPT on October 29, 1969 and thus the IAEA oversaw all declared nuclear activity within Iraq.[15]

Nevertheless, the possibility that Osirak would be a stepping stone to a nuclear weapon greatly worried Iraq's enemies. By 1980, Iraq and Iran were embroiled in a bloody conflict. Just nine days into fighting, the Iranian air force executed Operation Scorch Sword, an air raid attempting to destroy the facility. The raid dealt minor structural damage and failed to raze the reactor. Iran did not attempt further action.

Meanwhile, despite the safeguards, Osirak also concerned Israel. The key players within Prime Minister Menachem Begin's cabinet agreed that a nuclear-equipped Iraq was a threat to Israel. However, the cabinet differed on their short-term solutions. Hawks urged an attack as a preventive measure. Doves believed that a strike could trigger an anti-Israeli alliance of Arab countries (Perlmutter, Handel, and Bar-Joseph 2003, xl). Moreover, the Osirak reactor was in its infancy, and thus Israel had no need to rush to a decision.

After much debate, the Israeli cabinet approved counter-proliferation measures in October, 1980. The strike occurred eight months later, on June 7, 1981. Six F-15As and eight F-16As departed from Etzion Airbase,

---

[15] Iraq officially signed the NPT on July 1, 1968, two weeks before the Ba'ath takeover.

located toward the southern tip of Israel. The fighters flew through Jordan and Saudi Arabia before heading to Osirak. Once there, the F-16s dropped their payloads and scored numerous hits on the reactor's dome, completely demolishing it. Iraqi resistance proved ineffective; anti-aircraft fire failed to damage any of the planes, and all the pilots returned to Israel safely. Eleven died on the ground – one French technician and ten Iraqi soldiers.

International condemnation was universal. The United Nations Security Council unanimously passed Resolution 487 twelve days later, without veto from the United States. The resolution noted Iraqi compliance to IAEA inspections and its right to peaceful nuclear technology, criticized Israel for not adhering to the NPT, and called for restitution to Iraq. Israel offered no such concessions but compensated for the lone French casualty. Ultimately, Israel suffered no real sanctions from the attack. On the contrary, Washington expressed gratitude by the time the Persian Gulf War broke out in 1991, as Saddam Hussein could not deter the United States with a nuclear weapon.

Indeed, Iraq's nuclear program was never the same. Iraq initially vowed to rebuild the site. However, as Proposition 3.1 illustrated, rising states cannot effectively build if their rivals have credible preventive war threats. Israel had credibly demonstrated its willingness and ability to destroy Osirak-like reactors. Consequently, the Iraqi nuclear program went underground so as to deny Israel an effective preventive war option. However, these methods were unproductive. By the fall of Saddam Hussein in 2003, Iraq still had no nuclear weapons.

Much of Iraq's nuclear woes came from the international fallout from the attack. Although UNSC Resolution 487 supported Iraq on paper, Saddam found himself without a viable technological partner. France's initial response was to rebuild the facility, but Paris withdrew shortly thereafter. Saudi Arabia offered billions in support, but that money was useless without a seller.

While this overview establishes the players and their actions, it lacks a complete understanding of the parties' motivations and their strategic dilemmas. Even though almost four decades have passed since Operation Opera, details from within the Iraqi regime remains rudimentary. Still, there is little doubt the Iraqi nuclear program saw technological advances as a prerequisite to a nuclear bomb and not as an end in itself. Claims to the contrary – that Osirak was for research – only came after Operation Opera and trace back to an Iraqi nuclear scientist (Cooley 2005, 159). Meanwhile, Washington, Tehran, and the IAEA at the time

TABLE 8.1. *Timeline of the Osirak Reactor and Operation Opera*

Jul 14, 1958	Iraqi monarchy overthrown
Aug 17, 1959	Soviet nuclear assistance to Iraq begins
Jul 17, 1968	Ba'ath party comes to power
Oct 29, 1969	Iraq deposits accession to NPT
1969	First reactors come online
Aug, 1974	Iraq turns to France for nuclear assistance
Nov 18, 1975	France agrees to build Osirak
Apr 9, 1979	Original Osirak reactors destroyed in French hanger
Jul, 1980	Uranium shipments to Iraq begin
Sep 22, 1980	Iran–Iraq War begins
Sep 30, 1980	Iran attacks Osirak, fails to destroy the reactor
Oct 28, 1980	Israeli cabinet votes in favor of attack
Jun 7, 1981	Operation Opera
Jun 19, 1981	UNSC Resolution 487 unanimously condemns Israel
Aug 2, 1990	Iraq invades Kuwait
Feb 24, 1991	Coalition forces invade Iraq

believed that Iraq sought a nuclear arsenal. Conventional wisdom today concurs. Moreover, the types of reactors Iraq sought to purchase from France are consistent with a nuclear weapon being the end game, not nuclear energy (Kirschenbaum 2010, 51; McCormack 1996, 47–49).

Unfortunately, with Saddam Hussein's execution in 2004, we may never have a complete portrait of Iraq. As a result, the following subsections offer one possible explanation for why Israel and Iraq were unable to come to terms on the eve of Operation Opera, despite the existence of mutually preferable settlements.

8.3.2 The Osirak Reactor: An Open Secret

To separate the role of incomplete information versus the previous chapter's focus on imperfect information, this section must first establish that the presence of the Osirak reactor was an open secret. This is the easiest step to verify. Iraq's nuclear program was a matter of public record, and Saddam had been open about his nuclear weapons ambitions (Braut-Hegghammer 2016, 46 and 63). In fact, Iraq publicly sought nuclear assistance, and the French parliament openly debated whether to provide assistance (Perlmutter, Handel, and Bar-Joseph 2003, 47–49). The NPT protected Iraq's right to nuclear technology at the time, and the existence of the Osirak facility was in the IAEA's records. Although the IAEA did not have complete access to the site, it still reported on Iraq's nuclear technological progress.

Moreover, Iraq believed that Israel was deeply opposed to the nuclear facility. Perlmutter, Handel, and Bar-Joseph (2003, 53–63) detail a number of covert operations aiming to derail Iraq's progression toward a bomb. France scheduled its shipment of the original reactors for April 9, 1979. But two days beforehand, there was a mysterious explosion at the hanger that destroyed both reactors. Although the French media pinned responsibility on a domestic ecological terrorist group, French intelligence believed Mossad was responsible.[16]

The next operation took place on June 13, 1980. Iraq commissioned Yahya El Meshad, an Egyptian nuclear scientist, to inspect French equipment for delivery to Osirak. French police found him in his hotel room the next day, a victim of a brutal murder. Debate over the responsible party persists. Mossad again was the initial presumption, though French intelligence believed the reckless execution suggested otherwise. The alternative theory is that Syrian agents, working on behalf of the Soviet Union, had broken into El Meshad's room to obtain documents on the progress of Osirak. These agents bribed a prostitute to keep him occupied, but El Meshad ignored her advances.[17] He then entered the room mid-operation, at which point the agent panicked and killed him.

The final operations occurred two months later, on August 7, 1980. Iraq had coopted Italy to provide chemical-separation technology vital to the enrichment process. But on that evening in August, three bombs exploded simultaneously in Italy, two at an Italian company providing the sensitive assistance and one at its general manager's apartment. Mossad was the likely culprit.

Around this time, the French–Iraqi relationship became a major news story in the Israeli media. Israel's official position was unsurprising: a nuclear Iraq posed an unacceptable threat to Israel's security, and Israel was prepared to deploy the appropriate countermeasures. Perhaps Israel did not know about Iraq's decisions earlier on, and perhaps this led Iraq to make investments it would not have otherwise. But by this point, Iraq

---

[16] Given the lax security around the hanger, some suspect French intelligence aided the assailants. According to the theory, elements within France's government did not want to give Saddam Hussein nuclear technology and saw the sabotage as a convenient half-measure that would not harm French–Iraqi relations.

[17] Police questioned the prostitute, Marie-Claude Magal, on July 1. She mysteriously died in a hit-and-run eleven days later.

understood Israel's knowledge of the program.[18] Iraq was far away from actually developing a bomb, so there was still time for Iraq to drop the project. Instead, Iraq marched on, again in plain sight. Thus, imperfect-information explanations do not have much leverage over explaining this case.

What is missing, however, is a clear indication of Israel's resolve. All Iraq had observed at this point was cheap talk to the Israeli press and low-risk, low-cost, covert, anti-proliferation operations. Whether Israel would actually intervene militarily remained in doubt. And as the next section illustrates, Iraq had good reason to be optimistic.

8.3.3 Iraqi Optimism

The next task is to show that Iraq could have plausibly believed that the construction of Osirak would not result in an Israeli strike. Indeed, despite Israel's efforts to stall Osirak's development, Iraq had many reasons to be optimistic that a full-scale military assault was impossible for practical reasons or unlikely for political reasons. In turn, Iraq's decision to push forward on the reactor appears rational.

To start, the Iranian attack a year earlier proved fruitless. Damage to the reactors was superficial, thus raising Iraq's belief that further attacks would be more nuisance than destruction. Furthermore, the assault alerted Iraq that such aerial bombardments were possible. To deter further Iranian attacks on the site, Iraq invested $1.7 billion in anti-aircraft defense in the following months (Perlmutter, Handel, and Bar-Joseph 2003, 65). Israel would need superior aim and evasion skills for a military operation to be viable.

Second, Israel faced severe tactical constraints. Unlike Iran, Israel does not share a border with Iraq. Thus, any successful attack would have required Israeli jets to travel around 2000 miles round trip and fly over Syrian, Jordanian, or Saudi airspace, increasing the likelihood that Iraq would have an early warning.[19] The distance and foreign airspace created additional problems. Israeli fighter jets could not make the round trip without refueling – but tanker aircrafts required to refuel would have had

---

[18] In terms of a noisy signal model like Debs and Monteiro 2014, Israel had received confirmation of Iraq's decision.

[19] Israel chose the Saudi route. Reports indicate that King Hussein of Jordan saw the planes fly past him shortly after takeoff (Nakdimon 1987, 21–22). Communication problems prevented him from contacting Iraq in time.

to fly over a foreign country, leaving them vulnerable to air defenses.[20] Also, if anything went wrong, Israeli pilots would have needed to set down in an unfriendly location.

Third, Israel had to worry about international backlash. After all, France assisted Iraq in constructing Osirak, and many French workers supervised the facility. Any attack on Osirak would surely strain relations. Thus, preventive war against Iraq was also at least partially a conflict against France.

Moreover, Israel had signed the Camp David Accords with Egypt only two years earlier. An attack on another Arab state risked prompting Egypt to withdraw from the Accords. Perhaps worse, the United States induced Israel to sign the Accords in exchange for a generous stream of aid (Arena and Pechenkina 2016). The United States intended its military aid to Israel to be for defensive purposes only (Muller, Castillo, and Morgen 2007, 214). Preventive war would not qualify. The United States therefore had the means and contractual forewarning to punish Israel should it disapprove of a preventive strike.

This is not to say that Saddam was certain that Osirak would go untargeted. The model predicts that in the absence of a deal a rising state cannot be sure whether it is facing a strong type willing to intervene or a weak type bluffing strength. Indeed, Saddam warned of a possible Israeli attack, perhaps even a nuclear strike (Brands and Palkki 2011, 155). Rather, the point is that Saddam had some reason to be optimistic.

As it turned out, Iraqi optimism was appreciated within the Israeli cabinet. Only a slight majority consented to what would become Operation Opera, and the opposition was vocal. For reasons I outline in the next section, Prime Minister Menachem Begin ultimately followed the majority. If bargaining broke down here as a result of information problems, we should expect precisely such a close vote within Israel – after all, close votes should be more difficult for foreign entities to anticipate than blowouts.

8.3.4 Preventive War Versus Disadvantageous Peace

The remaining question is whether Israel preferred bearing the costs of preventive war to an efficient but disadvantageous peace. A power shift – especially a nuclear power shift – would have left Israel in a vulnerable

[20] This continues to be an issue for Israel today with a potential strike on Iran (Raas and Long 2007, 23–27).

position. Israel is a small country with few large cities. Just a handful of Iraqi nuclear weapons would have the potential to functionally destroy the country (Muller, Castillo, and Morgen 2007, 213). Although the Israel could respond in kind with its own nuclear weapons, the possibility alone would have drastically shifted bargaining power to Iraq.

Moreover, the prevailing wisdom within the cabinet believed that Saddam was belligerent enough to press his luck in the shadow of mutually assured destruction. To that end, in 1978, he announced on public radio that his regime's goal was "an all-out military struggle, aimed at uprooting Zionism from the area" (Perlmutter, Handel, and Bar-Joseph 2003, 39). Although the practicality of such a declaration is questionable, this nevertheless concerned Israel. Further exacerbating the problem, Israel grew convinced that Osirak would eventually yield a bomb regardless of IAEA safeguards and French assurances (Kirschenbaum 2010, 53).

Dissenters in the cabinet argued that Israel should hold back and wait in the hope that Iraq would yield to other foreign political pressure. But it was unclear how waiting would have benefitted Israel. At best, Israel could hope that Francois Mitterrand, elected President of France on May 10, 1981, would withdraw nuclear assistance. But two weeks later, despite sympathy for Israel's plight, the Mitterrand administration announced it would honor its preexisting commitments to Iraq (Nakdimon 1987, 202–203).

Failing that, Israel understood how distant its policy positions were from Iraq. No third country was willing to provide payment. Iran, the other major rival in the region, was already at war with Iraq. The United States, traditionally the leading nonproliferation advocate, was only two years removed from the Iranian hostage crisis and sought a better relationship with Saddam Hussein. All other states lacked a large enough stake in the outcome to provide substantial bargaining leverage.

This left Israel as the only state left to initiate a butter-for-bombs deal. But Israel stood firm. And as this chapter's model demonstrates, Iraq could not directly differentiate whether this was because Israel planned a preventive strike or because Israel was bluffing. Waiting would not resolve Iraq's unfounded optimism, as the lack of a butter-for-bombs offer is consistent with both weakness and strength.

Meanwhile, the waiting game only gave Iraq more time to conduct nuclear research. Thus, Israel struck at an opportune moment. According to a former Mossad agent, an Iraqi contact had placed a beacon within Osirak a few days before the attack, which allowed IAF pilots to score two direct hits to the reactor (Westerby 1998, 25–32). Delay would have given Iraqi counterintelligence more time to uncover the plot, remove the beacon, and reduce the effectiveness of the assault. So Israel pushed forward with Operation Opera and saw a resounding success.

In doing so, Israel banked on a subdued response from its trade partners, particularly the United States. The cabinet was correct – backlash against Operation Opera proved inconsequential. Twelve days after the attack, the United Nations Security Council unanimously approved Resolution 487, which condemned the operation. But the real punishment was minimal; although the United States failed to veto Resolution 487, it promised to do so on any subsequent resolutions to sanction Israel. Washington did punish Israel on its own for using American-supplied aircraft on the mission (Muller, Castillo, and Morgen 2007, 216), but the two-month suspension on sales amounted to a slap on the wrist.

For the cost paid, Israel sent a powerful message to Iraq's nuclear patron. Paris knew Saddam planned to eventually obtain a nuclear weapon but provided atomic assistance anyway to secure access to Iraq's vast oil reserves. Primier Jacques Chirac successfully quelled opposition from within his own administration at the start of the project (Perlmutter, Handel, and Bar-Joseph 2003, 51). Israel's bold attack bolstered the critics' position. France subsequently withdrew its assistance following Opera.

Militarily, Iraq produced no response. This was foreseeable, as the Iran–Iraq War was ongoing at the time; Iraq could ill afford to initiate a two-front fight. Thus, in pure military costs, Operation Opera only consumed jet fuel and the bombs the planes dropped on the reactor. And as the model shows, intervention is likely when the declining state's true cost of war is low.

Not to be stopped, Iraq multiplied its nuclear technology budget – with Saddam immediately investing $1 billion into new techniques (Albright and Kelley 1995, 56) – and went underground. This is consistent with the information-based mechanism described here. Iraq initially choose a cheaper method to acquire nuclear know-how under the assumption that Israel would be unlikely to attack. After Operation Opera, Iraq updated its beliefs about Israeli willingness to intervene and strategically altered its path to proliferation.

But the further investment proved futile. Throwing money at the problem could not provide a solution given that indigenous nuclear know-how was insufficient to produce a bomb (Kreps and Fuhrmann 2011,

171–172; Hymans 2012, 84–93). This forced Iraq to look for partners. But Israel believed Operation Opera was worthwhile in part to signal other countries to stay away (Perlmutter, Handel, and Bar-Joseph 2003, 79). The effort succeeded – after France pulled out, no other nuclear provider stepped in. Iraq instead had to rely on the A.Q. Khan nuclear black market, and much of the extra spending went toward hiding the program from the eyes of the nonproliferation regime. A decade later, at the start of the Persian Gulf War, Iraq still lacked a bomb despite no further direct intervention on its nuclear program.

Note that the causal logic at work here is not whether Operation Opera was a long-term success. Decades later, this remains a point of debate. Reiter (2005), for example, argues the strike only pushed the Iraqi program underground and contributed to the Iraq War in 2003.[21] While this debate is important for policy prescription, the task here was to show that Israel believed that preventive war was better than the alternatives for the purpose of explaining the causal mechanism. To that end, tracing the Israeli cabinet's decision-making process is sufficient.

Nevertheless, this may be an interesting path for future research. For the reasons described in the previous chapter, going underground makes building the cost of weapons greater. Under those circumstances, Israel may not have known whether or what to bomb. The possibility of secret arms production combines elements of the previous chapter with the current chapter and could reveal new dilemmas that potential proliferators face.

8.4 CONCLUSION

This chapter showed how incomplete information can interfere with butter-for-bombs bargaining. If the rising state is unsure whether the declining state is weak or strong, weak declining states have incentive to mimic the strong type's behavior to convince the rising state not to proliferate. However, this causes the rising state to sometimes call the declining state's bluff and invest in nuclear weapons. When the declining state is truly strong, it launches preventive war; when it is weak, it permits the rising state to proliferate unimpeded. The result is inefficient because of the unnecessary proliferation and unnecessary war.

---

[21] Part of the reason Iraq chose an overt route initially was due to a lack of covert options. At the time, Iraq's technological capacity was low. It therefore had to seek nuclear cooperation agreements, making it harder to hide the paper trial.

The model contributes to our understanding of how incomplete information promotes or inhibits proliferation behaviors. Referring back to the conventional wisdom from Chapter 1, rising states acquire nuclear weapons if declining states will not prevent and the gains from bargaining outweigh the investment cost. Incomplete information would then seem to *decrease* the likelihood of proliferation; rising states might opt not to proliferate if they are unsure whether a declining state will intervene. However, because butter-for-bombs agreements work, incomplete information permits proliferation by sabotaging the bargaining process.

Substantively, the model and case study of Operation Opera provide insight on the preventive strike on Syria and Israel's recent gambit with Iran. Although reliable diplomatic histories for Operation Orchard are not yet available, the same mechanism gives one plausible explanation – Syria underestimated Israel's tactical advantage, leading to the construction (and ultimately destruction) of the facility. The model also suggests that Israel's red line with Iran was inherently unbelievable. In sum, communicating the threat of preventive war is not straightforward.

Israel's succession of attacks highlights an incentive that this chapter has only partially explored. When facing a string of potential proliferators, declining states have an incentive to develop a reputation for intervention. For example, Israel's actions in Iraq and Syria may lead other Arab states to believe that attempting to build a nuclear weapon will induce a similar preventive strike. But this in turn justifies Israel's initial decision to intervene regardless of whether an attack is the most cost-effective nonproliferation strategy for any single case. In effect, nonproliferators face a chain-store paradox (Kreps and Wilson 1982).

Investigating such reputational effects may prove fruitful for future research. Whereas this book's models have only included bilateral negotiations, Coe and Vaynman (2015) view the nonproliferation regime as a cartel, with powerful states capable of paying costs to stop client states from developing nuclear weapons. In contrast, this chapter's framework only has two actors but allows for endogenous concessions and uncertainty about the declining state's willingness to pay costs to intervene in a program's progress. Marrying these assumptions may produce interesting new results.

Finally, this chapter utilizes a research design that may prove fruitful for future work on war. From the beginning, Fearon (1995) noted that the many mechanisms for costly conflict may not operate in isolation. More recent research has taken this seriously by integrating shifting power with uncertainty over the declining state's cost of war (this chapter), rising state's cost of war (Wolford, Reiter, and Carrubba 2011), the probability of victory (Streich and Levy 2016), or the decision to shift in general (Debs and Monteiro 2014). These models are more difficult to solve than those with a single bargaining problem due to the extra moving parts, but the interesting results they provide are worth the price.

8.5 APPENDIX

This appendix covers the formal claims from the chapter.

8.5.1 Proof of Lemma 8.1

Let ψ be R's posterior that D is the strong type. Consider how R responds to an offer y. With probability ψ, D is strong, and R earns $p'_R - c_R$ for the rest of time for rejecting. With complementary probability, D is weak, and R earns $p'_R - c_R$. These are the same payoffs, so R simply earns $p'_R - c_R$ if it rejects. Accepting generates y regardless of D's type. Thus, R accepts if $y \geq p'_R - c_R$ and rejects if $y < p'_R - c_R$.

Note that D's payoff if R accepts is identical regardless of its cost of war. As such, D's optimal acceptable offer equals $p'_R - c_R$. The strong type prefers making this offer to inducing rejection if $1 - p'_R + c_R > 1 - p'_R - c_D$, which holds. Likewise, the weak type prefers making this offer to inducing rejection if $1 - p'_R + c_R > 1 - p'_R - c'_D$, which also holds. Consequently, both types of D offer $y = p'_R - c_R$ and R accepts. $\qquad\square$

8.5.2 Derivation of the Cut-Point in Proposition 8.2

To see how to derive the critical value of q, note that R earns $p_R - c_R$ for accepting that offer size. In contrast, if both types of D pool on $p_R - c_R$ and R builds, R earns $p_R - c_R$ with probability q and $(1 - \delta)(p_R - c_R) + \delta(p'_R - c_R)$ with probability $1 - q$; either way, it pays the investment cost $(1 - \delta)k$. Under these conditions, R would want to accept if:

$$p_R - c_R > q(p_R - c_R) + (1 - q)[(1 - \delta)(p_R - c_R) + \delta(p'_R - c_R)] - (1 - \delta)k$$

$$q > 1 - \frac{(1 - \delta)k}{\delta(p'_R - p_R)}.$$

This is the critical point seen in the proposition.

Given this, the weak type cannot profitably deviate. Offering any less than $p_R - c_R$ reveals that D is weak. R then builds, which leads to a payoff less than $1 - p_R + c_R$ for the weak type. The same is true if the weak type offers $x \in (p_R - c_R, p'_R - c_R - (1 - \delta)k/\delta)$. R accepts if $x \geq p'_R - c_R - (1 - \delta)k/\delta$, but the weak type could induce acceptance at a lower price by pooling on the offer $p_R - c_R$.[22]   □

8.5.3 Proof of Proposition 8.3

For showing uniqueness of equilibrium strategies given the off-the-path assumptions, the following lemma will prove invaluable:

Lemma 8.2. *No PBE exist in which D offers* $x > p'_R - c_R - k(1 - \delta)/\delta$.

Proof: The proof follows similarly to a portion of the proof for Proposition 3.3. For $x' > p'_R - c_R - k(1 - \delta)/\delta$, both types of D can profitably deviate to the midpoint between x' and $p'_R - c_R - k(1 - \delta)/\delta$.

Consider R's best response to x'. If R accepts, it earns x', which is greater than its pre-shift war payoff $p_R - c_R$. (Proposition 8.1 covered the "too cold" situation where this is not the case.) If R builds, then D does not prevent in R's best case scenario. R earns $(1 - \delta)x' + \delta(p'_R - c_R) - (1 - \delta)k$ for this outcome. This is worse than accepting outright if:

$$x' > (1 - \delta)x' + \delta(p'_R - c_R) - (1 - \delta)k$$

$$x' > p'_R - c_R - \frac{k(1 - \delta)}{\delta}.$$

So R accepts any such x'.

Now consider D's payoff for offering any such x'. R accepts and D earns the remainder, or $1 - x'$. But D could profitably deviate to offering

$$x = \frac{x' + p'_R - c_R - \frac{(1-\delta)k}{\delta}}{2}.$$

---

[22] Although these are the unique equilibrium outcomes for the assumptions above, it is worth noting that PBE supports more strategies. Indeed, the strong and weak types can pool on *any* demand size on the interval $[p_R - c_R, p_R + c_D]$ as part of a perfect Bayesian equilibrium. However, the PBE on the interval $[p_R - c_R, p_R + c_D]$ require that R believes D is likely to be weak if it offered a smaller amount at least as great as $p_R - c_R$ off the equilibrium path of play. In essence, R must take a surprisingly aggressive offer as a sign of weakness, not strength. (It also allows for wildly different payoffs for D for slight changes to the informational structure of the game. More specifically, recall that with complete information and D strong, D earns $1 - p_R + c_R$. But if we introduce incomplete information and allow D to be weak with some arbitrarily small probability ϵ, D's payoff could drop as low as $1 - p_R - c_D$ in a PBE.) The above assumption on off-the-path beliefs prevents R from making these types of inferences, and Proposition 8.2 describes all PBE that survive it.

This amount is still strictly greater than $p'_R - c_R - k(1-\delta)/\delta$, so R accepts. But because

$$\frac{x' + p'_R - c_R - \frac{(1-\delta)k}{\delta}}{2} < x',$$

D keeps strictly more for itself. Thus, offering x' cannot be a part of any PBE. □

Now for the full proof for Proposition 8.3. To begin, consider the full equilibrium strategies and beliefs:

- **Strategies**

  - Strong type of D offers $x = p_R - c_R$
  - Weak type of D offers $x = p_R - c_R$ with probability

  $$\frac{q}{\left(1 - \frac{(1-\delta)k}{\delta(p'_R - p_R)}\right)(1-q)} - \frac{q}{1-q}$$

  and offers $x = p'_R - c_R - (1-\delta)k/\delta$ with probability

  $$1 - \frac{q}{\left(1 - \frac{(1-\delta)k}{\delta(p'_R - p_R)}\right)(1-q)} + \frac{q}{1-q}$$

  - Depending on off-the-path beliefs, R rejects or builds given $x \in [0, p_R - c_R)$
  - R accepts given $x = p_R - c_R$ with probability

  $$\frac{(1-\delta)(p_R - p'_R - \frac{k}{\delta})}{\delta(p'_R - p_R)}$$

  and builds with probability

  $$1 - \frac{(1-\delta)(p_R - p'_R - \frac{k}{\delta})}{\delta(p'_R - p_R)}$$

  - R builds given $x \in \left(p_R - c_R, p'_R - c_R - (1-\delta)k/\delta\right)$
  - R accepts given $x \in \left[p'_R - c_R - (1-\delta)k/\delta, 1\right]$
  - Strong type of D prevents if R builds if $c_D < x_t(1-\delta) + p_R - \delta p'_R + \delta c_R$ and advances otherwise
  - Weak type of D prevents if R builds if $c'_D < x_t(1-\delta) + p_R - \delta p'_R + \delta c_R$ and advances otherwise

- **Beliefs**

  - Given $x \in [0, p_R - c_R)$, R is free to have any belief (off the equilibrium path)

- Given $x = p_R - c_R$, R believes D is strong with probability $1 - (1 - \delta)k/[\delta(p'_R - p_R)]$ and is weak with probability $(1 - \delta)k/[\delta(p'_R - p_R)]$ (via Bayes' rule)
- Given $x \in (p_R - c_R, p'_R - c_R - (1 - \delta)k/\delta]$, R believes D is weak with probability 1
- Given $x \in (p'_R - c_R - (1 - \delta)k/\delta, 1]$, R is free to have any belief (off the equilibrium path)
- In the second period, R believes D is weak with probability 1

Bayes' rule trivially validates the on-the-equilibrium-path beliefs, so this appendix focuses on proving the rationality of the strategies given the equilibrium beliefs.

First, note that R and the weak type of D mix. Thus, they must be indifferent between their pure strategies at each of these information sets. Let σ_A be R's probability of accepting given that D offers $x = p_R - c_R$. The following derives the weak type's indifference condition:

$$1 - p'_R + c_R + \frac{(1-\delta)k}{\delta} = \sigma_A(1 - p_R + c_R) + (1 - \sigma_A)[(1 - \delta)(1 - p_R + c_R)$$
$$+ \delta(1 - p'_R + c_R)]$$

$$\sigma_A = \frac{(1 - \delta)(p_R - p'_R + \frac{k}{\delta})}{\delta(p'_R - p_R)}$$

This is R's equilibrium mixed strategy. Note that the dominator is strictly positive. For σ_A to be valid, it must also be that $p_R - p'_R + \frac{k}{\delta} > 0$ so that the numerator is as well. This implies $k > \delta(p'_R - p_R)$, which the assumptions verify.[23]

Likewise, R must be indifferent between accepting and building. Let s be the probability D prevents in response to R building. The following derives R's indifference condition:

$$p_R - c_R = s(p_R - c_R) + (1 - s)[(1 - \delta)(p_R - c_R) + \delta(p'_R - c_R)] - (1 - \delta)k$$

$$s = 1 - \frac{(1 - \delta)k}{\delta(p'_R - p_R)}.$$

Note s is not D's strategy but rather a posterior belief that D will prevent. Let σ_B be the probability the weak type bluffs by offering $x = p_R - c_R$. Because the strong type always offers $p_R - c_R$ and is the only type

---

[23] As Proposition 3.3 showed, k must be greater than this to ensure that D prefers making butter-for-bombs offers to taking the entire good up-front.

to prevent if R builds in response, Bayes' rule gives the value of σ_B which makes R indifferent between accepting and building:

$$s = \frac{q}{q + (1-q)\sigma_B}.$$

From before, $s = 1 - (1-\delta)k/[\delta(p'_R - p_R)]$. Thus, the following substitution gives the solution for σ_B:

$$1 - \frac{(1-\delta)k}{\delta(p'_R - p_R)} = \frac{q}{q + (1-q)\sigma_B}$$

$$\sigma_B = \frac{q}{\left(1 - \frac{(1-\delta)k}{\delta(p'_R - p_R)}\right)(1-q)} - \frac{q}{1-q}.$$

This is D's equilibrium mixed strategy.

Now check for profitable deviations. To begin, consider R's response to receiving $x = p'_R - c_R - (1-\delta)k/\delta$. R believes D is weak with probability 1. If R builds, it earns $(1-\delta)\left(p'_R - c_R - (1-\delta)k/\delta\right) + \delta(p'_R - c_R) - (1-\delta)k = p'_R - c_R - (1-\delta)k/\delta$, which is not a profitable deviation. For rejecting to be optimal, it must be that $p'_R - p_R < (1-\delta)k/\delta$, which Proposition 8.1 prohibits. Thus, accepting is optimal.

Next, suppose R receives $x = p_R - c_R$ instead. The indifference condition ensures R earns the same amount for accepting as it earns for building. Note that R also earns $p_R - c_R$ for rejecting as well, so rejecting is not a profitable deviation. In turn, R's equilibrium strategy here is optimal.

Now consider D's strategies. The optimality of the strong and weak types' decision to prevent or advance follows directly from Proposition 3.1. Thus, I check whether either type of D can profitably deviate by changing its offer.

First, consider the weak type of D. In equilibrium, its payoff equals $1 - p'_R + c_R + (1-\delta)k/\delta$.[24] If the weak type offers $x \in [0, p_R - c_R)$, equilibria exist in the subgame for all of R's possible beliefs. Regardless of the specific belief, accepting cannot be optimal for R; R could reject and earn $p_R - c_R$ instead. If rejecting is the best response to the belief, the weak type earns its pre-shift war payoff, which is worse than the butter-for-bombs offer. If building is the best response, then the proof for Proposition 3.3 shows that D is again better off with the butter-for-bombs offer because $k > \delta(p'_R - c_R)$. So deviating to $x \in [0, p_R - c_R)$ is not profitable.

---

[24] This is because it is indifferent between offering $x = p_R - c_R$ and $p'_R - c_R - (1-\delta)k/\delta$. In the latter case, R accepts, thereby granting the weak type a payoff of $1 - p'_R + c_R + (1-\delta)k/\delta$, the equilibrium amount.

Next, consider deviations to $x \in (p_R - c_R, p'_R - c_R - (1 - \delta)k/\delta)$. According to equilibrium beliefs, R believes that D is weak with probability 1. Because R must receive at least $p'_R - c_R - (1 - \delta)k/\delta$ to not find investment profitable and the weak type does not prevent for $x < p'_R - c_R - (1 - \delta)k/\delta$, it builds. D does not prevent because $k > \delta(p'_R - p_R + c'_D + c_R)/(1-\delta)^2$. So D earns $(1-\delta)(1-x)+\delta(1-p'_R+c_R)$. This is not a profitable deviation if:

$$1 - p'_R + c_R + \frac{(1-\delta)k}{\delta} > (1-\delta)(1-x) + \delta(1 - p'_R + c_R).$$

Because $1 - \delta + \delta(1 - p'_R + c_R) > (1-\delta)(1-x) + \delta(1 - p'_R + c_R)$, we may instead prove this by showing:

$$1 - p'_R + c_R + \frac{(1-\delta)k}{\delta} > 1 - \delta + \delta(1 - p'_R + c_R)$$

$$k > \delta(p'_R - c_R).$$

As before, this holds.

Lastly, the weak type could deviate to $x > p'_R - c_R - (1 - \delta)k/\delta$. However, this is clearly not optimal – R accepts $x \geq p'_R - c_R - (1 - \delta)k/\delta$, so giving any more is an unnecessary concession. Therefore, the weak type has no profitable deviations.

Now consider deviations for the strong type. In equilibrium, the strong type receives a convex combination of $1 - p_R - c_D$ and some amount greater than that. Thus, the strong type earns some amount strictly greater than its war payoff.

First, suppose the strong type offers $x \in [0, p_R - c_R)$. Equilibria exist for all of R's possible beliefs. Accepting remains suboptimal for R because it could reject and earn $p_R - c_R$ instead. So R either builds or rejects. If R builds based on its belief, then Condition 8.1 ensures that the strong type will prevent in response. Thus, regardless of R's decision, D earns its war payoff. But this is strictly worse for the strong type than earning a convex combination of its war payoff and some strictly greater amount. Therefore, the strong type cannot profitably deviate to offering $x \in [0, p_R - c_R)$.

Second, suppose the strong type offers $x \in (p_R - c_R, p'_R - c_R - (1 - \delta)k/\delta)$. Then R believes D is weak with probability 1 and therefore builds. The strong type then prevents and earns its war payoff. But again, this is strictly worse than offering $p_R - c_R$ and earning a convex combination of its war payoff and some strictly greater amount.

Consequently, the strong type cannot profitably deviate to offering $x \in (p_R - c_R, p'_R - c_R - (1 - \delta)k/\delta]$.

Finally, suppose the strong type offers $x \in [p'_R - c_R - (1 - \delta)k/\delta, 1]$. R believes D is weak with probability 1 if $x = p'_R - c_R - (1 - \delta)k/\delta$ and is otherwise free to have any belief but accepts regardless. However, the strong type earns strictly less than its war payoff and therefore fares worse than had it offered $x = p_R - c_R$. As such, the strong type has no profitable deviations. $\square$

9

Lessons Learned

Recall that John F. Kennedy once feared a world with up to twenty nuclear powers. Given the attractiveness of nuclear weapons, this was understandable. Yet with fifty additional years of retrospect, it appears that the proliferation paranoia was overstated. Although the world is full of nuclear-competent countries, only a handful have built a nuclear deterrent. Why?

This book reveals a clear answer: proactive negotiations convince potential rising states to forgo nuclear-weapons programs. Even if technologically feasible, such weapons are still costly. Declining states can therefore shift the distribution of benefits to accommodate those potential rising states. Doing so alters the opportunity cost of proliferation. Whereas proliferation seems highly desirable when the status quo is disadvantageous, the net benefit of proliferation diminishes as rising states grow more satisfied. As a result, declining states can reach credible nonproliferation settlements with their rivals.

Bargaining is not always easy. Existence of mutually acceptable agreements does not imply that states will actually reach those agreements. Indeed, later chapters showed how credible commitment problems and information problems can lead to bargaining failure. As a result, despite the mutual gains that come from reaching an agreement, the so-called "butter-for-bombs" deals may fail. But this is the exception to the rule.

Uncovering the incentives behind nonproliferation revealed a number of implications for both researchers and policymakers. I conclude by summarizing the more important findings.

PROLIFERATION IS A BARGAINING PROBLEM. At present, the rational choice paradigm has a strange disconnect between its models of war and its models of weapons construction. Since the publication of "Rationalist Explanations for War," we have recognized that bargaining is a critical determinant of war and peace. Thus, if we are to explain war, we must also explain why bargaining proves ineffective.

Yet our existing models of costly weapons investment tend to focus on how declining states leverage a credible threat of preventive war to stop potential proliferators. Positive inducements take a back seat. Presumably, this is due to an implicit assumption that anarchy makes such deals unreliable to the point of irrelevance. However, the baseline model presented in Chapter 3 rejects this notion – deals are possible and credible even with obstacles like imperfect information.

Going forward, any explanation for nuclear proliferation should explicitly state why actors choose the inefficient means of resolving their conflict when more efficient agreements are available. Put simply, proliferation is a bargaining problem.

IN THE MODEL, RISING STATES ARE ALWAYS WILLING TO ACCEPT NONPRO-LIFERATION SETTLEMENTS.   The key is generosity in bargaining. Proliferation can only grant a rising state so many concessions. Consequently, if declining states offer most of those concessions prior to proliferation, the relative return on investment diminishes. Give enough concessions, and it is simply no longer profitable to proliferate. As a result, rising states can always credibly commit to nonproliferation settlements. Apparent commitment problems in this regard hold no bite.

From a policy perspective, this means that the United States should actively seek to engage potential proliferators before the first nuclear flash. By and large, the United States and the nonproliferation regime as a whole have succeeded with proactive negotiations. Yet, in tough cases, skeptics worry that rising states will break agreements and proliferate anyway. Thus, the skeptics recommend a heavy-handed approach. But this leads to a self-fulfilling prophecy. Cutting the rising state's share of the status quo *increases* the relative return on investment and therefore incentivizes proliferation.

DECLINING STATES CANNOT ALWAYS COMMIT TO THOSE SETTLEMENTS OR MAY NOT WANT TO OFFER THEM.   Rising states are only willing to accept nonproliferation agreements because the deal is sufficiently good and they expect to continue receiving those concessions in the future. Both of these conditions can cause problems for the declining state. First, declining states may intentionally short-change rising states to bluff the threat of preventive war. Second, they might cut off concessions when preventive war becomes a credible alternative mechanism to shut off proliferation – whether due to fading war exhaustion or leadership turnover. Alternatively, if the ability to build nuclear weapons and then use them is not sustainable – whether due to an unreliable supplier or civil uprisings – a similar commitment problem appears. As a result, bargaining can rationally fail. Countries like the United States therefore need to consider their own strategic shortcomings and not immediately pin bargaining breakdown on the proliferators.

THE NON-PROLIFERATION TREATY IS NOT ONE-SIDED. At first, the Non-Proliferation Treaty appears to stack the deck against potential rising states, as it established the nonproliferation regime, erected barriers to nuclear development, and paved the way for a nuclear taboo. These factors increase proliferation's burden on those rising states, potentially hurting their bargaining power derived from the nuclear outside option.

Nevertheless, those additional burdens lead to *mutual* gain. When the costs of proliferation are too low, declining states prefer abandoning bargaining for short-term gains at the expense of long-term goals. But this benefits no one, as it introduces wasted investment costs in proliferation. Thus, increasing the rising state's burden brings the parties to the bargaining table. Rising states win by receiving the concessions they want without having to go nuclear.

From a research design standpoint, this book's modeling process provides a useful framework for analyzing institutional design. The baseline model investigated what happens when countries interact with one another. In a couple of different cases, one set of parameters led to an outcome worse for both parties than another set of parameters. Under such circumstances, there is mutual gain for creating institutions that can manipulate the incentive structure slightly – in this case, by increasing the cost of nuclear weapons.

THE NON-PROLIFERATION TREATY REFLECTS SATISFACTION WITH BARGAINED OUTCOMES. Indeed, the previous point does not imply that the Non-Proliferation Treaty *causes* nonproliferation behaviors in isolation. Rather, it reflects satisfaction with the bargained outcomes facilitated through the Non-Proliferation Treaty and through bilateral bargaining. Cutting these concessions can therefore lead to a state's withdrawal from the treaty. If the nonproliferation regime wants to see continued compliance, it cannot rest on its laurels.

POTENTIAL POWER COERCES CONCESSIONS. States do not fully need to make outside options available to have an effect on negotiations (Voeten 2001). In the absence of sufficiently attractive offers, rising states will take costly actions to sway bargaining power in their favor. Working backward, declining states are sure to pacify rising states, extracting the inefficient cost of investment in the process. Consequently, potential power acts as an "invisible fist" in international relations. A status quo is not stable because it reflects the balance of power (Powell 1996; Reed et al. 2008) but rather because it reflects the balance of power and the balance of power in what a future world would look like without an agreement.

WEAPONS INSPECTIONS BENEFIT ALL PARTIES. Initially, inspections appear to help declining states control rising states' proliferation ambitions. Yet modeling the bargaining process yields a more nuanced result. Inspections need not be about information gathering exclusively. Instead, shutting down the most efficient avenues of proliferation is sufficient to induce rising and declining states to sit down at the bargaining table. Once there, butter-for-bombs agreements convince rising states not to proliferate. Despite the lack of effective monitoring, declining states can rest assured that nonproliferation will hold as rising states no longer find the cost of bombs worthwhile.

Again, this process is risky. Inspections may not be successful, especially when not coupled with sufficiently attractive offers. They may also not reveal all information. But inspections certainly matter in some instances, resulting in less proliferation behavior and fewer preventive wars. The efficiency preserved in these cases is worth the cost of occasional failure.

Modeling the second-order effects of weapons inspections raises a more general point. International relations scholars have come to recognize information provision as important for reducing inefficient conflict. However, the causal logic often just compares Fearon's (1995) complete-information game to his incomplete-information game. Information is trickier than that; when fully modeled, adding information can lead to *more* conflict both when information acquisition is exogenous (Fey 2014; Bils and Spaniel 2018) and endogenous (Arena and Wolford 2012).

The point is two-fold. First, my argument about weapons inspections should not mean that information provision is always helpful. And second, information-gathering may not always have the obvious effect. Including features of institutions as a part of a broader model of interstate behavior is a useful way to sort through the mechanisms.

THEORIES OF PREVENTIVE WAR SHOULD ACCOUNT FOR ENDOGENOUS ARMS CONSTRUCTION. In thinking about extensions to the model, one critical component is the rising state's endogenous choice to build weapons. Exogenous power shifts rule out bargaining over proliferation by assumption, which means the researcher cannot answer questions about why rising states develop nuclear weapons.

But beyond that, the endogenous choice reinforces an earlier point from Chadefaux (2011) and Debs and Monteiro (2014). When the declining state has a credible threat to intervene, the rising state internalizes the disutility of preventive war and chooses not to proliferate – at least under complete and perfect information. If the source of a power shift is truly in the hands of the players, then excluding that move from the analysis essentially forces preventive war to occur *by assumption* of the model's game form.

This is not to say that *all* models of shifting power should have endogenous armaments. But if they do, the researcher must be careful in his or her interpretation of the results. Such an assumption only has empirical leverage over cases that are truly exogenous, perhaps shifting demographics as an example. The results definitely do not apply to arms programs like nuclear weapons, which require active investment and management.

THE MAIN THEORY IS NOT UNIQUE TO PROLIFERATION. Although the focus of this book is on nuclear weapons, the formal model applies to other topics as well. Indeed, the model describes any interaction in the shadow of coercive bargaining, preventive war, and costly arms construction. Nuclear weapons have received a great deal of scholarly attention and media coverage largely due to their destructive power. Consequently, focusing on nuclear weapons served as a useful starting point and illustration for bargaining over weapons.

However, this is only a first step. Certainly, the main model applies to other weapons systems. For example, the United States has long desired a missile-defense grid in Eastern Europe, ostensibly to shoot down Iranian bombs. Russia has continuously protested the system. The sides reached a tentative truce in 2009; Washington suspended the program, and Russia allowed NATO access to Russian shipping lanes to supply the war effort in Afghanistan. As in the butter-for-bombs model and the theme of this book, accommodation led to this concessions, not realized power. Similar agreements likely exist elsewhere.

The model could also have applications outside of a costly weapons framework. For instance, empire and tribute follow a similar story to the one presented here. Parent countries extract great rents out of their subject states despite having a minimal military presence. Why don't revolutionaries resist the local governors? Recasting the declining state as the subject state and the rising state as the parent state provides an explanation. To rule the subject state directly, the parent state would have to pay for a costly mobilization. Subject states, realizing this, buy off their parents. However, the subject states can extract some of the surplus created by not inducing the parent state to mobilize.

Future research ought to consider the implications of butter-for-bombs agreements in these non-nuclear bargaining situations.

THE BASELINE MODEL IS ADAPTABLE. Put differently, the basics of butter-for-bombs bargaining are theoretically powerful but relatively simple to express formally. Not all interesting strategic interactions are parsimonious, however. Fortunately, my structure is simple enough that a modeler could add those additional kinks while still keeping the model tractable. This was the common theme in Chapters 6, 7, and 8.

Yet these were only three extensions. In fact, this book's extensions focused mainly on how bargaining interplays with the threat of preventive war. Chapter 6 featured a changing value of preventive war; Chapter 7 introduced an information problem that complicated the declining state's threat to intervene; Chapter 8 allowed the rising state to be uncertain about the credibility of the declining state's threat to intervene. Bargaining over weapons programs is undoubtedly more complicated than what this book has covered. Additional research could consider other obstacles to reaching nonproliferation settlements.

One obvious route would be to manipulate the declining state's information about the value of nuclear weapons to the rising state. Indeed, I have assumed throughout that the declining state knows how costly building a nuclear weapon will be for the rising state and how quickly the project will finish. Both assumptions may not always hold. The conflict literature stresses that a state's resolve is often private information (Fearon 1995), which in turn affects how much a rising state is willing to spend. Meanwhile, intelligence estimates about nuclear timetables are notoriously inaccurate (Montgomery and Mount 2014). Building these sources of uncertainty into a model of nuclear negotiations may prove fruitful.

Despite the cause for optimism, the road ahead for the nonproliferation regime may not be easy. Technological proficiency has expanded rapidly in the nuclear era. More countries will cross the minimal capacity thresholds over the next few decades. As Figure 1.1's yawning gap illustrated, these countries are not destined to become nuclear-weapons states. However, it may take a concerted effort from the nonproliferation regime to maintain the nuclear status quo.

References

Adelman, Kenneth L. 1990. "Why Verification Is More Difficult (and Less Important)." *International Security* 14 (4): 141–146.

Akiyama, Nobumasa. 2003. "The Socio-Political Roots of Japan's Non-Nuclear Posture." In *Japan's Nuclear Option: Security, Politics, and Policy in the 21st Century* Eds. Benjamin L. Self and Jeffrey W. Thompson. Washington: Henry L. Stimson Center.

Albright, David. 1994. "South Africa and the Affordable Bomb." *Bulletin of the Atomic Scientists* 50 (4): 37–47.

Albright, David and Robert Kelley. 1995. "Massive Programs, Meager Results." *Bulletin of Atomic Scientists* 51 (6): 56–64.

Allison, Graham. 2012. "The Cuban Missile Crisis at 50: Lessons for US Foreign Policy Today." *Foreign Affairs* 91 (4): 11–16.

Arena, Philip and Daehee Bak. 2015. "Diversionary Incentives, Rally Effects, and Crisis Bargaining." *Foreign Policy Analysis* 11 (2): 233–250.

Arena, Philip and Brian Hardt. 2014. "Incentives to Rebel, Bargaining, and Civil War." *International Interactions* 40 (1): 127–141.

Arena, Philip and Anna O. Pechenkina. 2016. "External Subsidies and Lasting Peace." *Journal of Conflict Resolution* 60 (7): 1278–1311.

Arena, Philip and Scott Wolford. 2012. "Arms, Intelligence and War." *International Studies Quarterly* 56 (2): 351–365.

Aronson, Shlomo. 1978. *Conflict and Bargaining in the Middle East: An Israeli Perspective.* Baltimore: Johns Hopkins University Press.

Axelrod, Robert. 1984. *The Evolution of Cooperation.* New York: Basic Books.

Bahgat, Gawdat. 2007. "The Proliferation of Weapons of Mass Destruction: Egypt." *Arab Studies Quarterly* 29 (2): 1–15.

Bailey, Michael A., Anton Strezhnev, and Erik Voeten. 2017. "Estimating Dynamic State Preferences from United Nations Voting Data." *Journal of Conflict Resolution* 61 (2): 430–456.

Baliga, Sandeep and Tomas Sjöström. 2008. "Strategic Ambiguity and Arms Proliferation." *Journal of Political Economy* 116 (6): 1023–1057.

Bar-Joseph, Uri. 1982. "The Hidden Debate: The Formation of Nuclear Doctrines in the Middle East." *Journal of Strategic Studies* 5 (2): 205–227.

Barnett, Michael N. 1992. *Confronting the Costs of War: Military Power, State and Society in Egypt and Israel*. Princeton: Princeton University Press.

Bas, Muhammet A. and Andrew J. Coe. 2012. "Arms Diffusion and War." *Journal of Conflict Resolution* 56 (4): 651–674.

2016. "A Dynamic Theory of Nuclear Proliferation and Preventive War." *International Organization* 70 (4): 655–685.

2017. "Give Peace a (Second) Chance: A Theory of Nonproliferation Deals." *International Studies Quarterly* 62 (3): 606–617.

Beal, Tim. 2005. *North Korea: The Struggle Against American Power*. Ann Arbor: Pluto Press.

Beardsley, Kyle and Victor Asal. 2009. "Winning with the Bomb." *Journal of Conflict Resolution* 53 (2): 235–255.

2013. "Nuclear Weapons Programs and the Security Dilemma." In *The Nuclear Renaissance and International Security* Eds. Adam N. Stulberg and Matthew Fuhrmann. Palo Alto: Stanford University Press.

Benson, Brett V. and Quan Wen. 2011. "A Bargaining Model of Nuclear Weapons: Development and Disarmament." In *Causes and Consequences of Nuclear Proliferation* Eds. Robert Rauchhaus, Matthew Kroenig, and Erik Gartzke. New York: Routledge Press.

Berinsky, Adam J. 2009. *In Time of War: Understanding American Public Opinion from World War II to Iraq*. Chicago: University of Chicago Press.

Bils, Peter and William Spaniel. 2018. "Policy Bargaining and Militarized Conflict." *Journal of Theoretical Politics* 29 (4): 647–678.

Blainey, Geoffrey. 1988. *The Causes of War*. New York: New York Free Press.

Blechman, Barry M. and Douglas M. Hart. 1982. "The Political Utility of Nuclear Weapons: The 1973 Middle East Crisis." *International Security* 7 (1): 132–156.

Bleek, Phillip C. 2010. "Why Do States Proliferate? Quantitative Analysis of the Exploration, Pursuit, and Acquisition of Nuclear Weapons." In *Forecasting Nuclear Proliferation in the 21st Century, Volume 1* Eds. William C. Potter and Gaukhar Mukhatzhanova. Palo Alto: Stanford University Press.

Blix, Hans. 2004. *Disarming Iraq*. New York: Random House.

Bolton, John. May 2, 2010. "Get Ready for a Nuclear Iran." *The Wall Street Journal*.

Bowen, Wyn Q. 2006. *Libya and Nuclear Proliferation: Stepping Back from the Brink*. New York: Routledge.

Brands, Hal and David Palkki. 2011. "Saddam, Israel, and the Bomb: Nuclear Alarmism Justified?" *International Security* 36 (1): 133–166.

Braut-Hegghammer, Malfrid. 2016. *Unclear Physics: Why Iraq and Libya Failed to Build Nuclear Weapons*. Ithaca: Cornell University Press.

Brown, Jonathan N. and Anthony S. Marcum. 2011. "Avoiding Audience Costs: Domestic Political Accountability and Concessions in Crisis Diplomacy." *Security Studies* 20 (2): 141–170.

Buhite, Russell D. and William Christopher Hamel. 1990. "War for Peace: The Question of an American Preventive War against the Soviet Union, 1945–1955." *Diplomatic History* 14 (3): 367–384.

Bundy, McGeorge. 1988. *Danger and Survival: Choices about the Bomb in the First Fifty Years.* New York: Random House.

Burr, William and Jeffrey T. Richelson. 2000. "Whether to 'Strangle the Baby in the Cradle': The United States and the Chinese Nuclear Program, 1960–64." *International Security* 25 (3): 54–99.

Campbell, Kurt M. and Tsuyoshi Sunohara. 2004. "Japan: Thinking the Unthinkable." In *The Nuclear Tipping Point: Why States Reconsider Their Nuclear Choices* Eds. Kurt M. Campbell, Robert J. Einhorn, and Mitchell B. Reiss. Washington, DC: Brookings Institution Press.

Carroll, Robert J. 2013. "Making Peace on the Cheap." Manuscript, University of Rochester.

Carroll, Robert J. and Brenton Kenkel. 2018. "Prediction, Proxies, and Power." *American Journal of Political Science* Forthcoming.

Chadefaux, Thomas. 2011. "Bargaining over Power: When Do Shifts in Power Lead to War?" *International Theory* 3 (2): 228–253.

Chafetz, Glenn. 1993. "The End of the Cold War and the Future of Nuclear Proliferation: An Alternative to the Neorealist Perspective." *Security Studies* 2 (3): 125–158.

Chinoy, Mike. 2008. *Meltdown: The Inside Story of the North Korean Nuclear Crisis.* New York: St. Martin's Press.

Cirincione, Joseph. 2005. "Lessons Lost." *Bulletin of the Atomic Scientists* 61 (6): 42–53.

Cirincione, Joseph, Jon B. Wolfsthal, and Miriam Rajkumar. 2005. *Deadly Arsenals: Nuclear, Biological, and Chemical Threats.* Washington, DC: Carnegie Endowment for International Peace.

Clark, David D. and Susan Landau. 2011. "Untangling Attribution." *Harvard National Security Journal* 2 (2): 25–40.

Clarke, Kevin A. and David M. Primo. 2012. *A Model Discipline: Political Science and the Logic of Representations.* Oxford: Oxford University Press.

Coe, Andrew J. 2012. "Costly Peace and War." Manuscript, Harvard University.

Coe, Andrew J. and Jane Vaynman. 2015. "Collusion and the Nuclear Nonproliferation Regime." *Journal of Politics* 77 (4): 983–997.

Cohen, Avner. 1998. *Israel and the Bomb.* New York: Columbia University Press.

Cooley, John K. 2005. *An Alliance against Babylon: The US, Israel, and Iraq.* Ann Arbor: Pluto Press.

Cordesman, Anthony H. 1999. *Iraq and the War of Sanctions: Conventional Threats and Weapons of Mass Destruction.* Westport: Praeger.

Corera, Gordon. 2006. *Shopping for Bombs: Nuclear Proliferation, Global Insecurity, and the Rise and Fall of the A.Q. Khan Network.* Oxford: Oxford University Press.

Dai, Xinyuan. 2007. *International Institutions and National Policies.* Cambridge: Cambridge University Press.

Debs, Alexandre and Nuno Monteiro. 2014. "Known Unknowns: Power Shifts, Uncertainty, and War." *International Organization* 68 (1): 1–31.

Debs, Alexandre and Nuno Monteiro. 2017. *Nuclear Politics: The Strategic Causes of Proliferation*. Cambridge: Cambridge University Press.

Deyermond, Ruth. 2008. *Security and Sovereignty in the Former Soviet Union*. Boulder: Lynne Reinner Publishers.

Downs, George W., David M. Rocke, and Randolph M. Siverson. 1986. "Arms Races and Cooperation." In *Cooperation under Anarchy* Ed. Kenneth A. Oye. Princeton: Princeton University Press.

Drezner, Daniel W. 1999. *The Sanctions Paradox: Economic Statecraft and International Relations*. Cambridge: Cambridge University Press.

Dunn, Lewis A. 1990. "Arms Control Verification: Living with Uncertainty." *International Security* 14 (4): 165–175.

Edwards, Peter. 1997. *A Nation at War: Australian Politics, Society, and Diplomacy during the Vietnam War 1965–1975*. St. Leonards: Allen and Unwin.

Einhorn, Robert J. 2004. "Egypt: Frustrated but Still on a Non-Nuclear Course." In *The Nuclear Tipping Point: Why States Reconsider Their Nuclear Choices* Eds. Kurt M. Campbell, Robert J. Einhorn, and Mitchell B. Reiss. Washington, DC: Brookings Institution Press.

ElBaradei, Mohammed. 2011. *The Age of Deception: Nuclear Diplomacy in Treacherous Times*. New York: Metropolitan Books.

Ellis, Jason D. 2001. *Defense by Other Means: The Politics of US–NIS Threat Reduction and Nuclear Security Cooperation*. Westport: Praeger.

Endicott, John E. 1975. *Japan's Nuclear Option: Political, Technical, and Strategic Factors*. New York: Praeger.

Evron, Yair. 1994. *Israel's Nuclear Dilemma*. New York: Routledge.

Facon, Isabelle. 2012. "Ukraine: The Case of a Nuclear Inheritor." In *Over the Horizon Proliferation Threats* Eds. James J. Wirtz and Peter R. Lavoy. Stanford: Stanford University Press.

Fearon, James D. 1991. "Counterfactuals and Hypothesis Testing in Political Science." *World Politics* 169–195.

1994. "Domestic Political Audiences and the Escalation of International Disputes." *American Political Science Review* 88 (3): 577–592.

1995. "Rationalist Explanations for War." *International Organization* 49 (3): 379–414.

1996. "Bargaining over Objects that Influence Future Bargaining Power." Manuscript, University of Chicago.

2011. "Arming and Arms Races." Manuscript, Stanford University.

Feaver, Peter D. and Christopher Gelpi. 2004. *Choosing Your Battles: American Civil–Military Relations and the Use of Force*. Princeton: Princeton University Press.

Fey, Mark. 2014. "Learning to Fight: Information, Uncertainty, and the Risk of War." Manuscript, University of Rochester.

Fey, Mark and Kristopher W. Ramsay. 2011. "Uncertainty and Incentives in Crisis Bargaining: Game-Free Analysis of International Conflict." *American Journal of Political Science* 55 (1): 149–169.

Filson, Darren and Suzanne Werner. 2002. "A Bargaining Model of War and Peace: Anticipating the Onset, Duration, and Outcome of War." *American Journal of Political Science* 46 (4): 819–838.

Fly, Jamie and William Kristol. June 21, 2010. "A Period of Consequences." *The Weekly Standard.*

Fortna, Virginia Paige. 2003. "Scraps of Paper? Agreements and the Durability of Peace." *International Organization* 57 (2): 337–372.

2004 "Interstate Peacekeeping: Causal Mechanisms and Empirical Effects." *World Politics* 56 (4): 481–519.

Friedberg, Aaron L. 2000. *In the Shadow of the Garrison State: America's Anti-Statism and Its Cold War Grand Strategy.* Princeton: Princeton University Press.

Fuhrmann, Matthew. 2008. "Exporting Mass Destruction? The Determinants of Dual-Use Trade." *Journal of Peace Research* 45 (5): 633–652.

2009. "Taking a Walk on the Supply Side: The Determinants of Civilian Nuclear Cooperation." *Journal of Conflict Resolution* 53 (2): 181–208.

2012. *Atomic Assistance: How "Atoms for Peace" Programs Cause Nuclear Insecurity.* Ithaca: Cornell University Press.

Fuhrmann, Matthew and Sarah E. Kreps. 2010. "Targeting Nuclear Programs in War and Peace: A Quantitative Empirical Analysis, 1941–2000." *Journal of Conflict Resolution* 54 (6): 831–859.

Fuhrmann, Matthew and Michael C. Horowitz. 2015. "Leaders, Rebel Experience, and Nuclear Proliferation." *Journal of Politics* 77 (1): 72–87.

Fuhrmann, Matthew and Bejnamin Tkach. 2015. "Almost Nuclear: Introducing the Nuclear Latency Dataset." *Conflict Management and Peace Science* 32 (4): 443–461.

Gaddis, John Lewis. 1972. *The United States and the Origins of the Cold War 1941–1947.* New York: Columbia University Press.

1982. *Strategies of Containment: A Critical Appraisal of Postwar American National Security Policy.* Oxford: Oxford University Press.

1987. *The Long Peace: Inquiries into the History of the Cold War.* Oxford: Oxford University Press.

1997. *We Now Know: Rethinking Cold War History.* Oxford: Oxford University Press.

Gallagher, Nancy W. 2003. *The Politics of Verification.* Baltimore: Johns Hopkins University Press.

Galon, Galia. 2008. "A (Dubious) Conspiracy Theory of the 1967 War." *Diplomatic History* 32 (4): 669–673.

Garnett, Sherman W. 1995. "The Sources and Conduct of Ukrainian Nuclear Policy: November 1992 to January 1994." In *The Nuclear Challenge in Russia and the New States of Eurasia* Ed. George Quester. New York: M.E. Sharpe.

Garnham, David. 1986. "War-Proneness, War-Weariness, and Regime Type: 1816–1980." *Journal of Peace Research* 23 (3): 279–289.

Gartzke, Erik and Dong-Joon Jo. 2009. "Bargaining, Nuclear Proliferation, and Interstate Disputes." *Journal of Conflict Resolution* 53 (2): 209–233.

Gartzke, Erik and Matthew Kroenig. 2009. "A Strategic Approach to Nuclear Proliferation." *Journal of Conflict Resolution* 53 (2): 151–160.

Getmansky, Anna. 2017. "Who Gets What from IOs? The Case of the International Atomic Energy Agency's Technical Cooperation." Forthcoming, *International Studies Quarterly* 61 (3): 596–611.

Gilpin, Robert. 1981. *War and Change in World Politics.* Cambridge: Cambridge University Press.

Ginor, Isabella and Gideon Remez. 2006. "The Spymaster, the Communist, and Foxbats Over Dimona." *Israel Studies* 11 (2): 88–130.

Goemans, Hein and William Spaniel. 2016. "Multimethod Research: A Case for Formal Theory." *Security Studies* 25 (1): 25–33.

Goodman, Michael S. 2007. *Spying on the Nuclear Bear: Anglo-American Intelligence and the Soviet Bomb.* Stanford: Stanford University Press.

Gordin, Michael D. 2009. *Red Cloud at Dawn: Truman, Stalin, and the End of the Nuclear Monopoly.* New York: Farrar, Straus and Giroux.

Ha, Young-Sun. 1983. *Nuclear Proliferation, World Order, and Korea.* Seoul: Seoul National University Press.

Harrington, Daniel F. 2012. *Berlin on the Brink: The Blockade, the Airlift, and the Early Cold War.* Lexington: University of Kentucky Press.

Hartmann, Susan M. 1971. *Truman and the 80th Congress.* Columbia: University of Missouri Press.

Hayes, Peter. 1991. *Pacific Powderkeg: American Nuclear Dilemmas in Korea.* Lexington: Lexington Books.

Hewlett, Richard C. and Oscar E. Anderson. 1962. *The New World, 1939/1946.* University Park: The Pennsylvania State University Press.

Holloway, David. 1994. *Stalin and the Bomb: The Soviet Union and Atomic Energy, 1939–1956.* New Haven: Yale University Press.

Holmes, James R. and Toshi Yoshihara. 2012. "Thinking about the Unthinkable: Tokyo's Nuclear Option." In *Strategy in the Second Nuclear Age: Power, Ambition, and the Ultimate Weapon* Eds. Toshi Yoshihara and James R. Holmes. Washington, DC: Georgetown University Press.

Hong, Sung Gul. 2011. "The Search for Deterrence: Park's Nuclear Option." In *The Park Chung Hee Era: The Transformation of South Korea* Eds. Byung-Kook Kim and Ezra F. Vogel. Cambridge: Harvard University Press.

Horowitz, Michael. 2009. "The Spread of Nuclear Weapons and International Conflict: Does Experience Matter?" *Journal of Conflict Resolution* 53 (2): 234–257.

Howard, Michael. 1983. *The Causes of War.* Cambridge: Harvard University Press.

Hughes, Jeff. 2002. *The Manhattan Project: Big Science and the Atom Bomb.* New York: Columbia University Press.

Hymans, Jacques E. C. 2006. *The Psychology of Nuclear Proliferation: Identity, Emotions and Foreign Policy.* New York: Cambridge University Press.

2012. *Achieving Nuclear Ambitions: Scientists, Politicians, and Proliferation.* Cambridge: Cambridge University Press.

Ikle, Fred Charles. 1961. "After Detection – What?" *Foreign Affairs* 39 (1): 208–220.

Jackman, Simon. 2008. "Measurement." In *The Oxford Handbook of Political Methodology* Eds. Henry E. Brady, Janet M. Box-Steffensmeier, and David Collier. New York: Oxford University Press.

Jackson, Matthew O. and Massimo Morelli. 2009. "Strategic Militarization, Deterrence and Wars." *Quarterly Journal of Political Science* 4 (4): 279–313.

Jelnov, Artyom, Yair Tauman, and Richard Zeckhauser. 2017. "Attacking the Unknown Weapons of a Potential Bomb Builder: The Impact of Intelligence on the Strategic Interaction." *Games and Economic Behavior* 104: 177–189.

Jenkins, Roy. 2001. *Churchill: A Biography*. New York: Farrar, Straus and Giroux.

Jervis, Robert. 1980. "The Impact of the Korean War on the Cold War." *Journal of Conflict Resolution* 24 (4): 563–592.

——— 1989. *The Meaning of the Nuclear Revolution: Statecraft and the Prospect of Armageddon*. Ithaca: Cornell University Press.

Jo, Dong-Joon and Erik Gartzke. 2007. "Determinants of Nuclear Weapons Proliferation." *Journal of Conflict Resolution* 51 (1): 167–194.

Jones, Peter. 1998. "Iran's Threat Perceptions and Arms Control Policies." *The Nonproliferation Review* 6 (1): 39–55.

Jones, Daniel M., Stuart A. Bremer, and J. David Singer. 1996. "Militarized Interstate Disputes, 1816–1992: Rationale, Coding Rules, and Empirical Patterns." *Conflict Management and Peace Science* 15 (2): 163–215.

Jones, Rodney W., Mark G. McDonough, Toby F. Dalton, and Gregory D. Koblentz. 1998. *Tracking Nuclear Proliferation: A Guide in Maps and Charts, 1998*. Washington, DC: Carnegie Endowment for International Peace.

Karl, David J. 1996. "Proliferation Pessimism and Emerging Nuclear Powers." *International Security* 21 (3): 87–119.

Kassenova, Togzhan. September 28, 2009. "The Lasting Toll of Semipalatinsk's Nuclear Testing." *Bulletin of the Atomic Scientists*.

Kavakli, Kerim Can. 2012. "Leader Comebacks: Accountability in the Long Term." Manuscript, University of Rochester.

Keohane, Robert O. 1984. *After Hegemony: Cooperation and Discord in the World Political Economy*. Princeton: Princeton University Press.

Kessler, Glenn. "2003 Memo Says Iranian Leaders Backed Talks." *Washington Post*, February 14, 2007. www.washingtonpost.com/wp-dyn/content/article/2007/02/13/AR2007021301363.html (last accessed September 12, 2018).

——— "Cotton's Misguided History Lesson on the North Korean Nuclear Deal." *Washington Post*, March 13, 2015. www.washingtonpost.com/news/fact-checker/wp/2015/03/13/cottons-misguided-history-lesson-on-the-north-korean-nuclear-deal/ (last accessed September 12, 2018).

Kim, Hyung-A. 2011. "Heavy and Chemical Industrialization, 1973–1979: South Korea's Homeland Security Measures." In *Reassessing the Park Chung Hee Era, 1961–1979: Development, Political Thought, Democracy, and Cultural Influence* Eds. Hyung-A Kim and Clark W. Sorensen. Seattle: University of Washington Press.

Kirschenbaum, Joshua. 2010. "Operation Opera: An Ambiguous Success." *Journal of Strategic Studies* 3 (4): 49–62.

Koremenos, Barbara, Charles Lipson, and Duncan Snidal. 2001. "The Rational Design of International Institutions." *International Organization* 55 (4): 761–799.

Krass, Allan S. 1985. *Verification: How Much Is Enough?* Lexington: Lexington Books.

Krauthammer, Charles. June 19, 2009. "Hope and Change – But Not For Iran." *The Washington Post.*

Kreps, Sarah E. and Matthew Fuhrmann. 2011. "Attacking the Atom: Does Bombing Nuclear Facilities Affect Proliferation?" *Journal of Strategic Studies* 34 (2): 161–187.

Kreps, David M. and Robert Wilson. 1982. "Reputation and Imperfect Information." *Journal of Economic Theory* 27 (2): 253–279.

Kroenig, Matthew. 2009a. "Importing the Bomb: Sensitive Nuclear Assistance and Nuclear Proliferation." *Journal of Conflict Resolution* 53 (2): 161–180.

2009b. "Exporting the Bomb: Sensitive Nuclear Assistance and Proliferation." *American Political Science Review* 103 (1): 113–133.

2010. *Exporting the Bomb: Technology Transfer and the Spread of Nuclear Weapons.* Ithaca: Cornell University Press.

2012. "Time to Attack Iran." *Foreign Affairs* 91 (1): 76–86.

2013. "Nuclear Superiority and the Balance of Resolve: Explaining Nuclear Crisis Outcomes." *International Organization* 67 (1): 141–171.

Kydd, Andrew H. 2000. "Arms Races and Arms Control: Modeling the Hawk Perspective." *American Journal of Political Science* 44 (2): 228–244.

2005. *Trust and Mistrust in International Relations.* Princeton: Princeton University Press.

Lake, David A. 2009. *Hierarchy in International Relations.* Ithaca: Cornell University Press.

2010. "Two Cheers for Bargaining Theory: Assessing Rationalist Explanations for the Iraq War." *International Security* 35 (3): 7–52.

Lanoszka, Alexander. 2013. "Protection States Trust? Major Power Patronage, Nuclear Behavior, and Alliance Dynamics." Manuscript, Princeton University.

Laumulin, Murat. 1995. "Kazakhstan's Nuclear Policy and the Control of Nuclear Weapons." In *The Nuclear Challenge in Russia and the New States of Eurasia* Ed. George Quester. New York: M.E. Sharpe.

Lavoy, Peter R. 1993. "Nuclear Myths and the Causes of Nuclear Proliferation." *Security Studies* 2 (3–4): 192–212.

Leah, Christine M. 2016. "Deterrence Beyond Downunder: Australia and US Security Guarantees Since 1955." *Journal of Strategic Studies* 39 (4): 521–534.

Leeds, Brett Ashley and Jesse C. Johnson. 2017. "Theory, Data, and Deterrence: A Response to Kenwick, Vasquez, and Powers." *Journal of Politics* 79 (1): 335–340.

Levite, Ariel E. 2003. "Never Say Never Again: Nuclear Reversal Revisited." *International Security* 27 (3): 59–88.

Levy, Jack S. 1987. "Declining Power and the Preventive Motivation for War." *World Politics* 40 (1): 82–107.

Levy, Jack S. and T. Clifton Morgan. 1986. "The War-Weariness Hypothesis: An Empirical Test." *American Journal of Political Science* 30 (1): 26–49.

Lian, Bradley and John R. Oneal. 1993. "Presidents, the Use of Military Force, and Public Opinion." *Journal of Conflict Resolution* 37 (2): 277–300.

Lundgren, Carl. 2013. "What Are the Odds? Assessing the Probability of a Nuclear War." *The Nonproliferation Review* 20 (2): 361–374.

Martin, Curtis H. 2002. "Rewarding North Korea: Theoretical Perspectives on the 1994 Agreed Framework." *Journal of Peace Research* 39 (1): 51–68.

Mattes, Michaela. 2008. "The Effect of Changing Conditions and Agreement Provisions on Conflict and Renegotiation Between States with Competing Claims." *International Studies Quarterly* 52(2): 315–334.

Mattes, Michaela and Burcu Savun. 2010. "Information, Agreement Design, and the Durability of Civil War Settlements." *American Journal of Political Science* 54 (2): 511–524.

Mazarr, Michael J. 1995. *North Korea and the Bomb: A Case Study in Nonproliferation.* New York: St. Martin's Press.

McCormack, Timothy L. H. 1996. *Self-Defense in International Law: The Israeli Raid on the Iraqi Nuclear Reactor.* New York: St. Martin's Press.

McKoy, Michael K. and David A. Lake. 2012. "Bargaining Theory and Rationalist Explanations for the Iraq War." *International Security* 36 (3): 172–178.

Mearsheimer, John J. 1993. "The Case for a Ukrainian Nuclear Deterrent." *Foreign Affairs* 72 (3): 50–66.

Mehta, Rupal and Rachel Whitlark. 2017a. "The Benefits and Burdens of Nuclear Latency." *International Studies Quarterly* 61 (3): 517–528.

2017b. "The Determinants of Nuclear Latency." Manuscript, University of Nebraska.

Meirowitz, Adam and Anne E. Sartori. 2008. "Strategic Uncertainty as a Cause of War." *Quarterly Journal of Political Science* 3 (4): 327–352.

Meyrowitz, Elliott L. 1990. *Prohibition of Nuclear Weapons: The Relevance of International Law.* Dobbs Ferry: Transnational.

Mikesell, Raymond Frech. 1994. *The Bretton Woods Debates.* Essays in International Finance, vol. 192. Princeton, NJ: International Finance Section, Department of Economics, Princeton University.

Miller, Roger G. 2000. *To Save a City: The Berlin Airlift, 1948–1949.* College Station: Texas A&M University Press.

Miller, Steven E. 1993. "The Case Against a Ukrainian Nuclear Deterrent." *Foreign Affairs* 72 (3): 67–80.

1995. "Proliferation Dangers in the Former Soviet Union." In *The Successor States to the USSR* Ed. John W. Blaney. Washington, DC: Congressional Quarterly.

Mitchell, Derek J. 2004. "Taiwan's Hsin Chu Program: Deterrence, Abandonment, and Honor." In *The Nuclear Tipping Point: Why States Reconsider Their Nuclear Choices* Eds. Kurt M. Campbell, Robert J. Einhorn, and Mitchell B. Reiss. Washington, DC: Brookings Institution Press.

Monteiro, Nuno and Alexandre Debs. 2014. "The Strategic Logic of Nuclear Proliferation." *International Security* 39 (2): 7–51.

Montgomery, Alexander H. and Adam Mount. 2014. "Misestimation: Explaining US Failures to Predict Nuclear Weapons Programs." *Intelligence and National Security* 29 (3): 357–386.

Morgenthau, Hans. 1960. *Politics Among Nations: The Struggle for Power and Peace.* New York: Knopf.

Morrow, James D. 1999. "How Could Trade Affect Conflict?" *Journal of Peace Research* 36 (4): 481–489.

Muller, Karl P., Jasen J. Castillo, and Forrest E. Morgen. 2007. *Striking First: Preemptive and Preventive Attack in US National Security Policy.* Santa Monica: RAND Corporation.

Naimark, Norman M. 1995. *The Russians in Germany: A History of the Soviet Zone of Occupation, 1945–1949.* Cambridge: Harvard University Press.

Nakdimon, Shlomo. 1987. *First Strike: The Exclusive Story of How Israel Foiled Iraq's Attempt to Get the Bomb.* New York: Summit Books.

Nincic, Miroslav. 2012. "Positive Incentives, Positive Results? Rethinking US Counterproliferation Policy." In *Sanctions, Statecraft, and Nuclear Proliferation* Ed. Etel Solingen. Cambridge: Cambridge University Press.

Obama, Barack. 2009. Statements by President Obama, French President Sarkozy, and British Prime Minister Brown on Iranian Nuclear Facility. Washington, DC: Office of the Press Secretary.

Oberdorfer, Don. 2001. *The Two Koreas: A Contemporary History.* New York: Basic Books.

Organski, A. F. K. and Jacek Kugler. 1977. "The Costs of Major Wars: The Phoenix Factor." *American Political Science Review* 71 (4): 1347–1366.

Ostrom, Jr., Charles W. and Brian L. Job. 1986. "The President and the Political Use of Force." *American Political Science Review* 80 (2): 541–566.

Parsi, Trita. 2012. *A Single Roll of the Dice: Obama's Diplomacy with Iran.* New Haven: Yale University Press.

Paul, T. V. 1995. "Nuclear Taboo and War Initiation in Regional Conflicts." *Journal of Conflict Resolution* 39 (4): 696–717.

2000. *Power versus Prudence: Why Nations Forgo Nuclear Weapons.* Montreal: McGill-Queen's University Press.

Paznyak, Vyachaslau. 1995. "Belarusian Denuclearization Policy and the Control of Nuclear Weapons." In *The Nuclear Challenge in Russia and the New States of Eurasia* Ed. George Quester. New York: M.E. Sharpe.

Perlmutter, Amos, Michael I. Handel, and Uri Bar-Joseph. 2003. *Two Minutes over Baghdad.* Portland: Frank Cass Publishers.

Pickering, Jeffrey. 2002. "War-Weariness and Cumulative Effects: Victors, Vanquished, and Subsequent Interstate Intervention." *Journal of Peace Research* 39 (3): 313–337.

Pollack, Jonathan D. and Mitchell B. Reiss. 2004. "South Korea: The Tyranny of Geography and the Vexations of History." In *The Nuclear Tipping Point: Why States Reconsider Their Nuclear Choices* Eds. Kurt M. Campbell, Robert J. Einhorn, and Mitchell B. Reiss. Washington, DC: Brookings Institution Press.

Powell, Robert. 1987. "Crisis Bargaining, Escalation, and MAD." *American Political Science Review* 81 (3): 717–736.

1988. "Nuclear Brinkmanship with Two-Sided Incomplete Information." *American Political Science Review* 82 (1): 155–178.

1989. "Nuclear Deterrence and the Strategy of Limited Retaliation." *American Political Science Review* 83 (2): 503–519.

1990. *Nuclear Deterrence Theory: The Search for Credibility.* Cambridge: Cambridge University Press.

1993. "Guns, Butter, and Anarchy." *American Political Science Review* 87 (1): 115–132.

1996. "Stability and the Distribution of Power." *World Politics* 48 (2): 239–267.

1999. *In the Shadow of Power: States and Strategies in International Politics.* Princeton: Princeton University Press.

2004. "Bargaining and Learning While Fighting." *American Journal of Political Science* 48 (2): 344–361.

2006. "War as a Commitment Problem." *International Organization* 60 (1): 169–203.

Quester, George H. 1973. *The Politics of Nuclear Proliferation.* Baltimore: Johns Hopkins University Press.

1989. "Some Thoughts on 'Deterrence Failures'." In *Perspectives on Deterrence* Eds. Paul C. Stern, Robert Axelrod, Robert Jervis, and Roy Radner. Oxford: Oxford University Press.

2000. *Nuclear Monopoly.* New Brunswick: Transaction Publishers.

Raas, Whitney and Austin Long. 2007. "Osirak Redux? Assessing Israeli Capabilities to Destroy Iranian Nuclear Facilities." *International Security* 31 (4): 7–33.

Rabinowitz, Or. 2014. *Bargaining on Nuclear Tests: Washington and Its Cold War Deals.* Oxford: Oxford University Press.

Rabinowitz, Or and Nicholas L. Miller. 2015. "Keeping the Bombs in the Basement: US Nonproliferation Policy Toward Israel, South Africa, and Pakistan." *International Security* 40 (1): 47–86.

Reed, William, David H. Clark, Timothy Nordstrom, and Wonjae Hwang. 2008. "War, Power, and Bargaining." *Journal of Politics* 70 (4): 1203–1216.

Reiss, Mitchell B. 1988. *Without the Bomb: The Politics of Nuclear Nonproliferation.* New York: Columbia University Press.

1995. *Bridled Ambition: Why Countries Constrain Their Nuclear Capabilities.* Baltimore: Johns Hopkins University Press.

2004. "The Nuclear Tipping Point: Prospects for a World of Many Nuclear Weapons States." In *The Nuclear Tipping Point: Why States Reconsider Their Nuclear Choices* Eds. Kurt M. Campbell, Robert J. Einhorn, and Mitchell B. Reiss. Washington, DC: Brookings Institution Press.

Reiter, Dan. 1995. "Exploding the Powder Keg Myth: Preemptive Wars Almost Never Happen." *International Security* 20 (2): 5–34.

2005. "Preventive Attacks against Nuclear Programs and the 'Success' at Osiraq." *Nonproliferation Review* 12 (2): 355–371.

Reynolds, Celia L. and Wilfred T. Wan. 2012. "Empirical Trends in Sanctions and Positive Inducements in Nonproliferation." In *Sanctions, Statecraft, and Nuclear Proliferation* Ed. Etel Solingen. Cambridge: Cambridge University Press.

Reynolds, David. 2006. *From World War to Cold War: Churchill, Roosevelt, and the International History of The 1940s.* Oxford: Oxford University Press.

Reynolds, Wayne. 2000. *Australia's Bid for the Atomic Bomb.* Melbourne: Melbourne University Press.

Riabchuk, Mykola. 2010. "Ukraine's Nuclear Nostalgia." *World Policy Journal* 26 (4): 95–105.

Richardson, Lewis. F. 1960. *Arms and Insecurity*. Pittsburgh: Boxwood Press.

Rublee, Maria Rost. 2009. *Nonproliferation Norms: Why States Choose Nuclear Restraint*. Athens: University of Georgia Press.

Sagan, Scott D. 1993. *The Limits of Safety: Organizations, Accidents, and Nuclear Weapons*. Princeton: Princeton University Press.

1996. "Why Do States Build Nuclear Weapons?: Three Models in Search of a Bomb." *International Security* 21 (3): 54–86.

2011. "The Causes of Nuclear Weapons Proliferation." *Annual Review of Political Science* 14: 225–244.

Sagan, Scott D. and Kenneth N. Waltz. 2003. *The Spread of Nuclear Weapons: A Debate Renewed*. New York: Norton.

Schelling, Thomas C. 1960. *The Strategy of Conflict*. Cambridge: Harvard University Press.

1966. *Arms and Influence*. New Haven: Yale University Press.

Schiff, Benjamin N. 1983. *International Nuclear Technology Transfer: Dilemmas of Dissemination and Control*. Totowa: Rowman & Allanheld.

Schiff, Ze'ev. 2001. "Israel Today: Strategic Options." In *The Dynamics of Middle East Nuclear Proliferation* Eds. Steven L. Spiegel, Jennifer D. Kibbe, and Elizabeth G. Matthews. Lewiston: The Edwin Mellen Press.

Schoff, James L. 2012. "Changing Perceptions of Extended Deterrence in Japan." In *Strategy in the Second Nuclear Age: Power, Ambition, and the Ultimate Weapon* Eds. Toshi Yoshihara and James R. Holmes. Washington, DC: Georgetown University Press.

Schub, Robert. 2017. "Unfair Fights: Power Asymmetry, Nascent Nuclear Capability, and Preventive Conflict." *Conflict Management and Peace Science* 34 (4): 431–455.

Schultz, Kenneth A. 1999. "Do Democratic Institutions Constrain or Inform? Contrasting Two Institutional Perspectives on Democracy and War." *International Organization* 53 (2): 233–266.

Schumer, Charles E. 2015. "My Position on the Iran Deal." Press Release, August 6, 2015. www.schumer.senate.gov/newsroom/press-releases/my-position-on-the-iran-deal (last accessed September 15, 2018).

Schwartz, Stephen I. 1998. *Atomic Audit: The Cost and Consequences of US Nuclear Weapons since 1940*. Washington, DC: The Brookings Institute.

Scott, Len. 2011. "Intelligence and the Risk of Nuclear War: *Able Archer-83* Revisited." *Intelligence and National Security* 26 (6): 759–777.

Sechser, Todd S. and Matthew Fuhrmann. 2013. "Crisis Bargaining and Nuclear Blackmail." *International Organization* 67 (1): 173–195.

2017. *Nuclear Weapons and Coercive Diplomacy*. Cambridge: Cambridge University Press.

Sick, Gary. 2001. "Iran's Nuclear Program: Is There a Negotiated Alternative?" In *The Dynamics of Middle East Nuclear Proliferation* Eds. Steven L. Spiegel, Jennifer D. Kibbe, and Elizabeth G. Matthews. Lewiston: The Edwin Mellen Press.

Signorino, Curtis S. and Jeffrey M. Ritter. 1999. "Tau-b or Not Tau-b: Measuring the Similarity of Foreign Policy Positions." *International Studies Quarterly* 43 (1): 115–144.

Silverstone, Scott A. 2007. *Preventive War and American Democracy*. New York: Routledge.

Singer, J. David, Stuart Bremer, and John Stuckey. 1972. "Capability Distribution, Uncertainty, and Major Power War, 1820–1965." In *Peace, War, and Numbers* Ed. Bruce Russett. Beverley Hills: Sage.

Singh, Sonali and Christopher R. Way. 2004. "The Correlates of Nuclear Proliferation: A Quantitative Test." *Journal of Conflict Resolution* 48 (6): 859–885.

Slantchev, Branislav L. 2003. "The Principle of Convergence in Wartime Negotiations." *American Political Science Review* 97 (4): 621–632.

    2005. "Military Coercion in Interstate Crises." *American Political Science Review* 99 (4): 533–547.

    2010. "Feigning Weakness." *International Organization* 64 (3): 357–388.

    2011. *Military Threats: The Costs of Coercion and the Price of Peace*. Cambridge: Cambridge University Press.

Smith, Bradley C. and William Spaniel. 2018. "Introducing v-CLEAR: A Latent Variable Approach to Measuring Nuclear Capability." Forthcoming, *Conflict Management and Peace Science*.

Solingen, Etel. 2007. *Nuclear Logics: Contrasting Paths in East Asia and the Middle East*. Princeton, NJ: Princeton University Press.

Spaniel, William. 2015. "Arms Negotiations, War Exhaustion, and the Credibility of Preventive War." *International Interactions* 41 (5): 832–856.

Spaniel, William and Peter Bils. 2018. "Bargaining, Uncertainty, and the Calculus of Conquest." *Journal of Conflict Resolution* 62 (4): 774–796.

Spaniel, William and Michael Poznansky. 2018. "Covert Action, Investigation, and Punishment." *American Journal of Political Science* 62 (3) 668–681.

Stone, Randall W. 1996. *Satellites and Commissars: Strategy and Conflict in the Politics of Soviet-Bloc Trade*. Princeton: Princeton University Press.

    2011. *Controlling Institutions: International Organizations and the Global Economy*. Cambridge: Cambridge University Press.

Streich, Philip, and Jack S. Levy. 2016. "Information, Commitment, and the Russo-Japanese War of 1904-1905." *Foreign Policy Analysis* 12 (4): 489–511.

    2016. "Information, Commitment, and the Russo-Japanese War of 1904–1905." *Foreign Policy Analysis* 12 (4): 489–511.

Tannenwald, Nina. 1999. "The Nuclear Taboo: The United States and the Normative Basis of Nuclear Non-Use." *International Organization* 53 (3): 433–468.

Telhami, Shibley. 1990. *Power and Leadership in International Bargaining: The Path to the Camp David Accords*. New York: Columbia University Press.

Thayer, Bradley A. 1995. "The Causes of Nuclear Proliferation and the Utility of the Nuclear Non-Proliferation Regime." *Security Studies* 4 (3): 463–519.

Thucydides. 1972. *History of the Peloponnesian War*. Translated by Rex Warner. Baltimore: Penguin Books.

Trachtenberg, Marc. 1985. "The Influence of Nuclear Weapons in the Cuban Missile Crisis." *International Security* 10 (1): 137–163.

    1988. "A 'Wasting Asset': American Strategy and the Shifting Nuclear Balance, 1949–1954." *International Security* 13 (3): 9–49.

Treisman, Daniel. 2004. "Rational Appeasement." *International Organization* 58 (2): 345–373.

Truman, Harry S. 1955. *Memoirs by Harry S. Truman, Vol. 1: Year of Decisions.* Garden City: Doubleday.

Tsebelis, George. 1989. "The Abuse of Probability in Political Analysis: The Robinson Crusoe Fallacy." *American Political Science Review* 83 (1): 77–91.

Turner, Henry Ashby. 1987. *The Two Germanies Since 1945: East and West.* New Haven: Yale University Press.

Tusa, Ann and John Tusa. 1988. *The Berlin Airlift.* New York: Atheneum.

Uzonyi, Gary and Toby Rider. 2017. "Determinants of Foreign Aid: Rivalry and Domestic Instability." 43 (2): 272–299.

Voeten, Erik. 2001. "Outside Options and the Logic of Security Council Action." *American Political Science Review* 95 (4): 845–858.

Volpe, Tristan A. 2017. "Atomic Leverage: Compellence with Nuclear Latency." *Security Studies* 26 (3): 517–544.

Walsh, James Joseph. 2001. *Bombs Unbuilt: Power, Ideas, and Institutions in International Politics.* PhD Dissertation, Massachusetts Institute of Technology.

Way, Christopher R. and Jessica Weeks. 2014. "Making It Personal: Regime Type and Nuclear Proliferation." *American Journal of Political Science* 58 (3): 705–719.

Westerby, Gerald. 1998. *In Hostile Territory: Business Secrets of a Mossad Combatant.* New York: Harper Business.

Wolford, Scott. 2007. "The Turnover Trap: New Leaders, Reputation, and International Conflict." *American Journal of Political Science* 51 (4): 772–788.

    2012. "Incumbents, Successors, and Crisis Bargaining: Leadership Turnover as a Commitment Problem." *Journal of Peace Research* 49 (4): 517–530.

Wolford, Scott, Dan Reiter, and Clifford J. Carrubba. 2011. "Information, Commitment, and War." *Journal of Conflict Resolution* 55 (4): 556–579.

Wolford, Scott and Emily Ritter. 2016. "National Leaders, Political Security, and the Formation of Military Coalitions." *International Studies Quarterly* 60 (3): 540–551.

Xiang, Jun. 2010. "Relevance as a Latent Variable in Dyadic Analysis of Conflict." *Journal of Politics* 72 (2): 484–498.

Yergin, Daniel. 1977. *Shattered Peace: The Origins of the Cold War.* New York: Penguin Books.

Zagare, Frank C. and D. Marc Kilgour. 2000. *Perfect Deterrence.* Cambridge: Cambridge University Press.

Ziegler, Charles A. and David Jacobson. 1995. *Spying without Spies: Origins of America's Secret Nuclear Surveillance System.* Westport: Praeger.

Zubok, Vladislav and Constantine Pleshakov. 1996. *Inside the Kremlin's Cold War: From Stalin to Krushchev.* Cambridge: Harvard University Press.

Index